Integrative Person-Centred Counselling

Integrative Person-Centred Counselling

The Combined Model of Counselling and Psychotherapy

Rick Murphy

WILEY

This edition first published 2026

Registered Offices
John Wiley & Sons, Inc., 111 River Street, Hoboken, NJ 07030, USA
John Wiley & Sons Ltd, New Era House, 8 Oldlands Way, Bognor Regis, West Sussex, PO22 9NQ, UK

For details of our global editorial offices, customer services, and more information about Wiley products visit us at www.wiley.com.

The manufacturer's authorized representative according to the EU General Product Safety Regulation is Wiley-VCH GmbH, Boschstr. 12, 69469 Weinheim, Germany, e-mail: Product_Safety@wiley.com.

Wiley also publishes its books in a variety of electronic formats and by print-on-demand. Some content that appears in standard print versions of this book may not be available in other formats.

Library of Congress Cataloging-in-Publication Data Applied for:

Paperback ISBN: 9781394328970

Cover Design: Wiley
Cover Image: © Dedraw Studio/Shutterstock

Set in 10.5/13pt Minion by Straive, Pondicherry, India

Printed and bound by CPI Group (UK) Ltd, Croydon, CR0 4YY

C9781394328970_070825

Contents

Acknowledgements

My family, friends, colleagues, clients, and students have enormously helped me in writing this book. My two children, Oli and Nora, have been a constant reminder of the value of living and the profound excitement for role modelling to them that work can be playful. Thank you to my partner Lisa Dvorjetz, who has kindly read and re-read every word in this book, always with insightful feedback. She has contributed a chapter of her own, on existential therapy, from her background as a psychologist. I am grateful to my sister Hayley Knight, who has given ideas and vignettes to the book, as well as valuable feedback on draft chapters. I am indebted to Conny Kerman for her wisdom and clinical supervision, and she has made a valuable impact on the case discussions throughout the book.

I thank my good friend Savvas Eftychiou Pavli for illustrating the book and offering his generous creativity throughout the writing process. In addition, I thank my colleague Matt Schofield for contributing a chapter from his expertise on attachment theory. Of the many students who have supported this work, a special thank you to Charlotte Clark, Vanessa Edworthy, Humayra Hussain, Sarah Leather, and Nicky Woods for reading and giving feedback on the draft chapters. Your words were encouraging, and the book has changed because of your thoughtful ideas. One of my counselling students, Salma Mohamed, has contributed her own writing to Chapter 10, and I extend my thanks to her for the generosity in using her experience as learning for others. And finally, thank you to my clients who have agreed for their stories, transcripts, and poetry to be printed throughout the chapters. Though you are anonymous, I am extremely grateful to you personally for passing on your experience to the readers of this book.

Rick Murphy

1

Person Centred

Counselling is a modern talking therapy that improves how people feel. It was once based on the sole belief that some people suffer from a mental illness. When confronted with someone we struggled to understand, we said to ourselves "there must be something wrong here or else they wouldn't be behaving that way." But when they were examined, and others like them, they were not suffering from a physical illness. From this, people assumed they were not in a sound state of mind. They were not thinking and acting the way others did, and we thought they must have something wrong mentally. Doctors found that talking about the emotional underside of the problem helped people feel better.

Since the early days of the talking cure, counselling has moved from a single description of abnormal psychology to a vast library of models and theories. But along the way, counselling concepts have become estranged. One counsellor speaks of the unconscious, and another of the cognitive process. One therapist speaks of experience, and another of family dynamics. Today, psychotherapy is like a shredded book. Each theory provides a fragment of knowledge but remains detached from the bigger conversation.

The purpose of this book is to unite the psychotherapy literature into one model. We sketch the family tree of counselling, demonstrating through its history and relationships how it is one thing: the theory and practice of psychotherapy. In the beginning, we explore relationship-based counselling and argue for its rightful place as the foundation to all psychotherapies. Then, chapter by chapter, we take each of the most influential therapy models and combine them into a bigger picture: an integrative person-centred counselling model.

Integrative Person-Centred Counselling: The Combined Model of Counselling and Psychotherapy, First Edition. Rick Murphy.

The Relationship Cure

Before the invention of counselling, human cultures always had theories about mental health. Lydia Kang and Nate Pedersen wrote a funny yet insightful book called *Quackery: A Brief History of the Worst Ways to Cure Everything*. In it, they tell us of doctors prescribing mercury to patients with chronic health anxiety – corroding their skin, eyes, and teeth in the process! We learn that the ancient Greeks believed mental illness signalled anger from the gods. The Romans used chants and chamomile potions to cope with anxiety. Medieval doctors leaked blood from unanaesthetised mental health patients. There's even bone evidence of our neolithic ancestors, 7,000 years ago, attempting to cure psychological disease by drilling holes into people's heads.

Modern people find these so-called treatments bizarre, but how do we know any better? What do we know about human wellbeing, and how do we know it?

Historically these are questions for shamans and village elders, but the wisest people of antiquity were unable to give scientific answers. It would have seemed naïve to suggest swapping a goat sacrifice with a listening ear or to harness the curing power of empathy in place of the punishing seclusion of a mental asylum. If an ancient time traveller visited the 21st century, they would be astonished to find that something available to everyone could cure the psychological ills of their time. They might not believe that a trusting relationship and a strong dose of empathy would become the modern medicine for anxious and depressed people. But this turns out to be the truth.

Philosophers and healers existed for thousands of years without realising the true power of relationship. The talking cure was invented prior to understanding the role of empathy in overcoming psychological hardship. This wisdom arrived late in the human story, but in the 1940s it dawned on one quiet and wholesome man. He had thick circular glasses, a shy Illinois accent, and his name was Carl Rogers.

It is true that many others had sensed the human need for empathy, but it was Carl Rogers who elevated the role of human connection to the status of a psychological cure. He was the first person to redefine talking therapy not as an intellectual task but as a relationship treatment. He famously changed the doctor's question from "How can I fix or cure a patient?" to "How can I provide a safe relationship for people to fix and heal themselves?" From his work we learned that to accept another's experience without judgement, to relate to their pain and suffering without trying to fix them, flattens the peaks of their distress. Emotional presence helps people escape from troubling experience.

For Rogers, counsellors build therapeutic relationships from three core ingredients – empathy, congruence, and unconditional positive regard. For him, the foundation of psychotherapy became a trusting relationship in which the counsellor senses, feels, and understands the client's experience. The counsellor is honest, their intentions match their actions, and they support the client without judgement or interpretation. John Norcross and Michael Lambert recently reviewed the meta-analysis, case study data, outcome studies, and random control trials on the subject. They found each of these core conditions to correlate very well with successful outcomes.

We know from the evidence that Carl Rogers' ideas do stand the test of time. But we needn't get swept up by one man and one set of ideas. The heart of psychotherapy might be relationship, empathy, and acceptance, but how does this construction of therapy interact with other ideas? Don't other therapy models have the same support from the evidence (and sometimes more convincingly so)? No single model of therapy tells the full story, but authors tend to present their approach as all-encompassing and final. In this case, psychotherapy becomes like a carousel of ideas that changes with the season. The science behind therapy, if viewed more like a fashion than a secure body of knowledge, develops more slowly. In this book we try and demonstrate how much healthier it is to build psychotherapy from the ground up, combining the approaches into one solid structure.

We have learned from our intellectual ancestors not to be blinded by received wisdom. Having different ideas, having different tools, and being open to seeing in new ways can hugely benefit clients undergoing therapy. The relationship might be a universal law of psychotherapy, but what can the discoveries of other counselling and psychotherapy models contribute to the conversation? How do we avoid shutting our eyes to alternative theories and practices?

The purpose of this counselling book is to show the theory and practice behind the most *useful* conclusions in psychotherapy, building from the ground up. Instead of taking a one-sided view, we apply the findings from psychology and the counselling clinic into a modern integrated psychotherapy – mixing the science and the psychology of different approaches into one coherent model. Counsellors, trainees, and interested readers will become fluent in the language of general psychotherapy, and in such a way as to be more able to tolerate and connect with other people's emotional worlds. We use Carl Rogers' ideas as the foundation to our approach and integrate them with the main psychotherapy models. This chapter sets the foundation for a humanistic, person-centred counselling. In the chapters that follow, we build onto this Rogerian foundation a range of other psychotherapy ideas, brick by brick, until a final structure is in view, a model called Integrative Person-Centred Counselling.

Humanising Mental Health

The picture we have starts with the Italian Renaissance man, Francesco Petrarch, who saw beyond the ancient fog of mental health superstition. He saw that human beings have innate potential, a healthy state of mind that grows with the right encouragement. Without support for this natural human goodness, people self-sabotage and become emotionally unwell. This was one of the first models of human wellbeing that attached itself to human nature, and it's to this model we now turn.

Petrarch is known as the father of humanism, which was developed in Italy in the 14th century AD, though it wasn't named until 500 years later. Instead of a mythical account of mental health, humanism proposed that feelings come from real things like self-worth, dignity, and a capacity for making progress. If there was a metrestick for life satisfaction, which there is, he predicted it would measure how much health, purpose, acceptance, and freedom a person has – and his predictions are now confirmed to be accurate. When researchers designed the life-satisfaction survey in the early 1990s, they found that humanistic attributes like being valued and understood match life satisfaction. The World Health Organisation took on these humanistic values by defining positive wellbeing as people feeling good about life, coping emotionally, and realising their potential. Over time, Petrarch's humanism has become a normal part of public conversation, and it now feels intuitive to most people.

In psychotherapy, humanism came of age in the 19th and 20th centuries. During this time, society witnessed the birth of psychiatry, psychoanalysis, and scientific psychology. Most humanistic counsellors came from one of these professions. Probably the most famous person to fit this mould was Carl Rogers. Dissatisfied with the psychiatric view of mental illness, that clients are inherently flawed or sick, humanistic values spoke to his inner care for people. As a psychologist, he took to the unusual practice of calling his patients 'clients' to humanise them.

In 1940, Rogers took humanism and made it into a counselling model. He called it 'non-directive therapy' because, in this theory, people guide themselves to wellness. He reasoned that if people grow naturally from a supportive environment, then talking therapy shouldn't direct or instruct the client. Instead, counselling should provide a therapeutic setting for the client to change and mature on their own. Self-discovery and self-acceptance create self-change, rather than kind teachers or wise words educating people out of distress.

The counselling branch of humanism was developed in contrast to earlier psychotherapies. Behaviourism was a model that viewed mental health as determined by emotional triggers in the environment. It saw clients as trained into bad habits and negative thinking. A person doesn't think negatively out of the blue; they are taught to think negatively by the people and judgements around them.

Humanistic counsellors felt the behaviourist model belittled the notion of free will. Behaviourism was not necessarily wrong but did not consider each person's uniqueness, experience, and freedom to make choices. When the behavioural revolution had peaked, Rogers introduced humanity back into psychology, centring on the client's drive for achievement and fulfilment. He modelled negative thinking as a sign of social and emotional obstacles getting in the way of freedom and progress. As the behaviourist counsellor modelled negative thinking through the lens of environmental triggers, Rogers modelled negative thinking through the unique experience of each client. They aren't fundamentally contradictory but just different in what they emphasise as important about the client's situation. Hence both models of counselling work; they just emphasise different things.

Another contrast was between humanism and the earliest model of psychotherapy, psychoanalysis. Talking therapy began with the view that childhood sculpted the adult personality. Psychoanalysis modelled the client's issue using unconscious forces from childhood that reveal themselves in behaviour. In this way, the unconscious model is similar to the conditioning process; it leads to a view of human beings as being somewhat shackled by prior events. Negative thinking is inevitable if one's childhood neglects to install a sense of optimism. In response to the inevitability model, Rogers put moment-to-moment experience and freewill back into the conversation. He believed that an individual's behaviour related to the full range of experiences, from childhood onwards, but certainly current experience too. In this view, a person has the freewill to change who they are at any time in their life. Counselling is less about interpreting the unconscious or reconditioning the overthinker and more about providing safety for a new self to emerge.

The philosophy of Heidegger, known as phenomenology, hugely influenced the humanistic model. Heidegger noticed that people represent their world via language and behave accordingly. Instead of reacting to factual events, they react to experiences and psychological models of those events. As such, humanism borrowed from phenomenology the idea that people live in a world of interpretation, and their experience is shown through behaviour. Humanistic counselling based itself on the idea that clients are naturally good, able to make their own decisions, and are motivated to achieve – but only when they experience themselves as worthwhile and free to make choices.

Humanistic counselling was aptly named 'the third force' in psychotherapy, coming after the 'first force', psychoanalysis, and the 'second force', behaviourism. In humanistic counselling, mental health issues come about when obstacles get between the individual and personal growth. Like the behaviourists, many obstacles come from the environment. And like the psychoanalysts, many obstacles come from childhood. But the root of negative thinking to a humanistic counsellor is a need for acceptance, emotional tolerance, and a sense of meaningful agency. This humanises counselling, seeing clients as experiencing selves who strive towards fulfilment – a perspective not without its issues, which we will explore in this book, but one that is foundational to our current picture of psychotherapy.

Non-directive Therapy

Earlier we named Carl Rogers' work as non-directive therapy. Contrasting with psychoanalysis and behaviourism, the non-directive approach gets inside a person's experience without directing or analysing it. Rogers criticised therapy that teaches clients how to experience their psychological issues. He felt the best way to understand someone was not by complex theory, but by their internal frame of reference.

Consider a client who says:

> I don't want to go into work today; people are going to judge me.

This person might be analysed as having a negative supervising self, for example, an internalised father who criticises them. Or, they may have been conditioned to think about themself as capable of being judged and unworthy, meaning they avoid socialising with colleagues. These two lenses, one which is psychoanalytical and the other which is behavioural, would lead a therapist to take certain actions. Noticing the client repeatedly become the internal judge, the therapist works on clawing back power. They teach the client to spot the unconscious self-critic, empowering them with this insight.

Similarly, the behaviourist tries to psychoeducate the client. They teach them about the psychological pattern, to try out new behaviours and ways of thinking. And both models of the situation can create profound change by seeing something the other model misses.

The non-directive counsellor offers a third option, which is to emphasise and accept the current experience of the client:

> You don't want to go into work today, people are going to judge you . . . ?

Here the client's experience is accepted at the surface level and not interpreted. The voice of the therapist sounds curious, like an interviewer of an interesting person, and invites more experience to come through. The client says:

> Yes. People might see me as stupid, and I don't want to feel like that.

The non-directive therapist hears the words as a small portion of experience, wanting to experience more and more of the client's world. We start from a position of ignorance, of not understanding or grasping how it is to be the client, but slowly we learn their internal frame of reference:

> You don't want to feel stupid?

At each turn, a different therapist would take the client's words in a certain direction. Being non-directive means putting aside what we want, expect, or need from the client, and being in their experience with them. If we change the client's words or experiences, even slightly, we would no longer be in their world. Let's rewind to the beginning of the conversation to see how this works:

> I don't want to go into work today; people are going to judge me.

If someone says this to us, what are we tempted to say back? A good friend might say, "Don't worry about that," or "Who cares what they think!"

An experienced therapist might ask, "What is it that most worries you about judgement?" An inexperienced therapist might feel uncomfortable tolerating judgement and move to a rescuing question like, "What strengths can you hold in mind about yourself when you go into work?" Or, to dial up the rescuing some more, "Don't think like that, what good things can come out of being challenged at work today?"

Each one of the responses directs the client towards something outside of their present experience. The first therapist's question directs the client towards worries, and the other two towards strengths. What these three responses have in common is a movement away from the client's words to the therapist's sense of what's important. Non-directive therapy says, "Don't interfere with the client's emerging experience." Instead, we show the values from Petrarch and Rogers by trusting the client to discover worries and strengths by themself. Instead of subtly teaching the client where to go, we follow them, ultimately to a stronger frame of mind.

Humanising the Theory

In the Christian Bible, Jesus warns his followers against the blind leading the blind, fearing they will fall into spiritual oblivion. The therapist being blind to the client's experience, taking the strategy of being led by the client who is blind to their fuller experience, feels intuitively similar. Here we ask the question, are non-directive therapies and humanism really doctrines of the blind leading the blind?

In a sense the answer is yes and in a sense no. Humanism says that each person is unique. Because they are unique, we cannot develop a one-size-fits-all psychology. Instead, we get inside experience to understand people's frame of reference. The therapist has expertise in sitting with and encouraging the client's authentic experience without preloaded ideas about what the client experiences. That is, we lead from the back, with clients finding their way through their experience. We echo, highlight, amplify, and mirror their movements, thoughts, feelings, and words.

Many psychotherapy models work on the assumption that we are experts in disorders, defences, and weaknesses, but non-directive therapy works on the assumption that we are experts only in bringing out experience, not in defining or categorising it. Our expertise lies in knowing that people become weak, disordered, and defensive when life gets in the way of their sense of purpose and progress. We enter each therapeutic relationship blind to the client's experience, but, by using our therapeutic eye to slowly map out their experience, we help them see a better and more hopeful self.

The human drive for reaching potential is called self-actualisation. To self-actualise is to take current existence and improve it emotionally, physically, humorously, artistically, and intellectually. There is no pre-existing rulebook for what counts as fulfilling, only the knowledge that people tend towards a fulfilling life when given fundamental physical, social, and emotional support.

Positive Psychology

With humanistic intentions, the renowned psychologist Abraham Maslow took an unusual route in his professional career. Instead of studying the downtrodden, psychotic, anxious, or depressed person, he chose to study emotionally healthy people. He found that when somebody is stable, they strive for higher states of fulfilment in the arts, relationships, careers, and emotions, and their motivation levels stay strong. By focusing on goals, values, acceptance, and self-drive, healthy people create positive wellbeing and life satisfaction. For this reason, he changed the name from humanistic psychology to positive psychology.

Maslow did not find a genetic programme for self-fulfilment; he found a social pyramid for it. Self-actualisation requires layers upon layers of social, emotional, and physical support. In fact, people who do not have the lower layers of support think differently from healthy people. They have what's called deficiency cognition, in which they fixate on what they don't have as a way of striving for what they need. Somebody who complains about having no friends despite being around lots of people might strive for belonging without ever truly feeling it. Somebody who frustrates their partner for being untrustworthy, in the face of no evidence, might strive for safety without having experienced it. Trust, friendship, and safety might be available to the client, but unless they experience it, they struggle to access it.

The pyramid was described as a hierarchy of needs and still bears Maslow's name. Maslow's hierarchy of needs says the human goal of self-actualisation requires lower needs to be met. The first two layers are physiological needs and safety. Food, sleep, shelter, and similar needs are the bedrocks of human happiness. When we work with clients, children in particular, if these needs are neglected then counselling is usually delayed until they are met. In neuroscience this finding is confirmed by the early growth of the brainstem. Before infants can feel complex emotions and interpret them, there is growth in this lower brain region that controls survival needs like the heartbeat, breathing, and reacting to danger. Emotion and social awareness require a level of safety before developing in the brain. People without a base-level of care during childhood tend towards experiences of higher threat level and struggle to trust other people. Neurologically, they are wired to trust less and become defensive, rejecting, and needy in new relationships.

The non-directive counsellor is aware of this but doesn't judge where the client is on the pyramid. It's not possible to judge the client's experience early in the conversation. For instance, the client who says, "I don't want to go into work today; people are going to judge me," could be experiencing a primitive psychological need for safety. If this is the case, the unmet need for safety comes out in therapy, naturally. For example, the client might say, "It feels unsafe to feel judged, like I am going to get hurt in some way," directing the therapist's attention to safety. Being non-directive allows the counsellor not to step in too soon and disrupt the client by saying something like:

It sounds to me like you feel unsafe.

Some clients will accept or agree with the label 'unsafe' and fit it to their experience. Other clients will disagree and reword the statement, or worse, feel misunderstood and shutdown. The trick is to withhold questions that carry assumptions, trying to reflect the client's experience in full colour. This is important because Maslow highlighted a need above safety, which is a social need to feel a sense of belonging and love. A different counsellor with this in mind might say:

It sounds to me like you feel you don't belong.

The therapeutic error in both paraphrases is to assume knowledge about the client's current experience and to attempt to direct them towards this topic – safety or belonging. The wisdom of Maslow's hierarchy is not in labelling and defining the client's experience. This is often what a psychological theory does: it creates expertise that categorises different kinds of experience. The risk is that therapists unknowingly project their own needs onto the client. Instead, the wisdom is in trusting the client to convey their experience, knowing it will fit into the hierarchy of needs, if given time without obstacles.

Clients whose experiences are accepted and trusted connect better with their strengths. Hence, Maslow and the positive psychologists brought attention to the way the therapist nurtures positive emotions in the room, connecting them with gratitude, enjoyment, and happiness. By using empathy and acceptance to meet these basic psychological needs, positive states of mind are inevitable. This is important because some intellectuals characterise positive psychology as avoiding the client's traumas and suffering. Positive psychology can be heard as "avoidant positive thinking" or as burying your head in the sand. But the humanistic element of positive psychology strongly resists this caricature. Instead, we say that stomaching those awful and debilitating emotions in a safe relationship leads to more optimism, self-esteem, and self-determination.

The other layers of need in Maslow's pyramid (Figure 1.1) link with positive psychology, which are self-esteem needs, to be accepted and self-resilient; cognitive needs, to learn and be fulfilled intellectually; aesthetic needs, for nature, art, beauty, and style; and, finally, a need for self-actualisation – the state in which the person is fulfilling their potential.

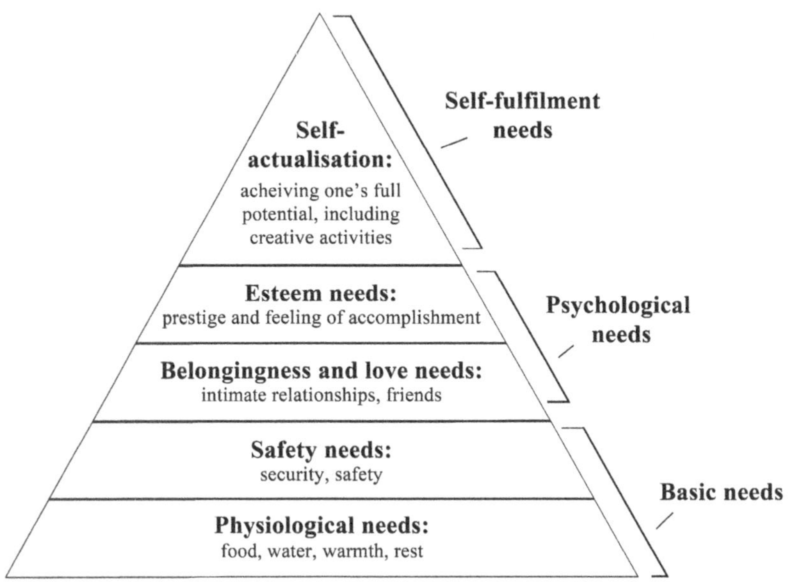

Figure 1.1 Maslow's Hierarchy of Needs

In saying, "You don't want to go into work today, people are going to judge you?," the therapist has no idea where the topic of conversation will go. But the therapist is sure the process will lead the client in the direction of greater connection with their experience. Non-directive therapy does not direct the kinds of experience the client can have, like a film director directing the scene. The non-directive therapist does, however, direct the client's attention to their experience and authentic self. In this limited sense, they are directive. But why is it beneficial for a client to be in greater contact with their experience? How will accepting thoughts and feelings be useful for reaching positive states of mind? Answers to these questions are tied up with Carl Rogers' theory of personality.

Person-Centred Theory

To grasp Rogers' theory of personality, try and imagine what would happen if we did **not** direct traffic at a busy intersection. Without traffic lights, pavements, and drivers trained in the highway code, there would be chaos. This is the situation many clients find themselves in. The busy intersection of thoughts racing against swerving and chaotic feelings, crashing into their boundaries; the never-ending roundabout of negative thinking; the lack of a red light to halt an accelerating emotion – in an unhappy person, the internal highway of emotion is frantic and disorganised.

To bring some order into the counselling room, implicitly to help clients become more organised in themselves, non-directive therapy evolved into *person-centred* therapy. The whole point of being non-directive was to centre the counselling process on the client. Hence, client-centred and person-centred are the main titles of the later books written by Carl Rogers and his colleagues. Shifting from non-directive to person-centred was about offering the counsellor a roadmap for their non-directive skills, a route through the client's winding experience.

Person-centred theory covers some broad terrain. It sees **the client as the centre of a world of frequently changing experiences**. The client does not respond to the world as it is; **the client responds to the world as they experience it**. If the world is perceived as dangerous, then the world *is* dangerous in accordance with the client's experience. Perception is reality. When a client feels anxious or excited when visiting their therapist, for example, the **emotion reveals something about the person's fundamental being**.

Person-centred therapy is humanistic because it interprets the client through the lens of Maslow's pyramid. This is the roadmap. Instead of non-directive therapy for its own sake, **the non-directive skill has the humanistic goal of supporting the client to enhance their experience and fulfil their potential.**

In theory, **the client behaves in a way that seeks to meet their needs**. A person who behaves paradoxically, who seems to self-sabotage, is probably trying to meet a lower-level need. They may reject you as the therapist because this feels safer than exposing themself to the possibility of your rejection. Person-centred therapy accepts the perception as the client's reality and reflects this without judgement. But when small experiences of safety shine through, these are reflected also, and the client's natural tendency is to grow from the safer experience.

How intense an emotion is for a client relates to the importance of protecting their reality, especially when they perceive their needs are being neglected. Some clients respond catastrophically to innocent questions when the questions are perceived as minimising their needs, for example. An experience I had was to ask a client if she was okay, at the start of the therapy session. She shouted at me, "Of course I am not okay, otherwise I wouldn't be here!"

An informal approach to greeting a client, such as my question, can be perceived in many ways, but the client's response is what's important. Before I theorise about the client's perception, I am invited by the person-centred approach to be curious. **Reality is better understood through the client's own internal frame of reference**, rather than through my experience or theory. How did the client experience my question?

When we add up all perceptions the client brings, leading to the total self-awareness of the client, this is their personality. In this theory, **personality is a basic range of perceptions that organise the client into routine ways of being** in the world. The 'me' or 'I' means not what others experience of me, but what I experience and accept as myself.

If I see myself as unworthy, when people interact with me, I will experience this judgemental reality even when the social signals contradict me. This forms part of my personality. If I see myself as loveable and essential to my friends and family, then I experience love in the social signals around me. This forms part of a different personality.

Person-centred theory states that the client's personality is an organised or common way of perceiving (and reacting to) events. **Values from the environment are fitted into the client's self-image, and they experience**

themself through those values. So being loveable or unlovable is a type of value. Being trustworthy or untrustworthy is another type of value. When mixed, like different colours in a paint tray, the personality emerges as a blend of values and experiences. Another name for this is the self-concept.

The Self-concept

The self-concept is the mental image a person constructs of themself. By interacting with others, we form beliefs, attitudes, values, habits, and self-knowledge. These things create a sense of self, and they colour how we perceive ourselves. **Each new experience brings a variety of possible responses**. We can perceive the experience and organise it into part of ourselves, like eating a slice of apple and tasting it before it becomes part of our body. Or, if we feel we belong, and we are invited to a dinner party, we experience this as confirming our self-image. We consume the dinner invitation into our being (symbolically!), and it is perceived and organised into our sense of self. On the other hand, if we have not achieved a sense of belonging, we experience the dinner invitation as pity or as forced. The invitation is organised into our sense of self, but this time of not belonging.

Experience confirms our self-concept repeatedly, by our taking on new experience as if it were old experience. A person without a sense of belonging could ignore the dinner invitation as if it didn't happen. A clinical example is where a client starts to feel accepted in therapy and suddenly connects with friends they ignored for years or starts an intimate relationship. The experience of being accepted was there for the taking, but the self-concept needed to change before the positive perception could be accepted.

This is like the situation where a child acquires a narrow range of acceptable foods. By about age two, most children are neophobes, meaning they struggle to accept new tastes and textures – leaving parents pulling teeth to find the right diet! Like their self-concept, they have a food-judging centre in which olives get a rejection letter while blueberries and yoghurt get a thumbs up. Over time the palate changes, when safely exposed to new experience, and children acquire tastes for previously unwelcome foods. When a food clashes with the palate, like when an experience contradicts the sense of self, the person rejects it, unless they are given slow and safe awareness of it over time.

People can flatly deny experience, too, if the experience conflicts with their sense of self. Denial means a client would swear in court that nobody values them. It's as pointless trying to convince the client of their worth as it is to force tomatoes on a sour-faced two-year-old. Non-directive person-centred therapy constantly returns experience back to the client, such that they become aware of their truer self. If they really are likeable, they will discover this during the process.

By denying experience, the client is thrust into psychological tension. They deny being likeable or deny being unlikeable, and in person-centred theory **the denial of experience makes a person experience anxiety, low mood, psychosis, and other forms of psychological alienation**. From the outside, we see their struggle and naturally want to send in the lifeboat. But the rescue mission fails because our actions only confirm their helplessness, and we reinforce the negative self-concept.

By hearing experience on playback, using the person-centred approach, the client adjusts to a fuller range of experience. In the therapeutic relationship the client's self-concept can change, particularly if unmet needs are attended to. It's like learning to read a new language. Beforehand, the squiggles on the page have no meaning. But overtime the lines transform into an alphabet with recognisable words and flowing sentences. Analogously, the client reads their life situation differently, like a new self-language. They learn to tolerate their unmet need for belonging or their unlikeable traits. They become better able to experience and relate to other people's experiences – and this starts to show in how they speak about the world and how they describe themselves. But **any perspective from the outside that contradicts the self-concept can be experienced as a threat**. Even well-intended praise can become uncomfortable. Saying "I am sure people like you" can be experienced as "I don't understand you" or, worse, as "people should like you, and if they don't, there's something wrong with you."

Threat is lower when the client doesn't feel the need to defend their self-image. Hence, the non-directive approach gets rid of the ordinary threats in conversation because the therapist is a present, non-judgemental, and accepting person. Therapy is not the only place where people revise themselves, but it lends itself to being effective by removing social obstacles like judgement, reassurance, ridicule, dismissiveness, panic, uncertainty, and frustration. **As the client accepts more of their experience, including being likeable and tolerable to others, their sense of self changes**. An important moment in therapy is when **the client begins to evaluate their beliefs and values for themselves, trusting themselves more, feeling more in touch and in control**

of their life. The client no longer requires therapy and **is healthy when they replace distorted values and experiences with genuine and accepted ones.**

Conditions of Worth

The previous two sections contained 19 assumptions about the development of the human personality, **highlighted in bold**. Rogers named these the 19 propositions that outline the humanistic theory of counselling. A healthy person is someone who can experience the fullness of life without creating a distorted or weak self-image.

Therapy clients perceive themselves in undermining ways. They believe they must fulfil social expectations to be valuable, or else be criticised. A distorted self-image isn't drawn from thin air. Environmentally, the distorted sense of self, which can work like a fun house mirror, displaying an enlarged, elongated, or confused self-reflection, is linked with the values people grow up around.

Carl Rogers referred to these expectations as conditions of worth. If a child must look after their parent's emotions, to be fed and comforted properly, the child learns that to look after other people is a condition of their worth. As an adult they avoid therapy and meeting their needs, feeling guilty about taking time out of work or burdening a therapist with their unworthy problems.

Conditions of worth are expectations people feel they must meet to be accepted, liked, or loved by others. They arise in the culture and in the family. For example, a female child might be more encouraged in the family to care for her parent's feelings. Cultural pressure comes from outside the family to bring up girls in this way, and the family raises children like this. But a parent with a self-image of being emotionally uncontainable will turn the notch of cultural pressure to the extreme and raise a child who is anxious to please everyone. Girls hiding anger, boys hiding upset, and so on, become cultural conditions of worth, which clients internalise.

A client once said to me that he was frustrated at his brother for frequently wanting to borrow money. Before I could pick up on the frustration, he covered it over by saying that it's probably for the best that his brother relies on him. Despite the client's frustration, his condition of worth, which is a feeling of having to be reliable, hid the frustration and caused him to reconsider another loan.

This type of emotional incongruence happens when people feel different from one of their conditions of worth. Being frustrated grates on the feeling of being reliable, and usually the condition of worth wins over. Clients work against their personal boundaries and feelings to meet a condition of worth.

External validation is vital for social survival. But if the person doing the validation is too needy, bossy, abusive, or uncontaining, external validation becomes tricky to achieve. The client's expectation of looking after others crystallises into a personality trait. Hence, person-centred therapy mirrors personality traits and accepts them alongside the frustration, allowing the client to experience themselves fully. Dimming down frustration is one way towards leading an anxious and restricted existence.

Carl Rogers said the relationship between the client and therapist is crucial for creating personality change. Being non-directive in a warm and accepting way is the route out of a distorted self-image. Positive psychology, self-belief, and determination happen organically through non-directive counselling. Rogers's three core conditions counterbalance the messy conditions of worth. At the start of this chapter, we named these as empathy, congruence, and unconditional positive regard. These core conditions change the personality, and they will be explored in the next chapter alongside some new ideas about psychological problems. But before we start our work in combining different therapy models, let's summarise the key points so far.

Summary

Person-centred therapy offers a way to understand human nature and the nature of presenting problems in psychotherapy. It views clients as people striving to fulfil their potential but challenged by physical, social, and emotional obstacles. Experience becomes hidden and confusing, and the person copes poorly by using anxiety, low mood, anger, and the full range of emotional extremes available to them. When experience is tuned into by a caring, present, congruent, empathic therapist, if given enough time, then experience is accepted. The person copes better with their troubles, and ultimately their experience becomes tolerable. Feeling safer, the person explores their potential for love, acceptance, or a career, and they reach higher states of life satisfaction. The therapist tries to be with the client, to sit in their experience, and to reflect what they hear, see, feel, and learn. The client's personality traits ultimately adjust towards being healthier, self-aware, and more positively fulfilling.

Further Reading

Faris, A. and Van Ooijen, E. (2012). *Integrative Counselling and Psychotherapy: A Textbook*. London: Routledge.

Huppert, F.A. (2009). Psychological well-being: evidence regarding its causes and consequences†. *Applied Psychology. Health and Well-Being* 1 (2): 137–164. https://doi.org/10.1111/j.1758-0854.2009.01008.x.

Kang, L. and Pendersen, N. (2017). *Quackery: A Brief History of the Worst Ways to Cure Everything*. New York: Workman Publishing.

Kelly, K. (2017). *Basic Counselling Skills: A Student Guide*. Warrington: Counselling Tutor.

Lapworth, P. and Sills, C. (2009). *Integration in Counselling & Psychotherapy: Developing a Personal Approach*. London: Sage.

Maslow, A.H. (1943). A theory of human motivation. *Psychological Review* 50 (4): 370–396.

Merry, T. (2014). *Learning and Being in Person-Centred Counselling, Ross on Wye*. PCCS Books.

Murphy, R. (2024). *A Systemic Approach to Integrative Counselling*. Abingdon: Routledge.

Norcross, J.C. and Lambert, M.J. (ed.) (2019). *Psychotherapy Relationships that Work: Evidence-Based Therapist Contributions*, 3e. Oxford University Press.

Pavot, W., Diener, E., Colvin, C.R., and Sandvik, E. (1991). Further validation of the Satisfaction with Life Scale: evidence for the cross-method convergence of well-being measures. *Journal of Personality Assessment* 57 (1): 149–161. https://doi.org/10.1207/s15327752jpa5701_17.

Rogers, C.R. (1951). *Client-Centered Therapy*. London: Constable.

Rogers, C. (1959). A theory of therapy, personality, and interpersonal relationships, as developed in the client-centered framework. In: *Psychology: A Study of a Science. Formulations of the Person and the Social Context*, vol. 3 (ed. S. Koch), 184–256. New York: McGraw Hill.

Russell, W., Breunlin, D., and Sahebi, B. (2022). *Integrative Systemic Therapy*. London: Routledge.

Sanders, P. (2003). *The Tribes of the Person-Centred Nation: A Guide to the Schools of Therapy Associated with the Person-Centred Approach*. PCCS Books.

Tudor, K. and Merry, T. (2006). *Dictionary of Person-Centred Psychology, Ross on Wye*. PCCS Books.

World Health Organization (2022). *Mental health: strengthening our response*. Geneva: World Health Organization https://www.who.int/news-room/fact-sheets/detail/mental-health-strengthening-our-response (accessed 8 October 2024).

2

Psychoanalysis

In the children's novel *Peter Pan*, the feeling of never growing up is the central fantasy. Being free from responsibility, looked after but not controlled, and taking more than one is expected to give appeals to people fearful of growing up. Dreaming of living in never-never land dissolves horrible feelings about ageing and ultimately about one's own death. Symbolically, the writer displaces unconscious wishes into creative activities – drawing and telling stories. In a similar vein, when traumatised children draw freely, without interruption, they depict horrific scenes of violence and slaughter. When presented with a toy scenario, like a child giraffe accidentally breaking a dinner plate, they play out scenes of abuse and domestic violence. Mum and dad giraffe shout and hurt the child giraffe, ending in disturbing conflict.

Storytelling, fantasy, and play reveal inner experience with supreme accuracy. People imagine fairies and rageful giraffes, but what they imagine alludes to a deeper unconscious process lurking behind the scenes. Reading the hidden meaning inside imaginings and creative behaviour involves interpretation. We translate the author's image of Peter Pan into their unconscious fear of growing up. It's why many film study experts and race analysts criticise White film directors like Quinten Tarantino for the gruelling racism enacted in their films. They translate the slavery-themes into unconscious White-supremacist motivations in filmmaking. Wanting to document progress in civil rights comes from a markedly different place than wanting to channel and enact fantasies of brutal racism. A film, a painting, or a five-year-old's proud fridge-drawing of their family unravels unconscious mental representations.

Integrative Person-Centred Counselling: The Combined Model of Counselling and Psychotherapy, First Edition. Rick Murphy.

Commonly the person is so unaware of their inner representational world that they forcefully deny its existence. In an article with Steve Rose in the *Guardian* newspaper, Quinten Tarantino says, "You wouldn't think the colour of a writer's skin should have any effect on the words themselves." The filmmaker sees no relevance of race to films about racism. Dubious inner drives from a script writer are denied as having no "effect on the words." A common unconscious tactic aside from denial is to project the forbidden inner world onto another person, as Tarantino does in this quotation: "As a writer, I demand the right to write any character in the world that I want to write. And to say that I can't do that because I'm white . . . **that is racist**."

Accusing someone of being racist for questioning a White person's fantasy of murdering and enslaving Black people is a primitive psychological defence. With abused children and counselling clients, this usually comes out in seeing the adult or therapist like an angry and abusive person (like how Tarantino sees racism in others and not himself). Unfortunately for the client, often the therapist starts to identify with the abusive persona and act abandoningly, dismissively, rejectingly, and angrily towards them. The client transfers unconscious assumptions onto the therapist who starts to identify with those characteristics.

Analysing the psychological themes in transference, storytelling, and everyday behaviour is the main feature of psychoanalysis. Strictly speaking, psychoanalysis is the examination of conscious and unconscious parts of the mind that bring hidden thoughts and feelings into awareness by making interpretations. The model of change is that uncovering buried thoughts and feelings stops the symptoms that result in the act of hiding them. Hence gaining insight into why someone has violent fantasies, why someone hides emotions, and why someone panics around strangers frees them from psychological problems.

Integrating Psychoanalysis

The main assumption in psychoanalysis is that unconscious thoughts, feelings, memories, and desires are critical to the client's presenting problem. In the previous chapter, we didn't pick up on this at all. We said that personality is a person's range of perceptions about the world, which causes them to act in habituated ways. We said that mental health is based on perceptions and obstacles to personal growth. How does the unconscious fit with this viewpoint? If humanism sees the client as aspiring to become better, isn't the theory of the destructive unconscious a contradictory view of personality?

Historically psychoanalysis and client-centred therapy have been separated by a steel fence. There is usually no route or communication between them, other than rumbling criticisms that vibrate from one side to the other. The psychoanalysts see therapists like scientists discovering the underside of an iceberg, probing the depths of the human mind. When one reaches into the unconscious, they pull out defence mechanisms, transferences, psychological needs, reality struggles, and authority phobias. Reflecting on these leads the client to discover inner motivations.

The humanists see things the other way around: the client is the expert and must teach the therapist how to perceive the world from their point of view. By experiencing love and safety, the client perceives the world as loving and safe. They invite more love and safety from their surroundings, thus maintaining their sense of self. This person would not need therapy. Without trust in others, however, the client leads the therapist through a different picture, a meandering, darkly lit roadmap. But in the process, they become more resilient to the gloominess and more trusting of their environment. The person-centred client is changed by leading the therapist, the psychoanalyst's client is changed by being led.

The person-centred camp sees psychoanalysis as losing its curiosity. Its pre-written human themes become facts. People are interpreted through a narrow set of specialised stories. And the stories give more power to the analyst than to the client. In the opposing psychoanalytical camp, person-centred therapy loses its knowledge and becomes overinvolved with the client. It risks projecting the emotions of the therapist onto the client and neglects to study the client's issues in relation to the past.

Teaching an integrative counselling course, an experienced trainee, Shamaila Nura, recently said to me, "I'm a dogmatic person-centred therapist" (she allowed me to use this in the book). What she was struggling with was how to remain sturdy in a person-centred way of working when taking on new ideas like those from psychoanalysis. If we broke down the steel wall that separates these ideas, would they end up destroying each other?

My request to Shamaila was for her to take from each counselling idea anything of value to her work. The theories for how to integrate between counselling ideas tend to imply that taking some part of one model and some part of another model, stitching them together, is theoretically okay. And I agree. We needn't treat psychotherapy theories like warring parents, taking one side at the expense of the other. It is okay to choose between approaches in different situations. I might go to a person-centred mum when I want to offload. To a cognitive dad when I want to process my behaviour. To a mindful sister when I want some chill-out time. And sometimes I want to be on my own and think for myself. In the therapeutic family of ideas, I choose my own relationships. I think anybody who struggles to make peace between counselling ideas is struggling psychologically, not rationally.

Theories of integration date back to the beginning of psychotherapy. Freud integrated neurology and hypnosis into a psychology of the mind. Rogers integrated humanism and phenomenology into a psychology of the self. Psychotherapies are built from earlier fragments that are practical and philosophical in nature. In the 1970s, psychiatrist Thomas Stephen Szasz warned against integrating different psychotherapy models. He called integrative therapists 'role-players' who want to be 'all things to all people' but are 'nothing' to themselves. Ouch! He intended on addressing a very real concern that integrative therapists become disorganised and chaotic – something important to avoid.

But these criticisms were about eclecticism in the 1960s, not really *integration* – that is, a concern for being inconsistent in the way counsellors work with clients. The eclecticism movement was one attempt to explain the fact that many therapists use a range of therapeutic ideas in their practice, not solely one model, and successfully. There must be some sense to this widespread phenomenon. Szasz was deeply affected by mental health hospitals, which were behaving more like prisons than care homes. His most famous book was called *The Myth of Mental Illness* – an attempt to transform psychiatry into a kinder, more humane institution. His criticism was that therapists who take their counselling menu à la carte might not have the strong foundations for helping clients. Though his criticisms turned out to be worthy of note, they didn't address the true ideas and benefits of integration.

Integrative models are varied. Some take principles from different psychotherapies and combine them into a single approach. For example, Clara Hill, a professor of psychology, describes a three-stage integrative model. First the counsellor explores the client's issues, then together they analyse the issues, and finally they work on taking actions to overcome the issues. In Hill's model, humanistic counselling is followed by psychoanalytic counselling, and then behavioural counselling. That is, therapies are integrated by seeing them as a series of steps in a whole counselling approach.

Other models integrate different psychotherapy approaches in the moment-to-moment therapy rather than in stages. For example, a different professor of psychology, Arnold Lazarus, set forward an integrative model called multimodal therapy. Here the therapist sees psychotherapy like a unified whole, with the client's full self, including their behaviour, emotions, physical health, sensations, diet, imagination, thinking, and social relationships, worked on together. As a result, therapy is thought of in the broadest terms and may include physiotherapy, psychotherapy, cognitive therapy, medication, and lifestyle therapy.

Another relevant example of merging therapy ideas into one approach is Richard Worsley's primer on integrative counselling. In it he intuitively shows how to think about counselling modalities from a person-centred point of view. There is no core theory of integration, but an engaging collection of psychotherapy models viewed through a person-centred lens.

But another way to understand integration is possible. The family therapist and systemic theorist John Burnham suggests separating the theory from the technique and either changing the technique or the theory to create an integration. Though simple to understand, this approach has profound implications for integrative psychotherapy. It makes it possible to construct a theory-and-practice-informed integrative person-centred counselling. Using psychoanalysis and person-centred approaches, Burnham's model gives us two options. One is to use analytical ideas and the skills of a person-centred therapist. The other is to use the ideas of the person-centred therapist and the skills of the analyst. I suggest a third way, and that is translating one theory into the language of the other theory. We will leave that third step for a future chapter.

Integration as Multi-description

In the previous section, I referred to the person-centred counselling primer. In it the author says, "I am not interested in tools, or tricks of the trade. I want nothing to do with therapy by protocol" (Worsley 2007, p. 54). I think it's a mistake to dismiss the relationship between theory and practice highlighted so elegantly by Burnham. Carl Rogers himself was sceptical of teaching techniques. This was because he experimented with teaching trainees how to use skills and found his trainees lacked a core humanistic presence. They were more like automatons paraphrasing and summarising clients' words devoid of any obvious human empathy. Rather humblingly, automatons have been shown in a recent German study by Martin Kocur and colleagues to be effective with changing negative beliefs of depressed clients . . . so maybe we shouldn't assume automatons are untherapeutic!

The point is that the practice of psychotherapy is primarily shown through technique. What is empathy without mirroring or meaningful shifts in voice tone? What is listening without actively repeating your understanding of the client? How would you show congruence other than through the technique of reflection, use of self, or showing acceptance? Though we talk about theory separately from practice, they are as one. Practice is theory in motion.

To explore how theory always implies practice (and vice versa), let's take an example from Richard Worsley, the author of the person-centred primer discussed earlier. Working with a client named Helen, exploring feelings of stupidity when she fears her manager Gerald, Worsley (2007, pp. 94–96) suggests, "you look quite scared when thinking about Gerald." Helen replies, "Do I? That feels silly."

If it were true that techniques were not coming into play, we could imagine a response that would not be an act of theory or skill. Consider how you would respond to the client's statement "Do I? That feels quite silly?" We could pick up on the client's "Do I" and explore whether the client does indeed feel scared (considering 'scared' was the author's word, not hers). This would involve the technique of self-reflection and open questioning. Also, we could decide to notice that looking scared feels quite silly to Helen. This would be a restatement skill. We could take the whole sentence and paraphrase it – another skill. And each of these microskills neatly attaches to a theory of reflecting the client's experience, to enhance it: a person-centred theory.

Now let's take a look at how Worsley himself responds after Helen says it feels silly to look scared:

Richard: Helen, I wonder if you can just let yourself feel how it is to be scared of Gerald. Where do you feel the scaredness?

Helen: Right here. In my throat. It's like a stone stuck there. I can't speak for it.

Richard: When you feel scared, it's like you can't speak. Your throat feels tight, so tight.

My sense is that rarely would the reader have chosen the same pathway as Worsley here. Not that the direction he takes is problematic, it seems entirely supportive of the client. The point to grasp is that in actively making a choice, by the very action of choosing, we employ certain techniques that divulge our theoretical orientation. The statement, "I wonder if you can just let yourself feel the scaredness," implies that scaredness exists and that Helen is censoring her feelings: silliness covers fear like laughter covers insecurity. This is partly a psychoanalytic statement because it alludes to unconscious decision-making, an interpretation like "you are not letting yourself feel your feelings." His following question, "Where do you feel the scaredness?", implies that locating feelings in the body is useful for the client's self-awareness. This is a phenomenological question. Worsley's next response, "When you feel scared, it's like you can't speak," is a person-centred restatement; it is the skill of active listening.

In the model of psychotherapy that I am slowly building, I want to accept the concern that some therapists have about the use of empty, showy, and gimmicky techniques. But techniques are a foundation of psychotherapy that distinguishes us from the ordinary listener, the kind friend, and the reassuring partner. We develop theory-informed skills, and I think becoming aware of, and practising, these skills is essential to therapy. Hence the aforementioned author uses multiple theory-informed skills despite not being interested in the "tricks of the trade."

Integrating between therapy models, as we have seen in the earlier example, is inevitable. We merge ideas together or we take a technique from one model and make it fit with the ideas of another model. This will become the most important theme in the book.

Wish Fulfilment

I am hoping to have convinced you of the importance of psychotherapeutic techniques. Sceptics of therapy techniques arose, quite rightly, from the illustrious history of psychoanalytic therapy. The early techniques of psychoanalysis were built from the position that clients were unaware of their unconscious selves. The analyst's job was to evoke the unconscious feeling and memories by using a blank face, or sometimes a couch for clients to lie on, to avoid responding emotionally to the client. The thinking was that reassurance and emotion would sooth the client's unconscious fears artificially and not lead to fundamental insight.

Thus, analytic therapy developed a reputation for being cold and detached. Subsequent experiments with secure young children showed that when a parent intentionally stops responding, the child becomes achingly distressed. A healthy child tries to reach out to the parent or tries to make them laugh. The child resorts to minor whimpers and confusion, but ultimately, they cry desperately for a response. A speed bump in the psychoanalytic tradition was that instead of viewing the therapist as part of the distress, the many thousands of patients who rejected this form of treatment were interpreted in the form of resistance. That is, psychoanalytical thinking struggled to learn and grow as a school of thought. Person-centred therapy was one of a variety of therapies that rejected the psychoanalytic blank screen for a more relationship-based approach.

Using integration, we address the psychoanalytic way of thinking that leads to therapy as a form of all-knowing authority, one in which the therapist becomes absent from the relationship. Unconscious interpretations can be rejected by the interpretant, often experienced like a hostile takeover. If we take a detour into the skills and techniques of the person-centred therapist, we can return to this way of thinking with a more open and empathic therapy approach. Person-centred therapy takes a position on the far end of the relationship spectrum, by rejecting interpretation as a practice. In the following section, I will attempt to show the reader how we can take a middle road between the two positions, being empathic yet knowledgeable and tentatively interpretative therapists. In fact, I will go further and suggest we cannot *not* interpret – we always interpret.

I want to go back and pick up the conversation about symbolism. Earlier we said that psychoanalysis interprets behaviour and thought as representing, that is, as symbolising, conscious and unconscious needs. Anything the client says or does has its origin in basic biological and psychological needs. These are similar to Maslow's hierarchy of needs, starting with the most basic survival needs like food, comfort, and shelter. A client who reports to us a behaviour, a thought, or even a dream, invites us into their symbolic world – their inner representations. Psychoanalysis says that the client symbolises their unmet needs through behaviour and fantasy. A research study in Canada corroborated this by showing that children who experience violence create stories with less safety, less care, and less resolution to conflict. Childhood unmet needs continue to try and be resolved through fantasy – by 'playing out' the need.

Dreams are interesting examples. Sigmund Freud, to his 'great astonishment', discovered that psychoanalysis translates dreams as though they were ordinary thoughts. He noticed that when a client tells a dream, and speaks their thoughts without interruption, a chain of associations is made that reveals unconscious desires. So significant was this finding that Freud declared dreams the "royal road to the unconscious." A dream, like any other mental activity, tries to achieve a goal, which he called a wish fulfilment.

In one example, Freud dreamed that his declining and seemingly untreatable patient was prescribed hazardous medicine by another doctor, thus unconsciously he wished for a world where he was not responsible for his client's poor condition. His dream of being a good doctor was fulfilled. Another example is dreaming of going to the toilet when needing to urinate in the night. Less clear are those dreams in which we are hurt, hunted, or even murdered. Freud theorised that nightmares and anxiety dreams fit his theory by virtue of the anxiety-provoking situation distorting the underlying wish.

It's simple to see that a daydream or fantasy is an example of wish fulfilment, even when it involves violence. People who are bullied daydream of humiliating bullies. People walking late at night fantasise about uppercutting a mugger or head-locking a wild tiger. For an imaginary moment, the wish for safety or revenge is granted. An international study headed by Rachele Mariani demonstrated that people with traumatic histories use imagination more to cope with reality. Their study found that people fantasise to defend against experiencing troubling emotions, at the unconscious level. I think the wish-fulfilment of daydreaming is quite intuitive, but what about dreaming of scenes that pose serious risks to the self?

Dream Interpretation

In *The Interpretation of Dreams*, Freud is challenged by a lady at dinner. She accosts him with an anxiety dream where she tries but fails to make a meal for her family and friends. Obviously wanting to host the meal, she presents a contradiction to Freud. After some free association, the process of listing thoughts without interruption, a chain of relevant associations is revealed.

Interestingly, the previous day, the woman's husband began treatment for obesity. After some careful analysis, it's clear that part of the wish in the dream is a wish to prevent herself from overfeeding her husband.

Psychoanalysis says that a person has instincts like hosting meals (being accepted socially) and eating, but these instincts meet a reality, such as the reality of too much eating leading to weight gain. A person becomes psychologically unhealthy when their needs clash harshly with reality.

Defences kick in, like fulfilling wishes by dreaming, writing literature, or denying aspects of experience. Learning about the unconscious mind can make us more self-aware and adjusted. This now starts to take us far away from anything we discussed in humanistic counselling. Although there is plenty more to cover about psychoanalysis, I want to pause here and integrate.

Integration means taking the idea or the technique of one counselling model and merging it with the idea or technique of another. Once the main counselling and psychotherapy models are sufficiently mixed in with humanistic counselling, we have an integrated person-centred model of counselling.

A client's presenting issue, so far in psychoanalysis, can be broken down into a theory of conflict between the conscious and unconscious mind, uncovered via the technique of free association (Table 2.1). Think of the conflict between the desire to host a dinner and the desire to support a husband's health.

Person-centred therapy, on the other hand, breaks down the client's presenting issue into a humanistic theory of basic needs, belonging, and self-actualisation, reached via the use of empathy, congruence, and unconditional positive regard.

To integrate psychoanalysis into person-centred therapy, we take its theory or its technique, and use or understand it humanistically. How would that look with a client's dream? Should we take on psychoanalytic theory or technique? (And just a reminder that we have a third option, to be explored later).

Table 2.1 Two Counselling Theories

Model	Theory	Technique
Psychoanalytic	The mind is made up of unconscious basic needs, the reality of the world, and the conscious and unconscious rules that govern the individual. When unconscious needs, reality, and inner rules conflict, the client becomes mentally unwell.	Free association
Person Centred	Humans strive to reach their potential and to self-actualise. Obstacles to self-actualisation cause incongruence and diminished experiences.	Active listening, open questions, paraphrasing, restatements

Free Association

For now, imagine a client has dreamt they are alone on the top floor of an unfamiliar multi-story house. They can sense "something weird is happening." A large and frightening cluster of zombies close in on them. Scared to fight, the client tries to phone a family friend but there is no signal. The zombies continue closing in, slowly, and they sing a song that the client interprets as "they have the power, and they know it."

Free association is one psychoanalytic technique that we can use humanistically with this dream. In short, free association is the practice of encouraging the client to speak without censorship, need to explain, or concern for coherence. The client is asked to talk about the chain of thoughts and associations they have with each of the dream elements. We needn't direct the client too much, but when they organically bring up a dream, we ask openly about the first few things that come to mind.

The first element of the dream is the image of being alone on top of a tall unknown house. The client's free associations begin with, "The house is something you see in a horror movie . . . This feels eerie . . .. Why isn't my husband here?"

Psychoanalysis explores the themes from the associations using the client's words. For instance, here the client connects her husband being away with eeriness and the fearful isolation depicted in horror movies. In fact, the real person who had this dream, when reflecting on this chapter, said her husband was away from home as he is in the Royal Marines.

Though we are discovering some important things, we have hit a stumbling block. In this short sequence, we begin to stray from person-centred therapy. We directed the client towards an activity and attempted to create a meaning from it. Free association probably does not fit the humanistic philosophy of being non-directive. Criticisms of free association techniques are concerned with the pressure a client experiences to make meaningful links between random associations, being led by the therapist's authority.

But being non-directive is in my view an impossibility. Or at least it cannot be the guiding theory of person-centred therapy, but a technique. This is because direction is constantly being given by the presence, response, statement, and question of the therapist. Some authors move to the extreme and argue that counsellors should not ask questions. This only masks the therapist's influence.

I would go as far as to say that the early Freudian idea of the blank screen is more non-directive than the humanistic approach. Ironically, this was

Freud's problem with relationship-based psychotherapies. We parachute the therapist's personality and needs into the therapy room, masking with empathy and understanding an otherwise insightful self-discovery. I am not going to defend either view but will claim that non-directivity is an illusion. Every aspect of psychotherapy positions the client in some way. Free association is the psychoanalytic way of removing the muddying influence of the therapist. By removing the therapist as a person, the client's unconscious processes are more visible.

For this reason, in the integrative person-centred model, we relegate non-directiveness to the status of a technique, not an overarching philosophy. With this in mind, we can rewind time to reconsider free association and dreamwork as a resource in humanistic counselling. For a person-centred analysis, we would take each dream element and openly encourage the client to free associate. For example, we use open questioning about the dream to create psychological insight. In doing so, unconscious conflicts and desires are brought to the surface. What we want to avoid in our model is becoming an all-seeing superpower who tries to teach the client how to interpret their experience. We ask the client openly about the elements of their dream. We treat working with symbolism no differently from working with any behaviour or experience.

We explore the next dream element as an open free-association question:

Rick: What are the first few thoughts or images that come to mind when you recall your statement, 'I can sense something weird is happening'?

Client: My mind is blank . . . Let me pause and think for a minute. Oh, I just got a flash of something that happened before and feel a bit of nausea. Wow. This is probably a bit too deep for me . . ..

Using a person-centred empathic response, we repeat back those significant utterances we have heard, "a memory came flashing back," "you felt sick," and "it took you somewhere that felt too much for right now." As the client explored the first dream images, she became connected with otherwise-unspoken and deeply troubling memories. These were disturbing and traumatic memories from childhood. Person-centred analysis is not an oxymoron. It means to view symbolism, dreams, and behaviour as having some unconscious component, which the client can make meaning from. Our integrative model uses this lens to bring the unconscious wishes, needs, and experiences into the therapy. Otherwise, we ignore a wealth of useful information.

After working on the dream images, treating each one like mini-experiences from a person-centred toolbox, the client started to rethink the dream's meaning, and this had significance for her self-concept. This is what she said next:

> At first, I thought the zombies were a threat, but now they're kind of singing to me, as a sign of safety, telling me they're not going to hurt me. It's like they're a protection, letting me know I'm safe.

In response, I offered a psychoanalytic idea, but as a curious open question:

Rick: Some people see dreams as fulfilling certain wishes, maybe wishes that are under the surface. Do you have any thoughts about this idea and your dream?

Client: Yeah, I think it is like me, where I see the world as hostile towards me . . . Even if it's safe. My husband says I attack myself. Like the zombies . . . they aren't attacking me. The dream wishes me to feel safer, like I'm not under siege all the time. Even though it feels like I am.

Psychoanalysis is taking place here but in a way that centres on the person's unique meaning making. I have included the Freudian idea in my open and curious question, having no sense of where the client would lead me. My purpose is not to direct her, and I am not analysing her dream for its objective meaning, which is stereotypically where humanism departs from psychoanalysis.

The integrative person-centred model takes two concepts from psychoanalysis, which are unconscious wish fulfilments in dreams and the idea that insight into unconscious needs creates change. Once I have taken those two elements, I humanise them by working in the present, subjective experience of the client. Though psychoanalysis talks in scientific, objectifying language, I think it does fit with the subjective theory in person-centred work. The model is more biological than psychological because it focuses on concepts like 'instinct' and 'drive'. However, in *The Interpretation of Dreams*, Freud, contrary to what many people think, says that meaning is created through the client's subjective experience.

The technique level, now we have unchained our need to be completely non-directive, is recognisably person centred. The dream framework is slightly directive, encouraging the counsellor to work on a dream; to explore meaning, fears, and wishes; to work on the content of the dream as a symbol for hidden psychological meanings; and to empathically assist the client in becoming more self-aware. But here the client makes a discovery, "My world is safer than I experience it to be," and this is a common person-centred outcome, where the client feels more agency in their situation. The early trauma causes her to live in a more hostile world than is true. The insight from this dream was a powerful moment – a way to rewrite her self-concept as someone who now lives in a safer world. The humanistic research is clear: when someone finds hope they problem-solve better and are more able to reach their potential.

Psychoanalysis as an Emotional Process

So far, I have attempted to demystify the psychoanalysis of dreams for the integrative person-centred reader. Further than this, I have implied how psychoanalysing any symbolic aspect of a person's life, including their behaviour, thoughts, feelings, interpretations, fashion, creative outlets, relationship patterns, writing, fantasies, and dreams can bring a client closer to awareness and self-discovery. The person-centred model misses an understanding of symbolism, of meaning, and of unconscious process.

One important thing I have not discussed is how modern science has scanned the sleeping brain and uncovered some fascinating findings pertinent to our discussion. The science of dreams, which is called oneirology, tells us the purpose and effects of sleep. The findings from dream studies are that dreams support emotional processing by encoding emotional memories deep in the brain's hippocampus. The images are not real events, but the emotional process is real, and this gives some credit to the psychoanalytic idea that dream images are symbols for unconscious thoughts and feelings, not specific memories. By developing a story, like an old photographer develops a film, our sleeping brain takes emotions from experience to form lasting memories.

If emotions go unprocessed, negative emotions and anxiety increase. The specific psychic material in the dream, the drama, the obscurity, is therefore a therapist's area of concern. Integrating dreamwork into person-centred therapy can help clients process unexpressed emotions. That is to say that what the dream means to the client in the moment is personal and unique. We use the experience of the dream like any other experience. We see a zombie in a dream like any phenomenon, and work in the present experience to encourage shifts in perspective. It is psychoanalytical in the sense that we are transparent with the client that fantasies, behaviours, and thoughts are the tip of a psychological iceberg. The emotional and perspectival depths are revealed when we probe beneath the surface.

The Freudian Mind

Our integration between psychoanalysis and humanism is that the unconscious mental life is not a fixed structure but a subjective 'potential' experience in the present moment. It isn't a potential experience in traditional person-centred therapy because there is no model of the unconscious. In the integrative model, we use psychoanalytical frames to interview clients, prioritising their sensemaking and experience. When Freud discusses survival needs, which he termed the *id*, our humanistic techniques take this frame and work with it. "What is the need beneath that feeling?" The next area of the mind to develop, the *ego*, can be worked with, too. This is the mostly conscious part of the mind that must face reality. When reality conflicts with basic needs, then psychological issues come about. If a client needs safety but her reality is hostile, she may dream of singing zombies. Or when a client cannot tolerate the reality of delayed gratification, they may demand more time and energy from the therapist and forget to pay the fees. Strictly speaking these are interpretations of a psychoanalytical kind, but the usage one makes as a person-centred therapist is in seeing these as frames for questions and curiosities. We aren't verbally psychoanalysing the client, but are opening space for psychoanalytical insight.

Freud models the client's presenting issues as stemming from a psychological battle, whereas Rogers models the client as in a state of incongruence. We could say that Freud's model of the battle suits his conflictual mental representation of the world. Rogers, too, has a mental representation of people in need – something personal to him. The underlying argument in both systems of thought is that people have needs that go unmet. Rogers saw the way out as tuning into present experience. Freud suggested another route, to notice how people symbolise the need through fantasy and behaviour. This unconscious process, of turning a need like a wish to never die into an image like Peter Pan, is not picked up in humanism but is integrated into our model. While we have started to scrape the surface, we will move a little further into the psychoanalytical way of thinking by considering how to work with defence mechanisms. Before this, let us summarise the key points so far.

Summary

This chapter has worked on the philosophy that, in counselling, it is not always the idea that is good or bad, but how the idea is used. In counselling, the 'used' part refers to what the therapist does in the room with the client. Therefore, the usefulness of a psychotherapy model is linked with how its theory is shown in therapeutic practice. Because some people use an idea in a detrimental way does not mean the idea is harmful. Marxism, which criticises capitalism as the cause of poverty and social injustice, has been used to justify the poverty and social injustice of dictatorships in countries like Romania and North Korea. What happens generally is the techniques involved in 'doing' the ideology, such as installing a dictatorship or blank-screening a client, end up undermining the ideology in the first place. In the same way, there are times when the ideology of humanism leads to avoiding obvious unconscious impulses and symbolic expression, something we have tried to include in our approach. Modelling the unconscious in our psychotherapy theory draws attention to important perspectives on the client's presenting issues. Psychoanalysis offers the integrative therapist a way of peering behind the surface behaviour, feeling, or fantasy, knowing that what is found can help the client reach psychological health.

Further Reading

Bischof, M. and Bassetti, C.L. (2004). Total dream loss: a distinct neuropsychological dysfunction after bilateral PCA stroke. *Annals of Neurology* 56: 583–586. https://doi.org/10.1002/ana.20246.

Farnfield, S. (2014). From preschool to school age: narrative story stems. In: *The Routledge Handbook of Attachment: Assessment* (ed. S. Farnfield and P. Holmes), 81–101. London: Routledge/Taylor & Francis Group.

Freud, S. (1913). *The Interpretation of Dreams*. London: MacMillan Co.

Freud, S. (2005). *The Essentials of Psycho-Analysis*. New York: Vintage Classics.

Gosselt, J., Van Hoof, J., Gent, B., and Fox, J. (2015). Violent frames: analyzing internet movie database reviewers' text descriptions of media violence and gender differences from 39 years of U.S. action, thriller, crime, and adventure movies. *International Journal of Communication* 9 (2015): 547–567.

Hill, C. (2009). *Helping Skills in Practice: A Three-Stage Model*. American Psychological Association [DVD].

Kiley, D. (1997). *The Peter Pan Syndrome: Men Who Have Never Grown Up*. New York: Dodd, Mead & Co.

Kocur, M., Dechant, M., Wolff, C. et al. (2021). Computer-assisted avatar-based treatment for dysfunctional beliefs in depressive inpatients: a pilot study. *Frontiers in Psychiatry* 12: https://doi.org/10.3389/fpsyt.2021.608997.

Langevin, R., Cossette, L., and Hébert, M. (2019). Emotion dysregulation in sexually abused preschoolers: insights from a story completion task. *Journal of Child Sexual Abuse* 29 (4): 468–489. https://doi.org/10.1080/10538712.2019.1678542.

Lapworth, P. and Sills, C. (2009). *Integration in Counselling & Psychotherapy*. London: Sage.

Lazarus, A.A. (1989). *The Practice of Multimodal Therapy*. Baltimore, MD: Johns Hopkins University Press.

Leichsenring, F., Hiller, W., Weissberg, M., and Leibing, E. (2006). Cognitive-behavioral therapy and psychodynamic psychotherapy: techniques, efficacy, and indications. *American Journal of Psychotherapy* 60 (3): 233–259.

Mariani, R., Musetti, A., Di Monte, C. et al. (2021). Maladaptive daydreaming in relation to linguistic features and attachment style. *International Journal of Environmental Research and Public Health* 19 (1): 386. https://doi.org/10.3390/ijerph19010386. PMID: 35010644; PMCID: PMC8751151.

Marzano, C., Ferrara, M., Mauro, F. et al. (2011). Recalling and forgetting dreams: theta and alpha oscillations during sleep predict subsequent dream recall. *Journal of Neuroscience* 31 (18): 6674–6683. https://doi.org/10.1523/JNEUROSCI.0412-11.2011.

Rose, S. (2015). The Quentin Tarantino race debate isn't black and white. *The Guardian* (22 October). https://www.theguardian.com/film/2015/oct/13/tarantino-race-debate-isnt-black-and-white (accessed 21 April 2025).

Tronick, E. (2003). Things still to be done on the still-face effect. *Infancy* 4: 475–482.

Worsley, R. (2007). *The Integrative Counselling Primer*. Monmouth: PCCS Books Ltd.

Wright, J.H., Owen, J., Eells, T.D. et al. (2022). Effect of computer-assisted cognitive behaviour therapy vs usual care on depression among adults in primary care: a randomized clinical trial. *JAMA Network Open* 5 (2): e2146716. https://doi.org/10.1001/jamanetworkopen.2021.46716.

3

Defence Mechanisms

Psychoanalysis models the client's presenting problem as a conflict between biological needs, reality, and an internal judge. This unconscious conflict causes people to hide their needs, ignore reality, and be consumed by guilt. Person-centred counselling gets around these issues by remaining present in the client's experience. Overtime the person is less defensive, more aware of their needs, and no longer so self-critical. Psychoanalysis is sometimes called psychodynamic therapy because it analyses the dynamics of the mind – the psychodynamics of needs, reality, and self-judgement. I think this model offers support for the person-centred model, helping the therapist centre on the client while being alert to unconscious conflicts.

In this chapter, we hold a conversation between these ideas, using two case examples. The aim is to mine psychoanalysis further than in the previous chapter, to show how concepts like the unconscious mind, transference, and defence mechanisms can be integrated into the person-centred counselling model.

The Stages of Process

Person-centred theory says that psychological development happens when the client moves from lacking autonomy to being more in control. This is done via a sequence of seven stages. The client may be more open and further down the stages on one visit to counselling, yet more closed off and lacking control in another. The stages are fluid and are defined in Table 3.1.

Integrative Person-Centred Counselling: The Combined Model of Counselling and Psychotherapy, First Edition. Rick Murphy.

Table 3.1 The Seven Stages of Process

Stage	Description
Stage 1	Rigidly closed off from feelings and blames others for their difficulties.
Stage 2	Slightly less rigid about feelings and can question their responsibility. Continues to view others as primarily responsible for their issues.
Stage 3	Accepts some responsibility for self but focuses more on the past rather than the present experience.
Stage 4	Describes feelings in the moment but tends to criticise or shutdown their feelings.
Stage 5	More clarity in their experience, accepting responsibility, being prepared to take action.
Stage 6	Sees growth and purpose as a result of gaining responsibility and clarity from experience. More care and love for self.
Stage 7	A secure self develops, open to changes and challenges, someone who accepts themselves and their situation.

Review the stages of process and see if you can tell roughly where a client is based on a session transcript. The client is consulting me for anxiety work, and she says, "I'm quite quiet, and I don't really speak to a lot of people. Having to approach people kind of scares me."

I say, in a non-directive way, "You're a quiet person, and having to speak to people feels scary?"

She replies, "Yeah. I'm afraid they might judge me .... Maybe make fun of me? And obviously I don't want that to happen. I think I'm more quiet because I want to avoid that sort of thing."

Although brief, the interaction demonstrates some fluidity between the stages of process set out in Table 3.1. The client describes her feelings in the moment and takes responsibility for her actions. She says, "I don't really speak to a lot of people. Having to approach people kind of scares me." She doesn't shut down her experience, but also does not consider taking action. For this reason, the client moves between stage four and five of Table 3.1.

The stages of process is a good model to highlight when a change occurs in the client's ability to experience and be self-directed. The transcript from later in the session shows this. Rather quickly, within about five minutes, she shows growth from her anxiety, showing more self-care and appreciation:

> My friends usually tell me that I'm more sociable than I think I am, and that motivates me to try harder.

Drawing from positive psychology, which is about nurturing strengths and positive emotions, I ask, "What are your friends seeing, when they describe you as more sociable?" The client says:

> I mean … a better version of myself. You know, a more confident, brave, happy, version of me, which I know I am, really. I found, if I tell myself I can do something, then I usually can.

Here the client imagines how her friends see her. As a result, she shows more willingness to 'try harder', which reinforces her positive traits. This is a movement towards stage five and six of Table 3.1 because she takes more responsibility. The stages of process are not finished here, but when therapy is nearer the end, we anticipate the client to be further down the stages for longer periods of time.

In this person-centred way of working, it is common for therapy clients to move towards self-improvement when we appreciate their words and value their perspectives. We restate, paraphrase, and show curiosity towards them, and they strengthen psychologically.

Technique Is Not a Dirty Word

Before we move onto a more complex example, and one that I think justifies integrating psychodynamic ideas, I want to reflect on the skills being used here. Listening to this example during a training session, a person-centred counsellor said she had always learned that "technique is a dirty word." My emphasis on techniques like paraphrasing and reflective listening felt incongruent for her.

For me, technique means the 'doing' and the action in therapy. Theory is how we think about what we do, but the physical activity in counselling is shown by technique. Some colleagues experience the intentional act as manipulative, as though the textbook always leads to robotic, unnatural therapy. But my experience challenges this, and I find that technique often brings me into better contact with the client than does my initial feeling.

I use techniques intentionally when something about me might interrupt the flow of the therapy. Sometimes I notice myself trying to persuade or rescue the client. In this case, I focus on technique. A triathlete friend of mine, when I was struggling with the most basic uphill jog, gave me some excellent advice. She said when she gets tired of running, she focuses away from the tiredness onto the running technique. By tuning into the form of running, how accurately the foot swipes the floor, or how steadily the posture carries the movement, she increases her ability to run. Being in the tiredness increases the tiredness and prevents progress, but focusing on technique reenergises her.

I think, in an unintended way, my friend highlighted an unspoken contradiction in Carl Rogers' core conditions, a friction between congruence and unconditional positive regard. We cannot always be congruent or honest with the client and non-judgemental at the same time. Often, we do judge them and feel the urge to take away their autonomy with advice. When I heard the client worry if people disliked her, I felt like saving her from the negative emotion: "Who cares what they think, you're great!" But rescuing her from the insecurity would have probably been unhelpful.

What helped me here was technique. When the client says, "I'm scared they might judge me … make fun of me," it is the technique of reflecting the client's anxiety that keeps me congruent with person-centred values, showing positive regard for the client. Once my internal rescuing feelings are attended to via the technique, I am more emotionally congruent with her, able to sit with and accept her anxiety.

Clients with Greater Complexity

Not all clients attend therapy at rung five on the stages of process (see Table 3.1), with insight into their experience. Critics of person-centred therapy question how appropriate the unstructured and optimistic model is with complex mental health and trauma. The theory that human beings are naturally good is contradicted by the disturbing actions of some clients, those who actively resist, reject, demonise, and taunt the therapist. I think person-centred theory and practice can respond to these concerns. But before we discuss that, I think it's possible to take both positions seriously, by integrating the concept of defence mechanisms into our person-centred model.

What do we do when a client struggles to connect with their experience? How do we respond when a client circles around their mind without being present in the room? Let's review some transcript to explore this.

In this scenario, I ask a client how it is to separate from her mother, as a young adult, in her first week at university. She says:

> We're kind of just keeping it very platonic, in a way …. I don't even know if I'm using this word right …. Like, I acknowledge she's my mum, but it ends there.

I respond by using the restating technique with her last line of dialogue, "You acknowledge she's your mum, but …." She continues, "But I'm just keeping it at a very normal point; I'm not doing anything about it."

I ask, "How is that for you?" and she replies, "I don't mind too much, to be honest. I have my little support system …. And I might be even flying to Spain soon. Yeah, because, tickets in this season are very cheap. It's literally cheaper to fly to Spain than to Northampton!"

The client in this interaction attends counselling due to symptoms of anxiety disorder and panic disorder. My attempts to empathise with her separation experience fall flat. I use the same two techniques as with the first client: I restate her sentence and ask an experience-based question. But her response is very different from the previous client.

Rogers' evaluates the client as occupying rung one, two, or three on the stages of process because the client is closed off from experience. Of course, one short example is unconvincing, so let's keep going in the conversation.

(2–3 minutes later …)

I ask, "Have you had a chance to speak with anyone about moving to university?" The client says, "Yes, the other night when I was feeling lonely, my sister was the one to tell me everything's going to be fine. And she said she was in the same position five years ago. I'm way more social than she is, and she took ages to find any friends at all. So, for her, it was even harder than for me. Plus, she's anti-social, and she does not like making new friends or having new people in her life. Although sometimes she knows she needs it …."

Here the client connects with her sister's experience, but her experience remains foggy. I try and centre back on the client using a summarising technique, choosing to summarise the empathic parts of the story: "So she thought it might be difficult for you, and she could understand why it's difficult when you're on your own …." The client said, "Yeah, even when she moved, she … like … very much struggled. Me, it's only been a week and I've made some connections. With her, that didn't happen for a couple of months, which is way slower than me."

The client is very much engaging in therapy, but her connection with her sister's struggle is greater than her connection with her own struggle. A route for the person-centred therapist is to keep being open and reflective of the fragments of experience that come through and build on them over time – to relate to the client and be present with her. Over time, the client will find more clarity and begin to use experience as a way of growing.

Instead, I invite reflection on the process, but am congruently using myself and not labelling her. I draw attention to the way she moves her feelings from awareness:

Rick: You've mentioned loneliness and you've mentioned positive ways you are coping with the change. I'm not sure whether you want to focus on the loneliness or on the positive coping?

Client: Well … the loneliness, I guess, it's kind of still there. But it's not taking over other emotions. It's still there because everything is still new, but I still don't have a very strong connection with it.

Rick: When you say the word 'lonely', there seems to be a feeling there.

Client: It is a feeling …. It's like a sulking emotion because I have everything in Northampton, and now I'm here and it's all so different. I guess I'm missing it in a way.

Rick: Missing? What are you missing?

Client: It's kind of like the friends I have, I guess. And my cat. He's too cute not to miss! My friends actually went to my house today, without me being there. They only went for the cat. Because he's so cute. If you saw him, you'd be in love! Even if you're not a cat person …. Every person that's not a cat person will tell me they don't like cats, then they'll meet my cat and be like 'never mind' (laughter).

The client brings a theme of separation, and I try to connect emotionally with the theme. The topic changes and the client's emotions remain unexpressed. Then, the client is invited to connect with the theme and the emotion, but this time she connects with her sibling's emotion and minimises hers: "It was harder for her than for me." Thirdly, I invited her back into an experiential and emotional conversation, and she moved the topic again and talked about the value and emotions evoked by her cat (who was very cute by the way!)

These are the facts of the process. How we make sense of the facts is the theory. For a moment I want to pause on the interpretation of these facts. Before changing the frame from a person-centred one to one that includes defence mechanisms, I want to describe a perspective on how theories develop more generally. So hold that thought for a moment.

Fishbowl Physics

A psychotherapeutic theory is an idea used to account for the known facts and justify a specific course of action. The theory we use justifies the techniques we employ to work with clients.

We interpret the client's words and actions by creating a model out of them. When we see via a model, we reconfirm the model as reality. So, when a client sidesteps an experience-oriented question, multiple times, and tends to be closed from experience, we fit this into our picture of psychology. In humanistic psychology, this means something like seeing the client as being incongruent with their self. If, to feel like a worthwhile person, she internalises a prohibition on emotions, then this condition of worth disconnects her from feelings. But this is purely a model-dependent assumption, a frame we lay over the facts to understand them.

The eminent and inspirational physicist, Stephen Hawking, invites us to question the impact of our theoretical models. In his book, *The Grand Design*, where he attempts to make a model out of the known laws of physics, he says that the value of a model is how useful it is in a relevant context. Using the example of a fish in a fishbowl, he says that a goldfish who happens to be a physicist could quite accurately conclude a different model of physics from people in the outside world. The fishbowl shape bends the outside world to make things appear bubble-like. Fishbowl physics isn't wrong, but it is just likely to create much more effort in interpreting the world. Doing physics from inside a fishbowl is harder. But our human model of physics in the outside world is just as strange to an eagle, an ant, or a snake.

The point here is that what counts as 'real' is dependent on the model we use. It is real to us that our client is in a state of incongruence and as such disconnects emotionally. But this is not what the world is telling us. It is a form of model-dependent realism – where reality depends on our theory.

We can change the model, or point of view, without changing the facts. In the same vein, each counselling model puts forward a different perspective on the facts of counselling. They aren't alternate universes.

With this in mind, the integrative person-centred model unpacks the usefulness of counselling concepts with different client scenarios. The psychoanalytic model, described in the previous chapter, has some useful descriptions for what is happening here. Therefore, we will use Hawking's fishbowl as a rationale for switching humanistic psychology with psychodynamic psychology because the model describes some problems like emotional detachment in greater depth.

Psychological Defence Mechanisms

In 1923 Freud introduced the idea of the superego into psychoanalysis. Already aware of the instinctive craving for meeting physical and psychological needs (the id), coupled with the conscious awareness of reality where many unconscious desires are unsatisfiable (the ego), the superego was introduced as a part of the mind that represses psychological needs. When the child learns that their needs are unrealistic, they internalise a system of rules and prohibitions on their wants and desires. A child with a harsh, uncontained, and selfish environment learns to inhibit their need for love, attention, food, dependence, and interaction. The callous facial expressions of an overwhelmed parent, the fear of a threatening voice that calls out when the child cries in hunger, and the agonising isolation that accompanies neglected children create an internal supervisor of the child's needs – a supervising ego, or a superego. Reacting to an environment, the child ultimately learns to self-police.

Psychoanalysis is a counselling model in which conflicts between the id, the ego, and the superego create psychological issues. If someone is angry, depressed, or anxious, they are likely to have discord in their needs, their reality, and their internalised judge.

Think of the client above, who has overwhelming anxiety and panic attacks. She has moved away from home to start university. Early in life, her mother moved from the family home to work in another country, leaving her in the care of her older sister until she was 12 when she could move abroad with mum. Her father moved even earlier to a different country, to be with his family after separating from the client's mother.

Although the mother moving away for work was part of the culture, the mother was experienced as detached emotionally throughout childhood, becoming overwhelmed with the client's physical and emotional needs.

Table 3.2 translates the client's background information into the psychodynamic model of the mind.

In the psychodynamic model, when a basic need arises, the superego shuts it down by using defence mechanisms. When the client feels sad,

Table 3.2 A Client's Anxiety Issue

Part of the Mind	Description	Example
Id	Basic needs and impulses	Need for secure relationship. Need to express and contain emotions.
Ego	The reality of the situation	Moved away from home. Sadness at separation. Feeling lonely.
Superego	The (mostly unconscious) values, beliefs, prohibitions, and self-standards	Sadness is wrong. Always shut down the need for other people.

she immediately represses her sadness by changing the subject, making a cat joke, or minimising her feelings. A panic or anxiety problem develops when the client is unaware of her basic needs, reinforcing her pattern of shutting down feelings. While the defence assists the client in becoming less disordered, because it protects her from being aware of the painful need, it does so at great cost.

The integrative person-centred model takes on these psychodynamic ideas. The first is the importance of childhood in the client's problem. The second is the unconscious process that occurs when the reality or belief system pushes back unmet needs from childhood. The third is that defence mechanisms are useful descriptions for times when the client unconsciously solves the internal conflict by minimising, hiding, distancing from, or rejecting emotional needs.

Revisiting the client's session from earlier, we can redescribe her words using a psychodynamic frame. Just a note that we have changed 'psychoanalytic' to 'psychodynamic' because this second term includes the dynamic between the id, ego, and superego. Psychoanalytic focuses on the interpretation we make of the client's behaviour, fantasies, and so on, discussed in the previous chapter.

Keeping in mind that a defence mechanism kicks in when a client has tension between needs (id), reality (ego), and values (superego), where is the defence mechanism in the following transcript? Can you spot it? What is the unconscious defence the client employs?

Rick: How is it to separate from your mother, in your first week at university?

Client: We're kind of just keeping it very platonic, in a way .... I don't even know if I'm using this word right .... Like, I acknowledge she's my mum, but it ends there.

Rick: You acknowledge she's your mum, but ...

Client: But I'm just keeping it at a very normal point, I'm not doing anything about it.

Rick: How is that for you?

Client: I don't mind too much, to be honest. I have my little support system .... And I might be even flying to Spain soon. Yeah, because, tickets in this season are very cheap. It's literally cheaper to fly to Spain than to go to Northampton!

For a client with painful experiences of separation, connecting with the emotion during a period of change is tough. There are several psychological strategies the client uses to avoid experiencing loss. First, I ask her an experience-based question, "How is it to separate from your mother?" She responds without an experience but with quite a vague reference to behaviour, "we're keeping it very platonic." When I refer to experience by asking "How is that for you?", she says, "I don't mind too much" and she changes the subject.

One hypothesis is that the client does in fact miss her mother. This is confirmed much later in the session (she states it directly). But we pick this up early via interpretation. That is, the process of denial and of changing the subject suggests she is repressing experience, a threatening thought that maybe she needs and misses her mother. Denial, in the form of "I don't mind," allows the client to block distressing thoughts from conscious awareness. Panic and anxiety swell up when the client uses energy to push down basic needs.

A psychodynamic interpretation does not have to mean coldly interpreting the client. It is useful here because the client repeatedly defends against the experience, and as the therapist I know to create safety around the theme of separation. A completely humanistic model or psychodynamic model could arrive at the same point, helping the client be more emotionally resilient. My reason for combining the two is in noticing the surface-level conversation and the feeling of going round in circles when I don't highlight and work with defence mechanisms, in more complex scenarios.

Notice the small joke or query the client made in the beginning, where the client said, "I don't even know if I'm using that word right ...," with a smile and a pause. The comment has shades of the defence mechanism called 'compensation'. Compensation is when a client pays more attention towards things that make them feel relief from anxiety. When the client cannot do well with the feeling, she attempts to do well with the wording. This is why reassurance in therapy can be problematic. Sometimes we support the client in covering over distressing feelings. It was tempting for me to say "that's the correct word, a good and accurate choice!" Here we would likely have moved away from going deeper into the emotion.

In this transcript, the client denies the emotional impact of change and separation. She represses feelings using humour, distraction, and storytelling. What makes this person centred is that I do not instruct her or interpret her out loud. Instead, I anchor my open questions to the psychodynamic themes.

I maintain the relationship as the top priority, exploring glistening Spanish holidays and adorable cat photos, and I roll with the defences. In person-centred integrative counselling, the therapist brings back the topic of separation, communicating "we can face this" as a humanistic principle. I highlight the defences with curiosity, "It feels like a choice to talk about the positive things or the loneliness." When psychological defences are removed, the client has more ability to face reality, manage separation, and increase resilience through change.

Six Conditions for Change

In 1957, Carl Rogers wrote a book about change in psychotherapy. He put forward the view that there are necessary and sufficient conditions for clients to become psychologically healthy. In integrative person-centred counselling, we take the view that the conditions happen on a skill and a behavioural level as well as at a value or belief level. At rung one, the first condition is that the therapist communicates empathy. While many authors have interpreted this not as a skill but a way of being, we pay equal attention to the word 'communicate'. I cannot show empathy unless the client sees, hears, or experiences it. Empathy is in the doing – the softness of my gaze, the tilting of the head. We oughtn't fabricate the body language of empathy mechanically. Instead, we see the body as a part of the therapeutic process.

To communicate an understanding of the client's frame of reference, to 'do' empathy, is linked with the therapist's actions. In the hierarchy of theory over practice, we use a psychodynamic theory of mental health while practising in an empathic way. The conditions for therapeutic change as seen by

Table 3.3 The Conditions for Change

Condition No.	Description
1	Therapist communicates an empathic understanding of the client's frame of reference.
2	Therapist experiences unconditional positive regard for the client (valuing and not judging the client).
3	Therapist is in a state of 'congruence' (internal harmony, being genuine).
4	Therapist and client are in psychological contact.
5	Client is in a state of incongruence, being vulnerable or anxious.
6	Client experiences the therapist's conditions (1, 2, and 3).

Carl Rogers are presented in Table 3.3. Try and imagine how each condition looks in the counsellor's techniques.

The conditions of change are one way to model how a client changes from being out of touch with experience to being in touch with it. Some authors have discussed integrating psychodynamic theory into this humanistic model, but in doing so have tended to choose one in favour of the other. As an example, Worsley states that psychodynamic and person-centred approaches are "not obviously compatible" (Worsley, 2007, p. 18). He refers to the fact that psychodynamic theory sees insight as leading to change, unlike Table 3.3, which sees empathy, congruence, and unconditional positive regard as leading to change. For me, this is fishbowl physics again. They both model a fact, such as that when clients no longer need therapy, they tend to have more awareness and act in self-fulfilling ways.

Deconstructing 'insight' into its theory and practice components can help understand the nuances. In theory, psychodynamic insight means being aware that we hide fear of separation with humour, or that we reject people to displace our fear of rejection. Change comes automatically the next time we laugh over a fear of separation because our awareness is raised. But this is exactly like the idea of incongruence. This is when the client is confused between their experiences and their self-image. If my self-image includes coping with separation, yet my experience tells me otherwise, I laugh or act awkwardly. Psychodynamic insight and increased awareness are ways of speaking about the same phenomenon.

I think the issue is not in how we package theory, but in how the two ways of modelling the situation produce contradictory actions. That is, psychodynamic therapists tend to interpret the client, risking a disconnection and judgement. Resistance for integration comes from lack of distinction between theory and practice.

At the skill, or let's call it the 'behavioural', level, my way with the client can be person centred though I am using a psychodynamic idea. In our model, this is what we suggest: when you struggle to connect with a client's experience despite clear open questions, restatements, and empathy behaviours, notice how the client avoids experience in their response. Ask yourself which theme is in motion, such as separation from a parent, and view this as an area to stick with and explore. Person-centred skills are anchored to psychodynamic theory, such that being empathic towards any avoidance brings about change.

I think to integrate means taking things and combining them together (e.g. integrating practice or technique into theory). Integrating across theory is more of a challenge because we try to avoid diluting either view.

Consider the situation of social integration in a local town or city. What integration often means is segregation. A wealthier middle-class group moves in to gentrify a historically poorer area. The less-well-off locals are priced out of coffee shops and gastro pubs. Integration would look more like equality of participation than a beard-wearing avocado-on-toast takeover. True integration means valuing the diversity of perspectives inclusively, such that no one person or idea holds more power or sway. This ideal is unlikely to ever be fully realised, but we can do better in our theories (and our towns and cities).

Integration means valuing psychodynamic and humanistic thinking for their joint underlying principles. While insight-oriented theory sounds obviously not compatible with growth-oriented theory, I think the incompatibility comes from the doing of the theory in practice.

A stereotype of person-centred therapy is that we merely reflect what the client says, to exhaustion. The issue is clear. People see the technique without the theory. Using the integrative person-centred model means being mindful of the relation between theory and practice.

Why do we restate what a client says?

In the person-centred approach, with the first client in this chapter, I restate their words because I want to highlight their present experience, to tolerate it and, as a result, for the client to become more self-reliant – which she does. In the integrative person-centred approach, with the second client, I reflect words and experiences in the theme of separation to support her to reduce internal conflict between needs. A humanistic interpretation is that this is simply working through incongruence. I agree with this, but finding the integration aspect, or using psychodynamic theory, gives me richer ideas to understand the client. Noting four defence mechanisms in a 30-second transcript is more specific than incongruence and matches the facts in the counselling room just as well. The person-centred view simply didn't see the defences.

Transference

When Freud worked with his patients, he found a lot of them resisting his techniques. They were angry or hateful towards him, or they were helpless and relied too much on him. Initially, Freud believed this was childish resistance. But then he realised that clients transferred feelings onto him from other significant relationships, mostly from parents. Interpreting the transference relationship, or the way in which a client reacts and feels towards the analyst, became the central task of psychoanalytical therapies.

Being a humble man, Carl Rogers never exactly said what he thought about this. But what he famously did say was that, in person-centred therapy, he does not experience transference. The resistance experienced in psychoanalysis, in his view, was due to their judgement of the client. In a sense, he was implying that Freud created his patient's defensiveness by attacking clients with interpretations – usually sexual interpretations.

Psychoanalysis historically uses the blank-screen approach. Patients experience little empathy from the therapist. The intention is to reveal defence mechanisms and transference, without artificially creating safety with empathy. But this practice was challenged by Tronik and colleagues in the 1970s and largely (but not totally) removed from psychodynamic therapies. Their famous yet disturbing still-face studies revealed that if a parent, a good parent, stops responding to a child, distress quite quickly takes over. In some ways, this validated Freud's ideas because emotionally neglected children demonstrated lower expectations for emotional care. When seeking support as adults, they revealed these expectations by resisting or overly depending on the therapist. But healthy children also became disturbed when a caregiver stopped responding, and hence transference is sometimes confused with the client's need to relate.

After the Tronik still-face studies, a further 80 have been carried out, reviewed by Judi Mesman and her colleagues. They concluded that a child's reaction to an uncaring face matches their level of sensitivity in the home. When the child reunites with a caring face, their ability to calm down and be comforted is linked with their early experiences of care. That is, by empathising it is true that we miss parts of a client's early relationship history, which otherwise would be evident in the room. But as stated in the opening chapter, the relationship is the bigger factor in positive outcomes and as such the modern picture advises us to take the humanistic approach. Nonetheless, both ideas, one of transference and one of being empathic, have some use in therapy.

While transference is evoked less in a non-directive setting, because each response is attuned to, I still think there is evidence of transference in non-directive therapy. But the crucial point in this final section is how that plays out in counselling. What does it look like to integrate the ideas in this chapter? Is the practice clunky and confusing? Can a client make changes as a result?

Therapists are capable of thinking psychodynamic theory and doing person-centred therapy. Earlier we reached a point in a session where the client distracted us from her experience of separation. After using defence mechanisms, which were repression, displacement, compensation, and humour, she said she missed her friends. Then, quickly, she changed the topic to her cat. Our psychodynamic lens taught us to see the defence as a window into a psychological theme, a window into the pain of separation. I said that, in the integrative model, we use open questions, empathy, paraphrases, and other core skills to stick with the theme. Let's return:

Rick: Just now, you mentioned the word 'missing' … ?

Client: Yeah. This week my friend went round to my house, because my mum was going to re-pot their plant. I didn't know all of my friends were going to go. I only thought one would go because it's his plant that my mum was repotting. Because he does not do well with plants (laugh, pause) …. Like, I didn't know that everyone was going to go, but yep, cool … (stops talking).

Rick: What was it like to know they'd all gone round?

Client: Well, it was very sweet to be honest. I didn't take that in a negative way … or be like 'oh I wish I was there' …. It wasn't one of those things …. Well, it was one of those things when they went to breakfast on Sunday. That was our tradition. Which, we used to go to breakfast on Sundays … (begins to cry).

(Pause)

Rick: And you were missing out on that ….
Client: (crying) Yeah.

The client starts to contact her emotions. She is getting in touch with her separation feelings and starting to experience them in the safety of our relationship. We aren't out of the woods because the defence mechanisms continue. She made side comments like, "he doesn't do well with plants," followed by a pause, which I found difficult not to show that I found this funny. Seeing the jokes and side comments as requests for an exit out of distress, I show her I can tolerate heavy emotions by leaving space and not laughing.

In terms of the stages of process from Table 3.1, the client moves up a stage. She shares feelings in the moment despite cutting them off before they erupt. We pay attention to unconscious conflict in needs and the ego, while being non-judgemental and accepting. Anxiety reduces as evidenced by the opening of emotions.

I continue to tolerate her experience:

Rick: Could you talk a bit about that experience?
Client: I guess, it's hard a bit at first … (turns head crying, but turns back to look at me, implying she is ready to tolerate the upset).
Client: It was a bit hard at first because I always, like, used to do that. I guess I didn't appreciate it at the time (continues crying) because it became like a routine. And, when I missed it, I was like, 'oh, I'm not going to tell them not to do it.' But, yeah … (wipes eyes).
Rick: So, when you were in the routine, it just felt normal, but …
Client: Now that I'm missing it, it just feels a bit odd …. God, I didn't know this is hitting me that hard (laughs) …
Rick: … You didn't know it was hitting you this hard?
Client: Yeah, because, I haven't cried about it, besides this. I thought I was okay about it, but, now that I've spoken about it, I guess I'm not as okay as I thought. It's a bit odd. I don't think it's fully hit me yet, even though I've started class and everything. But it's just hit me that I'm here. This is my new home I guess …. Making this the new normal, I guess, just takes time.

At the end of this section, the client is more congruent emotionally. She begins to realise that she is not as okay as she thought. It hadn't sunk in that she had separated from friends and family; she denied this change from awareness. As she processes the change, she feels less in psychodynamic conflict, not needing to push back the emotion. The internal judge softens, and it allows her to cry and feel sad about missing her close friends.

The psychodynamic idea tells me that there is a deeper issue to connect with. Speaking about missing friends is safer than speaking about missing mother. The complex web of feelings she holds onto about her mother will take some careful unravelling. For now, we see alignment in working with defence mechanisms and a person-centred approach. We describe and redescribe the situation from both perspectives, and doing so helps us overcome the stuckness of a purely person-centred route.

Summary

In this chapter, we have found some limits to a person-centred approach. Those are the exclusion of the unconscious process and the slight vagueness in realising important themes in the session. We saw that clients defend against experience-based questions, if they have good psychological reasons for not experiencing feelings.

Defence mechanisms were integrated into the person-centred model, primarily by using empathy, congruence, and unconditional positive regard as techniques. We saw that clients repress an emotion to prevent it becoming conscious. This involves denying reality or shifting awareness to humorous or unrelated topics, avoiding anxiety-inducing subjects. Some clients reject their thoughts or feelings by seeing them in others. We saw this process of projection when our client empathised with her sister's need for friends, while not being in touch with her own.

The theory of the mind we drew on, the psychodynamic theory, explained defences as a way to solve the conflict between emotional needs, external reality, and the internal judge. By denying a need, the person does not have to suffer the consequences of it going unmet. Using the therapeutic relationship and empathising with and listening to each micro-statement of the client, we supported her with self-discovery. She started by having no experience of separation, "I don't mind," and moved to being able to recognise the feelings under the surface:

> I haven't cried about it, besides this. I thought I was okay about it, but, now that I've spoken about it, I guess I'm not as okay as I thought.

Further Reading

Bisson, J.I., Roberts, N.P., Andrew, M. et al. (2013). Psychological therapies for chronic post-traumatic stress disorder (PTSD) in adults. *Cochrane Database of Systematic Review* 2013 (12): CD003388.

Burnham, J. (2005). *Relational Reflexivity: A Tool for Socially Constructing Therapeutic Relationships in 'The Space Between'* (ed. C. Flaskas, B. Mason, and A. Perlerz). London: Karnac Pubs.

Cooper, M. (2010). *Essential Research Findings in Counselling and Psychotherapy: The Facts are Friendly*. London: Sage Publications LTD.

Cuijpers, P., Driessen, E., Hollon, S.D. et al. (2012). The efficacy of non-directive supportive therapy for adult depression: a meta-analysis. *Clinical Psychology Review* 32 (4): 280–291. https://doi.org/10.1016/j.cpr.2012.01.003. Epub 2012 Feb 8. PMID: 22466509.

Ghafoori, B., Wolf, M.G., Nylund-Gibson, K., and Felix, E.D. (2019). A naturalistic study exploring mental health outcomes following trauma-focused treatment among diverse survivors of crime and violence. *Journal of Affective Disorders* 245: 617–625.

Hall, J., Kellett, S., Berrios, R. et al. (2016). Efficacy of cognitive behavioral therapy for generalized anxiety disorder in older adults: systematic review, meta-analysis, and meta-regression. *The American Journal of Geriatric Psychiatry* 24 (11): 1063–1073.

Joseph, S. (2017). *The Handbook of Person-Centred Therapy and Mental Health: Theory, Research and Practice*. Ross-on-Wye: PCCS Books.

King, M., Sibbald, B., Ward, E. et al. (2000). Randomised control trials of non-directive counselling, cognitive-behaviour therapy and usual general practitioner care in the management of depression as well as mixed anxiety and depression in primary care. *Health Technology Assessment* 4 (19): 1–83.

Merry, T. and Lusty, B. (1993). *What is Person-Centred Therapy?* Loughton, Essex: Gale Centre Publications.

Mesman, J., van IJzendoorn, M., and Bakermans-Kranenburg, M. (2009). The many faces of the Still-Face Paradigm: a review and meta-analysis. *Developmental Review* 30: 120–162. https://doi.org/10.1016/j.dr.2009.02.001.

Meyer, T.D. and Hautzinger, M. (2012). Cognitive behaviour therapy and supportive therapy for bipolar disorders: relapse rates for treatment period and 2-year follow-up. *Psychological Medicine* 42 (7): 1429–1439.

Rogers, C.R. (1951). *Client-Centered Therapy*. London: Constable.

Rogers, C.R. (1957). The necessary and sufficient conditions of therapeutic personality change. *Journal of Consulting Psychology* 21: 95–103.

Rogers, C. (1963). The actualising tendency. In: *Nebraska Symposium on Motivation* (ed. M. Jones). Lincoln, NE: University of Nebraska Press.

Rowan, J. and Jacobs, M. (2002). *The Therapist's Use of Self*. Berkshire: Open University Press.

Weinrach, S. (1990). Rogers and Gloria: the controversial film and the enduring relationship. *Psychotherapy* 27 (2): 282–290.

Worsley, R. (2007). *The Integrative Counselling Primer*. Monmouth: PCCS Books Ltd.

Wosket, V. (2002). *The Therapeutic Use of Self: Counselling Practice, Research and Supervision*. London: Routledge.

4

Jungian Analysis

The concept of the unconscious travelled across Europe, America, and eventually to most of the world. It was taken on by Carl Jung, a psychiatrist in Switzerland, who treated patients with disturbing fantasies and delusions. His clients described beliefs, fantasies, and experiences that reminded him of stories from other clients, revealing patterns in how people unconsciously make meaning from experience.

On learning about psychoanalysis, Jung immediately wrote to Freud and entered into an energising yet short-lived friendship. When they met, having each discovered an intellectual soulmate, the conversation lasted for 13 hours.

Freud explained that the unconscious mind develops from experience. Jung grew unsatisfied with this explanation because of the unconscious patterns he found with his clients. If experience explains the unconscious, then why would there be resemblances in the minds of people with different experiences? Maybe experience influences the degree to which people make meaning in the unconscious, but Jung believed experience had no impact on the actual structure of the mind.

Freud crowned Jung his intellectual "eldest son" and wanted him to inherit his fatherly role in psychoanalysis. But this did not prevent the two from butting heads, ultimately declaring the other as wrong. As the story goes, each psychiatrist ended up diagnosing the other with a mental disorder!

Freud continued to build psychoanalysis, and Jung started his own branch of psychotherapy, called analytical psychology. In this chapter, we think about where Jung took psychoanalysis and how his ideas integrate

Integrative Person-Centred Counselling: The Combined Model of Counselling and Psychotherapy, First Edition. Rick Murphy.

into the person-centred way of working. We establish connections between the Freudian and Jungian models and show how these ways of thinking improve empathy and growth in the counselling room.

Jungian Psychology

While Jungian psychology is rooted in the unconscious, it sees the mind as attempting to regulate itself, ultimately to help the individual. When a person is depressed, for example, this is the body's attempt to draw attention to a psychological imbalance.

Jung felt that Freud was too fixated on sex, aggression, and illness. In his view of the self, people strive for wellbeing. In fact, though Carl Rogers did not meet Jung, he is known to have been influenced by Jungian psychology. Both Carls modelled the client as capable of autonomous growth, with psychotherapy being the process for using a relationship to support a client's self-healing.

Where Jungian psychology differs from humanistic psychology is in its emphasis on insight. Self-awareness, in this model, leads to transformation because the client learns about their psychological imbalances. Self-actualisation happens when the person learns to consciously override and control unconscious desires. Hence, Jung has a little more in common with Freud than with Rogers, but all three model the client as capable of more autonomy and psychological wellbeing.

The Archetypes

When Jung looked deeply into the unconscious mind, he discovered some universal themes. Jung saw that these themes organise a client's experience. Instead of experiencing the world as it is, the client filters the world through a limited variety of perspectives – and these result from the precarious balance of psychological needs. As an example, let's meet a client whose anger and low mood are spiralling out of control. In the psychotherapy session, he tells us that his boss is out to get him. Because the manager is inadequate, the good work of our client only serves to highlight his shortcomings. Therefore, the client feels trapped in a situation where he cannot progress.

Humanistically, we have a client attempting to self-actualise, wanting to belong, yet experiencing an obstacle. In our frame, the obstacle is not the manager but the client's perception of the manager. Recalling that humanistic theory says that clients do not react to the world objectively; they react to the world as they experience it.

What Jung adds to person-centred work can be very insightful. With our client he would suggest that underneath the managerial conflict is a deeper universal theme. The client's experience may have fixated him onto this theme, but the theme was nonetheless simply a part of human nature.

Figure 4.1 is a diagram of Jung's archetypes. Though there may be infinite archetypes, these are the main kinds that show up in therapy. There are four core archetypes with twelve connected themes. See if you can connect the client's presenting issue with one or more of the themes. In the centre are four core elements to the unconscious mind, called 'cardinal orientations'. One, as Freud identified, is the ego. Its primary orientation is to leave

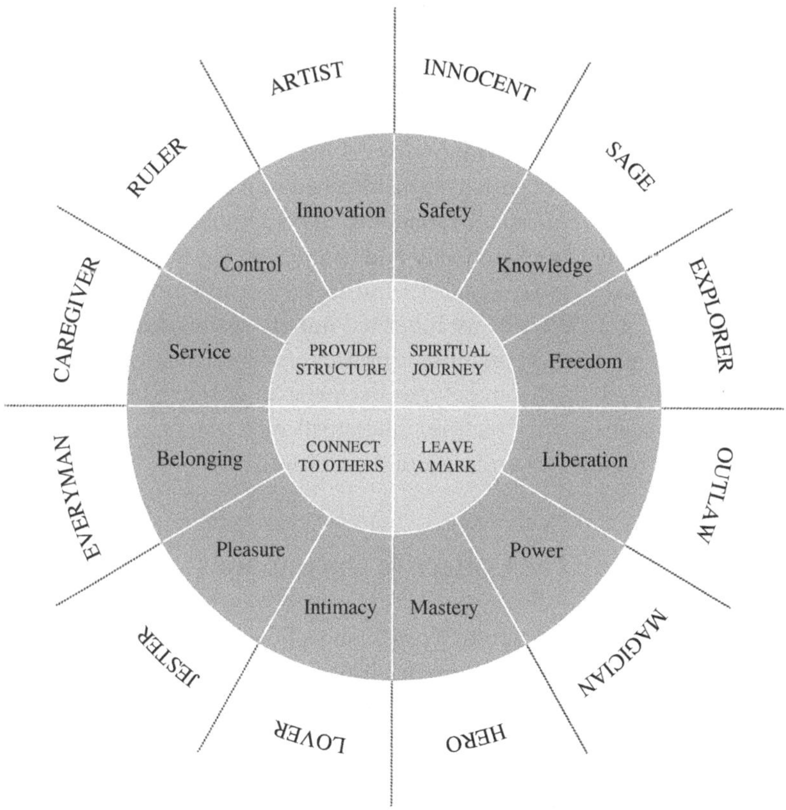

Figure 4.1 Jungian Archetypes

a mark on the world. Two is social, which is about connecting with other people. Three is the freedom aspect of the mind, which yearns for a meaningful life, termed a 'spiritual journey'. And fourth, a need for order, is to structure the world.

The client's story fits into multiple archetypes. Wanting to leave a mark on the world might show itself in anger when a manager blocks progress. Under the 'connecting to others' archetype, the client might resonate with a yearning for belonging. But the archetype that repeatedly comes up with this client is the one of control. In each session, the issue of control or of being ruled is the key theme.

When an archetype dominates a client's experience, Jung termed this a 'complex'. Our client has an 'authority complex' because his primary way of making sense of relationships is via authority. People who do not fixate on one archetype are not said to have a complex but a healthy balance between different ways of making sense of experience. In the transference with me, the authority complex shows itself by the client telling me my questions are wrong and inappropriate. For example, I asked him how his father views him and he said I was trying to take his father's side in an argument. An important feature of his childhood was his father being abusive, and this was part of a range of experiences that latched him onto this theme.

Archetypes are typically overlapping. The symbol of the father, for example, has elements of authority and belonging. These universal themes occur underneath a present concern and are deeper and more fundamental. The idea is that archetypes are inherited human stories, bound up in our evolutionary past, that organise experiences into themes. Experience determines which of the archetypes becomes an obstacle in our lives. By reverse-engineering this picture, humanistically, we can use a client's complex as a highway to understand their experience.

The Collective Unconscious

Jungian analysis unpacks archetypes to show how they create expectations that clash with reality. If, unconsciously, I come to expect order or belonging, or meaning or power, then my wellbeing is impacted by a lack of order, belonging, meaning, and personal agency. Here are the seeds of a humanistic outlook, but they are also saying something profoundly different.

The theory of mental health here is that people need to overcome their complexes to self-actualise. That is, the key obstacles to wellbeing are the client's expectations in an unsupportive reality. If our client is angry and low in mood, their awareness of the authority complex is part of overcoming it.

A huge implication of Jungian theory is that there is a layer beyond the personal unconscious. Rogers described present experience as the focus for psychotherapy. Freud described conscious experience, which is mostly the ego, like the tip of an iceberg. Underneath the iceberg is the unconscious, the heavier, more impactful part of the self. But Jung went a step further and said that this too is a tip of a deeper iceberg, merely a personal unconscious. Jungian archetypes point towards a social unconscious that spans the whole of humanity. He called this the collective unconscious.

In linguistics, Noam Chomsky found a similar thing. By looking at how children create new and grammatical sentences, he realised that children must be born with a language faculty, which he calls a universal grammar. That is, every sentence the child speaks is unique. Hence university and publishing systems uncover the amount of plagiarism in a written text by assuming that most text is unique to each writer. Although the words we use are in English, the underlying structure comes from an inherited linguistic capacity for understanding the world. We put sentences together in human terms whether we speak English, Urdu, Mandarin, or Welsh. This inherited capacity for producing unlimited sentences stretches beyond a child's experience of language. This is because their creativity with language far outweighs their training. Similarly with the archetypes, no matter what people experience, they do so within configurations that are universal across humankind.

In the archetypes, Jung noticed that people have an underlying meaning-making framework. Like language, which has some universal way of structuring words and phrases, the mind too has collective ways of structuring experience. Jung believed there was no fixed limit on the number of archetypes available to people because combinations are boundless. But some archetypes dominate human life, and these will be explored in the following section.

The Persona

Most people have some sense of self. Even though I am a different height, weight, and age; or that I have a different hairstyle, political orientation, and ability with language; or that where I live, who my friends are, and what people call me have changed since childhood, I retain the idea that I am one consistent person. Jung described the self as the core archetype that governs the human mind. We unify our unconscious and conscious minds into one thing, despite technically being multiple selves.

In our evolutionary history, we developed archetypes as unconscious templates to experience the world. There's a hawk–goose experiment that proves this for animals. In one version, chicks are shown a silhouette of a hawk (if moving to the right) and a goose (if moving to the left) (Figure 4.2). When the silhouette passes from left to right, the chicks get scared and begin to panic. Intriguingly, when the exact same silhouette passes from right to left, the chicks are unfussed. Experiments such as these, which are shown in many animals like chickens, birds, and dogs, are evidence of genetic memory. That is, people and animals are born with unconscious patterns that they recognise and respond to. One of the experiments in humans is with the dark. Fear response to the dark is shown not to depend on bad experience. Jung's argument is that the archetype of the self is like the chick's genetic memory of a hawk, a pre-loaded way of organising experience from birth.

The collective unconscious of chickens shows that hawks are dangerous and geese are not. These experiments were conducted before chicks met their mothers and so learned behaviour is not an adequate explanation. What's revealing here is that when social behaviour was looked into, the specific fear response was socially made. That is, whether the chick crouched, ran away, or sounded the alarm was linked with the social norm. Therefore, collectively inherited memories show themselves in culturally specific ways.

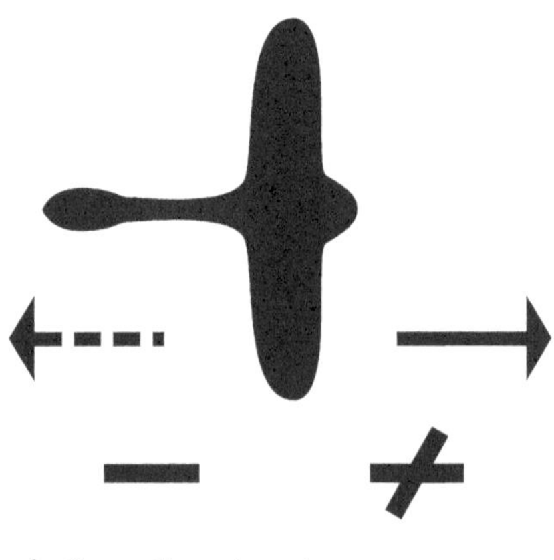

Figure 4.2 The Hawk–Goose Experiment

This is important because another of Jung's central archetypes is the persona. The real self gets obscured by a mask, a presentation of the self that feels socially acceptable. And hence, like the fear response in dogs or chickens, our specific behaviour is culturally made, yet our sense that we are a single self is universal.

A persona is a role played by us or the client. The role stands in for the self of the individual, often used as a guard between our ego and the outer world (Figure 4.3). That is, when we take on the persona of the teacher, receptionist, painter, or dinner host, we mask our self in ways that are normal to our culture. The American and the French persona of a waiter is a good example. American capitalism leads to a "customer is always right" greeting. In France, however, where workers' rights are more prioritised, the waiter commands more respect and is less attentive. When a French or American customer visits the other's country, they return home bemused by a "rude and arrogant" server or an "annoying and desperate to please" host.

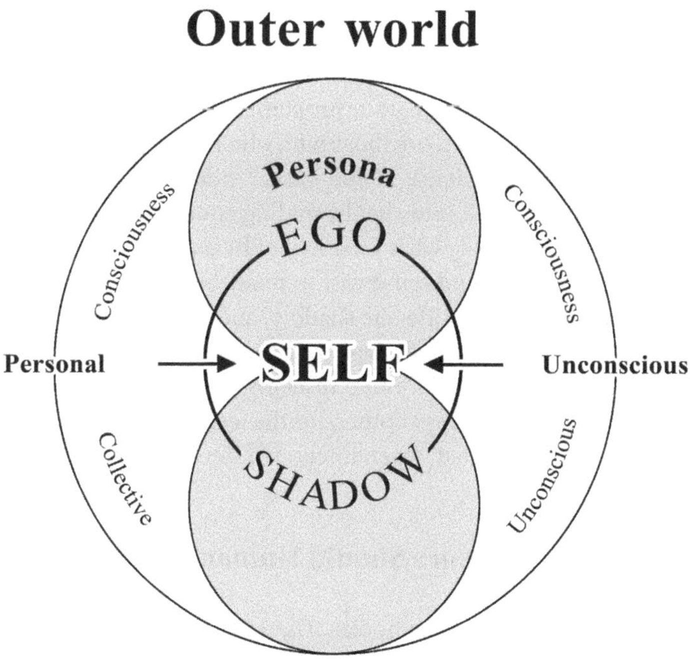

Figure 4.3 Jung's Model of the Self

Underlying these cultural elements is the fact that neither persona matches the self of the waiter. That is, despite being different, both situations show that a persona is at work. There is not always a conflict between the self and the persona, but often the persona leaves a false impression. In an extreme example, there are many awful crimes committed by people who seem like respectable and gentle people. In these cases, the respectable persona is a mask for manipulating others.

Mental health is affected by the persona, particularly when someone mistakes their persona for their real self. In fact, humanistic self-actualisation, which Jung discussed, is a way to distinguish the self from the persona. This is partly why counselling and psychotherapy courses require personal therapy. If becoming a therapist is a persona, in the sense of masking underlying psychological difficulties, the student can discover their more vulnerable self and learn from it.

Carl Jung wrote about the Grecian idea of the wounded healer, someone who heals others from their own pain. The therapist can heal others, as Jung put it, only to the extent that they have healed themself. This involves processing the deeper and darker sides to the unconscious archetypes. The concept of evil, or, more specifically, ideas and instincts to be violent, act immorally and punish others, are often separated from the self by the persona. If we become good therapists and incorporate that into our sense of self, without acknowledging our judgemental, vindictive, and violent impulses, we struggle to explore those with others. Even seemingly competent therapists, who specialise in the darker side of humanity, might be more likely to project that into clients, finding comfort in others' darkness, avoiding their own. This is what Jung meant by a psychotherapist needing to be sufficiently healed and self-aware to really help others grow.

Jung named this darker side 'the shadow', and in his analysis he encouraged clients to integrate their shadow with the self. Humanistically, this fits with the incongruence model of counselling. That is, the shadow is one concept, and incongruence is another, for the feelings and thoughts outside of the client's awareness that, when integrated into the self, inspire growth.

Theory Should Humanise

In one of Jung's most famous books, *The Undiscovered Self*, he says that theory cannot adequately describe experience. Despite being a theorist, he noticed that psychological theories are more abstractions than specific to individual cases. He gives the example of stones in a basket. If you took an average of all stones in a basket, you might find the average is 145 grams per stone. But you could spend all day weighing each individual stone and never find one that weighs exactly 145 grams. Psychological theory is like this. It takes an average across experiences that may not fit any individual. To learn about stones, we must explore each one of them individually.

Jung says there can be no knowledge about the self with theory. There can be a general guiding interpretation, but we cannot learn about Alex, Shamima, or Jo from theory. This is a deeply humanistic thought. In order to understand clients, we must lean into their frame of reference. Gathering insight from clients, we work backwards to fit these to our theories. That is where our skills and techniques come in. Fitting a client's experience into a model tells me something about the process and techniques of change.

Jung, like Rogers and Freud, says you must listen to the client's experience to understand them. Rogers was a phenomenologist who believed that the here-and-now experience was the gateway to psychological growth. Freud was a psychodynamicist who believed that underlying present experiences were unconscious impulses that open the gateway for psychological growth. Whereas Jung was a collective unconscious-ist (forgive my lack of imagination!), he believed that underlying experience and the unconscious mind was a collective unconscious spanning the whole of humanity – analysing and empathising with the archetypes that form the client's complexes that lead to change (Figure 4.4).

In this book I am making the argument that each theory of psychotherapy is different only in that it emphasises certain facts of life. When the

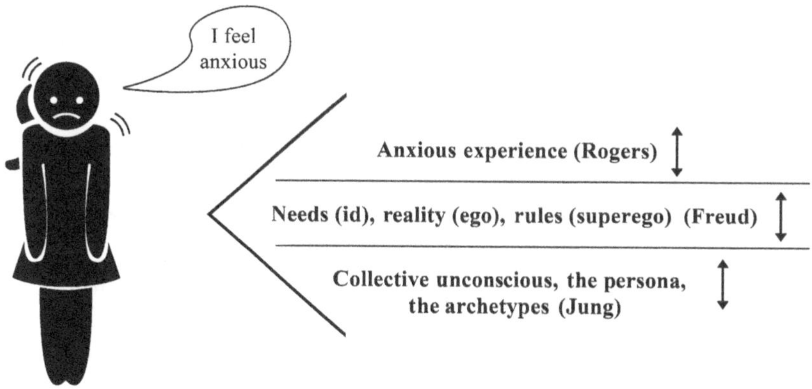

Figure 4.4 Level of Analysis in Psychotherapy

theory contradicts known facts, I have opted not to include it in the integrated person-centred model. None of these theories is necessarily in conflict as presented here, despite Jung and Rogers both articulating their theories as intentionally contradicting Freud. In the century-long catfight that is psychotherapy, my purpose is to join the dots in the collective knowledge of counselling and psychotherapy – minus the infighting.

Figure 4.4 outlines the current picture of integration. The double-sided arrows point towards counselling options. We can move up or down the levels of analysis according to the material brought by the client.

A Human Motif

Jungian analysis is similar to the idea of a musical motif. If I asked you to say a series of 'dos', say, six of them, you might struggle to connect them. Try it, "Do do do do do do." Usually, people have to go back and check how many they have said. But if we invited you to try this out using a musical melody, like the timeless melody of Happy Birthday, the sentence is easier and more engaging. Instead of "Happy birthday to you," try it in 'dos'. As in, "do do do do do do." This is easier for most people. The melodic motif provides a structure for the words in music like the archetype provides a structure for events in human experience.

Replace the motif of happy birthday with that of Jung's hero archetype, for instance. The hero archetype is a powerful human motif, formed in the collective unconscious. Its idea is that we ought to show our worth by overcoming great obstacles, saving, and inspiring other people with our powers. Then spawns a Wonder Woman, Captain America, Batman, Rocky, and Harry Potter (or even Barack Obama or Donald Trump for that matter). Each movie character or political figure faces enormous turmoil yet saves themselves and humanity from disaster.

In this way, the archetype is a soundtrack to experience. Academics in film school teach that a scene with a different soundtrack changes the audience's experience. Haunting music causes people to interpret the scene as scary. Inspirational music energises people to look for inspiration. This is even when the videos are exactly the same. Jungian analysis says that if I live a life without approval from others, which is a Rogerian condition of worth, then I put my energy into becoming a modern-day hero. I do things for validation, even causing harm to other people, so that I am credited with saving the situation (Figure 4.5).

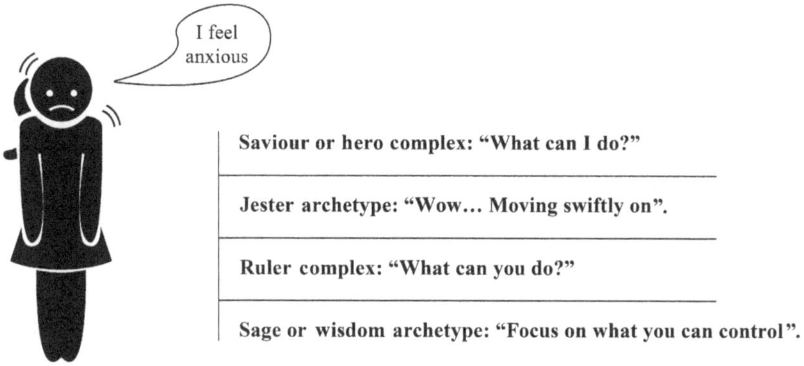

Figure 4.5 How Archetypes Change Experience

The point of the music analogy is that met and unmet needs create the playlist for experience. If I develop a hero or a saviour complex, then each scene in my life is interpreted as a time to fix and rescue. If I develop a Jester Complex, then each moment is a chance to find humour. As in Figure 4.5, the same event of someone being anxious changes according to how I fit the situation together into an archetype.

Therapy settings are ideally suited for thinking about these deep human motifs. A man came to my psychotherapy clinic because he was angry and depressed. In work, he did more hours than his colleagues, solved more of the problems, and picked up the slack, as he saw it, around him. At home, he did everything for his girlfriend, tidied the house, cooked, and asked for nothing, as he saw it, in return.

The client grew up in an abusive household. His mother would hit him, making sure he did as he was told. His father was an absent yet threatening presence, brought in for bigger and more severe punishments.

Exploring his *present* anger at work and home, he said his manager did not value his efforts and his partner did not see his sacrifices. He was not experienced by people around him as a hero, although there were plenty of friends and acquaintances who acknowledged his hero-status through his stories. In the therapy room, he was not experiencing his anger, either – it would just boil up one day and fade out the other. He talked in a monologue about the details of his lack of validation, rather than how it felt.

For Rogers, this client is in an early stage of the counselling process. He is not experiencing himself in the therapy room and is not taking account of his feelings. For Freud, the client is transferring the anger and distress from his inner child onto safer and more present people, his manager and girlfriend. What Jung adds, in his idea of the archetype, is that the motif of the hero, borrowed from humanity's vast unconscious library, fixates the client on a particular "melody" or hero complex. He plays the hero because he can't bear playing the villain. Those darker sides are pushed back, he only sees goodness in himself, and he makes others seem inadequate so that he can look good. This doesn't go down well socially because others' reality is very different from how he stitches it together.

From a Jungian perspective, counselling supports the client to tolerate other people's responsibility and choices, to use awareness instead of action, and to experience through a balanced variety of lenses. He can be many other things, not just a hero. The hero complex is not helpful to him because it creates a persona – a mask that covers his other sides. Having unexplained rage implies the uncontrollable release of coiled up anger. By seeing other people's power as a fact of the world, he may make his peace rather than live in a fictitious world where he is the only victor. Thus, the archetype of the hero is latched onto by a client who cannot bear or integrate traumatic experiences of powerlessness. Ultimately, he is someone who needed saving.

An example in the session might help make this clearer. When I sent the client an email for having missed one of our appointments, he said I had the date wrong, and it was not his fault. It's possible that I did have the wrong date, it's possible that I didn't. But in his return email he said that although it wasn't his mistake, he would pay me for the missed session. I felt annoyed – and there's the countertransference – because my sense is this was an issue of him not attending the session and then taking heroic credit for saving me from my mistake . . . and of course, we'll never know the truth!

The use I find in integrating this Jungian approach into the person-centred model is that it gives me a useful framework to remain client focused. Thinking there's a guy paying for my mistake is rather frustrating to me. But seeing that the hero complex develops out of an unmet need for approval and an intolerance of getting things wrong, even with people who create helpless situations to rescue others from, makes me care more for him. And that is ultimately how empathy works. I mentally model my client's experiences, and this sensitises me to him.

It is for this reason I think the theory is not to blame for analytical concepts running amok in counselling, but how analytical concepts are used to label and stigmatise clients. A person-centred approach could arrive at the same empathic moment, but the Jungian analysis provided a different and effective route. And I would have missed the pattern had I stuck in a purely person-centred frame. In the client-centred approach, the attention I pay to the current experience distances me from the overarching pattern.

Introverts and Extroverts

Carl Rogers defined experience as the total field of sensing and perceiving the world. Hearing, seeing, touching, feeling are all aspects of experience. One does not experience the past, so to speak. One remembers the past as a set of images, emotions, and sounds that are re-experienced in the present moment.

Person-centred therapy makes the distinction between self and environment, where the environment is part of how the self learns to experience, trust, and relate. Half a century before working out the experiential parts of non-directive counselling, Carl Jung contributed his own theory. He observed his patients closely and noticed an important pattern. Some patients spoke mostly about the world. They focused on people, the environment, making connections, and being social, and they were preoccupied with events outside the body. Other patients were at the opposite extreme. They were internally focused on thoughts and inner perceptions, being motivated by contemplating, imagining, and creating.

Ultimately Jung categorised these two types of people into introverts and extroverts. Clients who are energised by being alone, having time to think and process, may feel fatigued by social encounters (but energised by writing books!). These introverted people are likely to find wellbeing by creating lives that suit this type of neurological system. In the opposite way, extroverts are likely to feel low without social contact – their wellbeing is tied up with sharing feelings, experiences, and thoughts with other people. Without others to share experiences with, they feel less able to cope and manage.

Modern science has shown evidence for this. A study by Debra Johnson and colleagues in the *American Journal of Psychiatry* showed that introverts have more active blood flow in the thinking parts of the brain. Other researchers found that the grey matter in the frontal lobe, responsible for analytical thinking, is thinner in people who are extroverted. Equally, PET scans of the brain show that extroverts are less active in some dopamine centres, deep within the brain, meaning they require more social stimulation to remain energised and motivated.

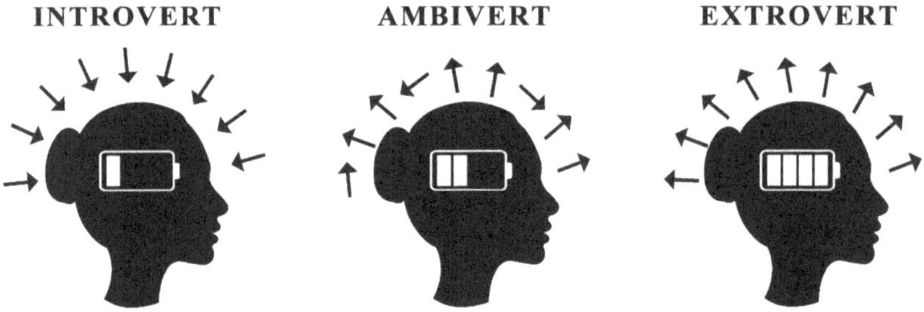

Figure 4.6 Introvert–Extrovert Diagram

Jung never intended to categorise people into crude boxes. His introvert–extrovert paradigm highlights important perspectives for therapists. Most people, as shown in Figure 4.6, are a mixture of introvert and extrovert, meaning they are ambiverts.

The reason for integrating this personality construct into the person-centred model is that it challenges us to think about the objective of therapy. We might see self-actualisation as the ultimate goal – when a client is congruent with themselves, not wearing a false persona, organically making progress. But progress looks different depending on the personality of each individual. Rogers has two similar concepts, (1) the external locus of evaluation and (2) the internal locus of evaluation, clearly influenced by extrovert and introvert personality types. But the locus of evaluation can imply an over-emphasis on helping clients to become more internally focused, particularly when it comes to evaluating themselves. The research above suggests that people's social battery is charged by different means, and therapists should remain non-directive in their view of what the client needs.

While most people are ambiverts, or a mixture of introverted and extroverted, Jung reminds us not to get caught up in our biased idea of change. Even if we use non-directive techniques, we run the risk of directing the client towards being an extrovert if our view on self-actualisation leans towards the social aspect. Clients who are not as sociable, which we may judge to signal a lack of 'progress', could (invisibly to our model) be improving on their introversion; listening more to their organismic need for withdrawal, pause, pace, and alone-time might improve their wellbeing. An extroverted counsellor makes judgements about progress differently from an introverted counsellor. Thus, Jung's mention of introversion and extroversion is a call for counsellors to align their change framework with the wellbeing of clients and their unique change. This expands the concept of self-actualisation, or the idea that counselling supports people to reach their potential, to value a client's inwardly focused and outwardly focused potential.

Summary

This chapter has integrated Jungian analysis into the person-centred model. We took Jung's idea of the collective unconscious to mean a set of genetic memories or meaning-making templates universal to human beings. These templates are seen in human behaviour, where people make meaning from experience in routine patterns. Those patterns are called archetypes, and there are archetypes that focus on meaning, on structure or power, on connecting with other people, and on leaving a mark on the world.

When we experience psychological unrest, some of these archetypes come to dominate our personality and our society. When this happens, we develop a 'complex'. In the hero complex, we explored how early trauma creates a need for validation, for justice, and for self-worth that ends up with a person seeing and creating the hero motif in everything they do. The problem with this is that the person is not really a hero. No one can be healthy if they are too fixed on certain archetypes because this pushes their needs and wants out of experience. They will develop a persona, a false mask that slowly becomes experienced as the true self.

Jungian person-centred therapy is about helping people tolerate other aspects of experience, sitting with their conflicting needs, being able to face and grow from experience. We ended by suggesting that the word 'grow' is problematic because each of us defines it based on our own values. If we are more externally focused, then 'grow' means being more sociable. If we are internally focused, then 'grow' means being more rational and thoughtful. The concepts of introversion and extroversion reminded us to reconnect with the client's experience, to use our relationship and discover empathy non-judgementally, such that our humanistic values are present in our therapeutic actions. Otherwise, we come to expect the client to develop in ways that are more about us than them.

Each chapter in this book will inevitably be a partial integration. Jung is a more complex character with hundreds of ideas not discussed here. Our suggestion is to use the principle of the integrative person-centred model by reading further into any authors explored here, finding your own routes to engage with their ideas in person-centred and humanistic ways. Provided the integrated concept is transferred via its theory or framework, or via its practice or techniques, then it can be thought about in person-centred terms.

Further Reading

Canty, N. and Gould, J.L. (1995). The hawk/goose experiment: sources of variability. *Animal Behaviour* 50 (4): 1091–1095. https://doi.org/10.1016/0003-3472(95)80108-1.

Fischer, H., Wik, G., and Fredrikson, M. (1997). Extraversion, neuroticism and brain function: a pet study of personality. *Personality and Individual Differences* 23 (2): 345–352. https://doi.org/10.1016/S0191-8869(97)00027-5.

Goss, P. (2015). Jung: A Complete Introduction: Teach Yourself. Hachette: UK.

Green, R., Carr, W., and Green, M. (1968). The hawk:goose phenomenon: further confirmation and a search for the releaser. *Journal of Psychology* 69: 271–276.

Johnson, D.L., Wiebe, J.S., Gold, S.M. et al. (1999). cerebral blood flow and personality: a positron emission tomography study. *American Journal of Psychiatry* 156 (2): 252–257. https://doi.org/10.1176/ajp.156.2.252.

Jung, C. (1923). *Psychological Types*. Harcourt, Brace.

Jung, C. (1958). *The Undiscovered Self*. London: Routledge.

Jung, C. (1995). *Memories, Dreams, Reflections* (trans. R. Winston & C. Winston). Fontana Press.

Raskin, N.J. and Rogers, C.R. (2005). Person-centered therapy. In: *Current Psychotherapies*, 7e, instr. ed. (ed. R.J. Corsini and D. Wedding), 130–165. Thomson Brooks/Cole Publishing Co.

5

Object Relations

Abraham Maslow's actualising principle says that people naturally gravitate towards self-improvement. They become healthy minded through a positive sense of belonging and self-esteem. Carl Rogers added that an accepting and empathic relationship supports self-actualisation against psychological obstacles. But ultimately, this is a model of individual psychology. Rogers, Freud, and Jung reference the relationship but do not model it in their theories. How does the relationship fit into a model of psychotherapy? Do we understand how or why the relationship is so significant to the humanistic model?

Object relations theory was one of the first psychodynamic models of the relationship. It had a significant impact on psychotherapists because it described how relationship experiences shape the mind of the client. The idea that one can model the relational experience of the client excited the field so much that it became instantly famous.

To understand the basics of object relations theory, imagine a person who sees herself as too emotional for others to contain. Just as she has a sense of self, she has a sense of other people. For her, other people are untrustworthy, overwhelmed, and fragile. Ultimately, this leads to distant and disappointing relationships (Table 5.1).

When the client sees herself as uncontainable, she treats people like they cannot accept or contain her feelings. In therapy she feels a sad emotion and buries it with an explanation. When explaining and analysing her situation, she seems stronger. We learned two chapters ago that the defence mechanism of repression is unconscious. It stops the person from having painful experiences, giving them a false sense of resilience.

Integrative Person-Centred Counselling: The Combined Model of Counselling and Psychotherapy, First Edition. Rick Murphy.

Table 5.1 Object Relations Example

How the client sees herself	Too emotional
	Uncontainable
	Strong when not emotional
How the client sees others	Untrustworthy
	Uncontained
	Chaotic
	Fragile
The types of relationship between self and others	Distant
	Frustrated
	Disappointing

After a client has buried enough emotion, it is probable that the therapist too becomes disconnected. This confirms the client's sense that other people cannot tolerate feelings. Moving from therapist to therapist, relationship to relationship, the client plays out the same patterns again and again.

The object relations view is that people are most comfortable in relationships similar to those they were brought up in. Childhood relationships that are invalidating and neglectful increase the expectation that others are emotionally unavailable. This normalises the client's expectation for neglectful partnerships. From an evolutionary perspective, this enables her to predict future responses, so her actions can ensure survival (Figure 5.1).

Experience of caregiving creates a self-image and an image of how others think and feel about us. With a loving and caring parent, we internalise a positive self-image. We believe ourselves to be loveable and worthy of care.

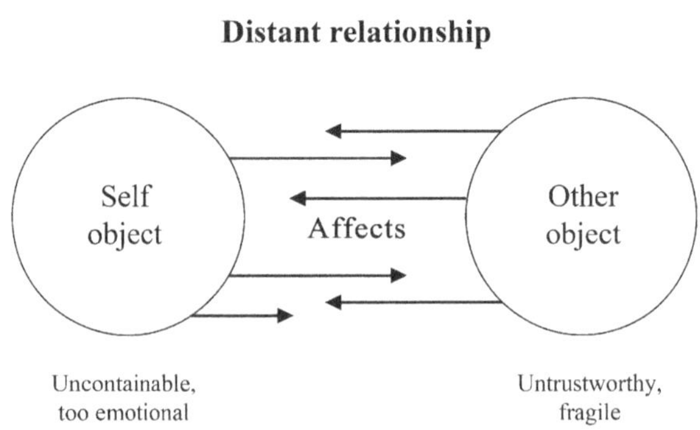

Figure 5.1 Object Relations Diagram

And we believe others to be caring and love-giving. Thinking about this in reverse, our client's relationship pattern teaches us something about her early experience. By feeling disconnected from her, we are led to consider how emotionally disconnected and uncontaining her childhood was. Freud conceptualised this as countertransference, any feeling the therapist has towards the client.

In object relations theory, the internalised self-image and the internalised caregiver are called 'objects'. In the original literature, 'object' meant a goal or a target, not a thing in the world. Influenced by Freud's psychodynamic theory, which says that psychological drives motivate behaviour, objects were thought of as a person's objectives. The self-image, for example, is an object that motivates the client to avoid help-seeking. The therapist is an internalised negative object of care, prompting the client to shutdown emotions.

Object relations theory is interested in the interactions between internalised objects. For example, how the negative self-image interacts with the negative internalised caregiver. Hence, it goes a step further than other theories because it considers the relationship between the client and their environment.

Good Object–Bad Object

Melanie Klein is the mother of object relations theory. She read Freud's work on psychoanalysis and pioneered its use with young children. Despite her enthusiasm for Freud, he publicly dismissed her work as a deviation from psychoanalysis. Her view, which is shared in this book, is that one can drop Freud's emphasis on biological and instinctual drives, which leads to an over-sexualised and aggressive interpretation of clients. Instead, we use his ideas to connect with subjective experience.

Freud's original theory of mental illness didn't seem to work for all clients. Interpretation became a one-trick pony for many people, and these ways of practising psychoanalysis brought out more defences than they overcame. This is why Klein extended – or, in Freud's words, deviated – from traditional psychoanalysis, to emphasise subjectivity in relationships.

In typical psychodynamic language, an object is a person or a thing that satisfies a conscious or unconscious need. Where Klein departed from this was in emphasising the relationship between unconscious needs, reflecting on how emotions, behaviours, and perspectives develop through human interaction.

An object can sometimes be a person, such as the mother. But usually, the infant experiences her symbolically divided into parts. The mother's voice, touch, absence, and breastmilk are internalised as 'part objects'. By associating the different parts of the mother with met or unmet needs the child internalises different aspects of the mother as good and bad objects.

For example, the mother's milk is a good object and her back, which the child sees when the mother leaves the room, is a bad object. Early neurological associations imprint themselves on the child's brain. And this is what we find in the neuroscience literature. A person's concept of, say, love, is made up from multiple (and usually early) divided experiences that span the depth and breadth of their brain. Love is made from an image of a candle-lit dinner, romantic music, arguments, handholding, kissing, divorce, kindness, commitment, sadness, holiday memories, rejection, birds in a nest, and lyrics from a song, to name a few. Love is constructed via a complex web of emotional experiences. When one is asked to relate to the word *love*, it'll bring about a significant range of things, only a handful of which are conscious, and many of which come from childhood.

As the saying goes, 'neurons that fire together, wire together'. Therefore, neurologically, when an experience of pain repeatedly kicks in with a mother leaving, this reinforces the internalisation of a 'bad object'. When satisfaction occurs with the mother's breastmilk, a positive association with being fed is made.

Freud's first case of child analysis was a child (his grandson) who repeatedly threw string through the bars of his cot, seeming anxious to pull it back in. The child made a mournful sound when he threw the string and a joyful sound when he pulled it back. Freud noticed that, symbolically, this spontaneous action mimicked his grandson's anxiety when his mother left him alone and came back into the room. Klein's child psychoanalysis was based on children like Freud's grandson playing out, and resolving, negative object relations. That is, Klein proposed a different perspective on psychological health.

The Paranoid-Schizoid and Depressive Position

In object relations theory, a child internalises their subjective experience of people and other things in their environment. There is no objective mother, but a subjective mother separated into parts according to how the mother is experienced.

Babies cannot have their needs met forever, and certainly not as soon as they need, so they must communicate. They show upset or aggression as a way of inviting the caregiver to resolve their suffering. Research in psychology shows that 12-week-old infants detect a range of facial expressions, with an ability to internalise the basic emotions, namely, happy, sad, excited, and angry, by six months. This supports the Kleinian view that good object–bad object representations are unconscious because they happen from a very early pre-memory age. By the age of two, a child's brain is 80% of its adult size, and hence much of the wiring in the brain occurs in early childhood.

In the communication process, the child is responded to in a variety of ways. Not only are they turning emotions and facial expressions into objects, but they are internalising how they are treated when they behave in certain ways. A child who is treated angrily as an infant learns to shut down their needs quicker than a child who is treated lovingly. But all children learn that the world cannot immediately and consistently meet their needs. The child's positive and negative emotions become linked with specific objects, be they the distressing sound of footsteps leaving the bedroom or the soothing sound of a returning mother's voice. Their emotions are not complex until around age four, and this immature state leads to a black-and-white view of life. The child divides experience into polarised internal representations. Things are either good or bad.

Klein called this the paranoid-schizoid position. The child represents experience in positive or negative ways. They cannot form relationships between good and bad representations. This means they are schizoid, in the sense that they form no relationship between safe and unsafe objects. Schizoid isn't meant to sound offensive. It means that the person detaches emotionally from perceived bad objects. Hence, if a child experiences the world as all 'bad', their personality becomes emotionally detached and dissociated.

Therapy clients are often stuck in a paranoid-schizoid position. They split you the therapist into a good object and themselves into a bad object; their mother is a good object and their father is a bad object; their boss is a good object and their colleague is a bad object. This is an early defence called *splitting*, where black-and-white thinking gets rid of anxiety. It's easier to tolerate a world where everything dangerous comes labelled with a bright hazard sticker. Tolerating the uncertainty of the real world is tough. Not knowing if someone is genuine or manipulative, for example, or sitting with the contradiction of love and hate caught in a relationship, leads to anxiety. The late Barry Mason, a well-known social worker and family therapist, called this 'unsafe uncertainty'. The paranoid-schizoid position provides some level of certainty.

Object relations theory offers a way out of such primitive defences. It studied children and adults to figure out what is needed for people to overcome this polarised perspective. And what they discovered is very relevant to integrated person-centred therapy. They asked the question, 'What needs to happen for clients to move beyond experiencing the world as black and white?'

Melanie Klein's research was very insightful. She saw that after the age of about six months, infants start to integrate good and bad things into whole objects. Instead of experiencing the mother as, for example, a good breast and bad abandoner, the child experiences mother as both. Klein called this the depressive position because the child realises the good and bad inherent in everything – which, when you think about it, is rather depressing. Some things have more of the good than the bad, but nonetheless reality is not black and white; all things are good and bad, even the things we love.

Figure 5.2 is a way to picture the change from the paranoid-schizoid position to the depressive position. First of all, positive and negative objects are split. Then, the awareness of positive and negative in the self and the other is acknowledged, resulting in a final integration.

When the child grows to the age of about three, and can distinguish their consciousness from other people's, they have already formed self-representations, or self-objects. They have also created instinctual objects, which are internalised blueprints for how others respond to their needs. This supports the Kleinian view, and the psychodynamic view in general.

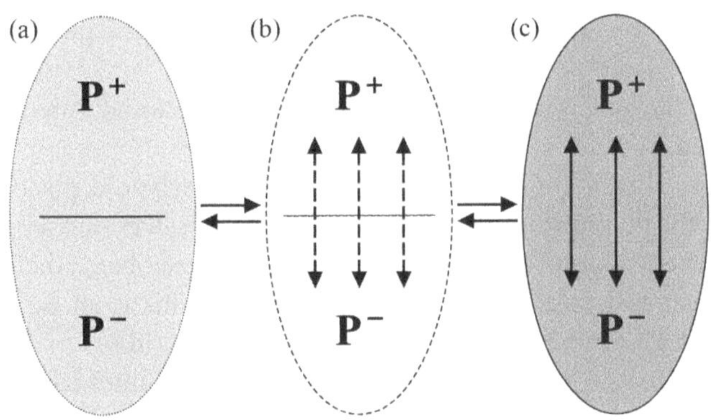

Figure 5.2 The Depressive Position. (a) Paranoid-schizoid position. (b) Transition to depressive position. (c) Depressive position.

Early childhood experiences clearly imprint into the child's physiology. The depressive position is a process in which the child learns to tolerate good and bad aspects but only when that is tolerable. If their environment is harsh, they may split more. Throughout life, people return to splitting as a way of coping and hence flip between the paranoid-schizoid and depressive positions.

A study by Rosemary Calverley and her colleagues looked into the impact of sexual abuse on object relations. As Klein predicted, they found that sexually abused young people are more likely to protect themselves via splitting. They found that, compared with non-abused young people, they were significantly more black-and-white in their thinking, very negative in their thinking, and represented themselves via mainly negative self-characteristics. Abused people were shown to be more mature than people who had not been abused. This is evidence that splitting is not a developmental delay but a defence that kicks in alongside traumatic experience. The maturation may itself be a defence – a forced 'growing up'.

While this research validates an object relations view, it also supports a humanistic style of therapy. Eugene Gendlin was a person-centred therapist and author. He noted that 'experiencing' is the primary focus of therapy. When a client splits the world into good and bad objects, they don't experience the objects fully. Or they are incongruent to their experience of certain objects, including the safety of therapy.

Gendlin encourages therapists to focus on experience in the verbal language, body language, and the therapeutic relationship. When the client speaks or interacts, they show how much or how little they tolerate experience by what they say and do. The process is captured in Figure 5.3. First, we name the experience (of the bad object) and intensify the present experience of it. It's important to acknowledge the experience and to face it. Then we try to tolerate what the client brings, without rescuing or directing their attention to other less-present things (such as the good parts of the

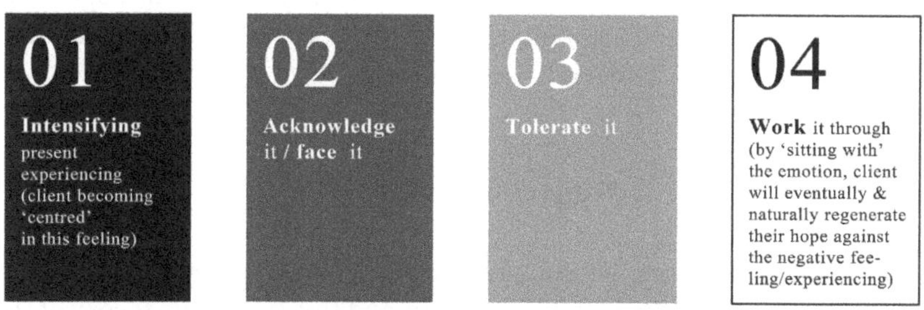

Figure 5.3 Gendlin's Stages of Experience

object). Only then can the experience be worked through. By sitting with the experience, the client naturally and spontaneously generates hope against it, experiencing the good together with the bad. The client takes a more realistic position.

As an example, a client was feeling anxious at work. She was sat around the table with younger people, feeling as though she had nothing to contribute. She had created a 'bad object' out of ageing. We intensified the present experience using open questions, "What is the feeling you have when thinking about the meeting?" and "Where is the anxiety in your body?." The client said she felt overwhelmed and "couldn't explain" why the anxiety was so powerful.

We faced the power of the anxiety using probing questions, "How much power does the anxiety have over you?," "Can you tell me how the anxiety is impacting you?." In the work context, the client judged herself as bad in the present day but good as a younger person, and hence she was splitting. The black-and-white thinking labelled youth as good and middle age as bad. But once she tolerated the anxiety, she began to describe other memories from the meeting.

First, she remembered being the most knowledgeable around the table, and others seemed to look up to her. She also felt she had taken on a new role in her life, one she had looked forward to – being a more senior member of the company. Once she connected with these experiences – once she no longer split the situation into good and bad, and tolerated both – she said she felt calm. Her hope against the negative feeling was organic, and she found calmness herself by us sitting with the anxiety. Gendlin comes from a person-centred view, but the object relations view highlighted the client's splitting. In doing so, this helped me to know which experience was important to tolerate. The integration is in noticing and processing the client's splitting from a person-centred orientation. That is, we integrate the object relations idea as though it is a theme in the client's experience. Although the client doesn't name it this way, they show it through what Gendlin describes as 'manifestations' – the body language, spoken language, and response to the relationship.

Aggression and Grief

Object relations theory developed from observing infant aggression. Infants show aggression towards specific objects, and this is how the theory of the bad-object good-object was made. The idea is that the child has very few options for how to express their experience. Black-and-white emotions represent black-and-white experience. Thus, at a cognitive and emotional level, the child is unable to make sense of the breast being absent. Hence, aggression matches the mother's (bad-object) absence and satisfaction matches the mother's (good-object) breastmilk. As usual in psychotherapy, the biological facts are modelled into a psychology. Here the paranoid-schizoid position helps us model what's happening at a biological level. It helps us notice when a client is splitting, when they match aggression exclusively to some things and love exclusively to other things. With 'good enough parenting', a term developed by object relations theorist Donald Winnicott, the child's aggression is accepted and enables them to assimilate contradictory experiences of care.

Clinically, splitting can mean a client shows negative feelings to others while idealising the therapist. I have sometimes asked clients to describe the things they dislike about therapy with me, anything that bothers them about my approach, and to invite criticism. As well as being a humbling experience, this is one route to encouraging unspoken (depressive-position) feelings. Often clients have deeper feelings about the work together, many of which are painful and bring out frustration or aggression, but their current experience does not show that. Being curious about fringe experiences supports the client to adopt the depressive position – which in humanistic language is more like 'tolerance' and 'acceptance'. It isn't that all people and objects should elicit a 50–50 balance of good–bad feelings. But that when the balance is 100% in any direction, usually the client is showing a struggle with being congruent with their feelings. For some clients, pausing to reflect on the positive aspects of the work, not just the bad, might be equally important.

As an example, Carl Rogers famously refused to give his client Gloria advice when she wanted to know how to parent her daughter. Carl highlighted the present experience, "you would really like me to tell you what to do," and Gloria said, "I was afraid you were going to say that." In Gendlin's person-centred model, Carl was highlighting the present wish. In the object relations model, Carl was not accepting the idealisation of himself as the expert, which could split Gloria into the bad helpless object and him into the good all-knowing expert. Both models take the same facts and view them differently. Retaining a person-centred interview, while seeing from an object relations perspective, would have encouraged Carl to explore the present experience of being 'afraid'. Rogers could ask a question like, "What is it like for me not to give you advice?," as a way of helping Gloria towards the depressive position. This question might help Gloria to learn to tolerate the good and bad in everything – including Carl himself.

When the client integrates good and bad objects, like the good yet non-advice-giving therapist, the client takes the accepting, depressive position. Here the client usually experiences grief for the lost ideal. Living in a world where the therapist is a saviour is hopeful. Living in a world where the therapist cannot be ever present, where they sometimes fumble, and where they don't meet your needs, is more difficult. This is why literature and films often use splitting. As well as the Jungian archetype of the hero and the villain, we can also interpret cinema through the good-and-bad-object perspective.

Many films keep good objects and bad objects separate, though some do resolve characters into the depressive position. For instance, in action films the good tends to get rid of the bad. This is splitting. The same is true for romantic films. But in the film *The Grinch*, based on the popular Dr. Seuss Books, the evil Christmas monster becomes a more complex and sympathy-worthy character, who ends up still belligerent yet kind. Similarly, clients in therapy discover nuance in their internal representations, integrating good and bad aspects of therapists, people, and events. Our client who is anxious of ageing takes a more Dr. Seuss–like perspective, seeing how ageing is belligerent yet wisdom-giving.

Carl Rogers sees the client's change as leading to congruence and self-actualisation. The person is more able to take responsibility. And this is the same conclusion in object relations theory. The client, by integrating good and bad, takes more responsibility for their actions, having more choice over how they perceive and interact with others. But the key difference is in how the client forms a more hopeful model of the other. The terminology for this in object relations theory is 'depressive position functioning'. Here the client sees people as three dimensional. They experience people more vividly as having separate consciousnesses, histories, wishes, beliefs, and perspectives. As with *The Grinch*, when clients see people as whole objects, as separate and complex, they relate better to them – they no longer use splitting.

Transitional Objects and Peekaboo

The child psychologist, Jean Piaget, studied how children experience real objects, before they are internalised. He found that when an object is hidden from an infant, they do not understand that it still exists. Object permanence is the understanding that an object or a person still exists when it is hidden or out of sight. This cognitive reasoning happens around four to seven months.

Object permanence is a cognitive milestone that sows the seeds for symbolic understanding, memory, imagination, and language. Knowing an object exists when out of sight requires an infant to have a mental image of that object stored in their memory. Object relations theory says that objects are not stored neutrally but are stored inside positive or negative emotions. So emotional development is part of object permanence, and it is the beginning of a child's emotional understanding of the permanency of the caregiver.

We talked about play and its ability to safely work through psychological difficulties. This is true with difficulties of separation and object permanence. The most universal childhood game, peekaboo, is a profound example of this. Why is this game so common in early infancy? What are the psychologically interesting factors in this game's success?

The answer is that peekaboo helps children learn object permanence. When the parent's face disappears behind a pair of hands, the parent has vanished. Hence, the child fixates on the hands, with enthralling anxiety. The child is relieved to humorous effect when the hands open and reveal the parent's beaming smile. Magically, the parent has reappeared!

Piaget hid balls under blankets and crayons in tins. He found that when children start to look under the blanket or inside the tins for the crayons, they demonstrate knowledge of object permanence. Before this, children assume the crayons have gone. Experience through touch, taste, sight, and sound is how children develop knowledge about objects, and hence the internal representations, while positive and negative, are also multisensory. Thus, foul tastes, soothing sounds, threatening images, and soft textures store in the infant's mental representations, way ahead of language development. Hence many clients struggle to verbalise some emotional memories – they carry sensory object representations from before they could speak.

When children discover object permanence, they also discover separation anxiety. The child becomes aware of things that keep them alive and comforted and their ability to be gone. When those things, usually parents, leave, it puts life in jeopardy. But this separation anxiety is on a symbolic level, which we know from Donald Winnicott. He explained the phenomenon of the transitional object. By having a symbolic object like a teddy or a blanket, children separate better from a caregiver. The object helps the child feel safe and secure. The comfort blanket, for example, is transitional in terms of being used in transition from being with a parent to being away from them. But it is also a transition into a more independent way of being.

In this way, the start of self-actualisation, the move to independence, happens when the child first begins to move away from the parent. The research is clear on this because around 60% of babies have transitional objects at nine months old, the time they usually begin to crawl. Hence object-relations adds a developmental timeline to self-actualisation as well as range of concepts for why experience becomes incongruent (black and white) during periods of stress.

Relations Between Objects

So far we have presented the basic model of object relations theory. A child represents experience by linking parts of objects with positive or negative emotions. When the child reaches around six months, they can integrate the positive and negative into whole objects, seeing the world as more complex, but only if the caregiver is containing enough to tolerate the child's needs. Over time they revert to black-and-white thinking to tolerate anxiety, though a healthy person is one who remains mostly in the real and more complex world.

The next area of object relations theory is the relationship between the internal representations. In Figure 5.4, we have a representation of the self and a representation of an object.

In the diagram, we see that the self-representation is divided into positive and negative objects, and so is the object representation. Otto Kernberg, an Austrian psychoanalyst soon to reach his 100th birthday, noticed that people internalise themselves and their world separately. He called these two representations 'object relations dyads'. The person internalises the good and bad self and the good and bad object as separate from one another. Hence with the therapist, the friend, the mother, and the father, they evoke a different sense of self based on the paired internal representations.

In serious mental health conditions, like psychosis, the person is fuzzy in how they differentiate the self from the environment. That is, there is no distance between the object relations dyad. In healthier people, they represent the self and the environment much more clearly. The research confirms this theory. Those with a diminished sense of others, including through autism and schizophrenia, are shown to have a less developed representation of other minds. In Kernberg's work, he shows that a mental health issue is

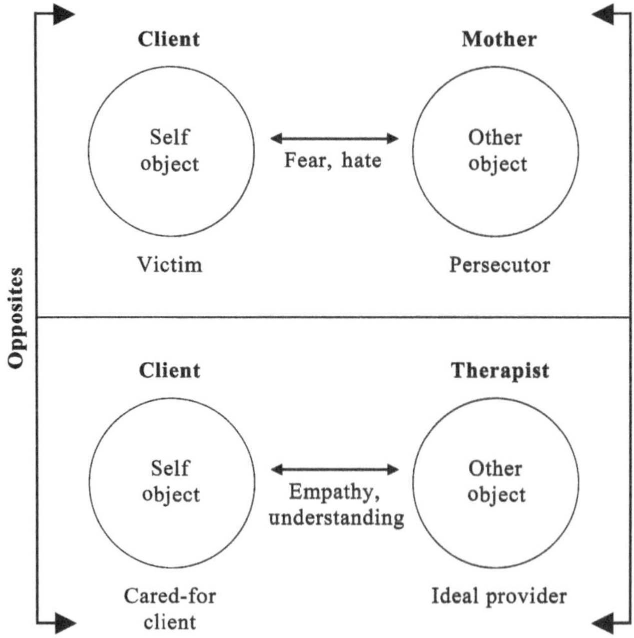

Figure 5.4 Object Relations Dyads

linked with negative self-representations and a healthier person with positive self-representations. We meet again with the humanistic outlook that a healthier person is more self-accepting yet reflective. The object relations view deepens our understanding of how clients represent experience via positive and negative splitting and by distinguishing themselves (or not) from their environments. When clients feel incongruent or detached from experience, their internal self is blurred. As a therapist, this re-emphasises the importance of working with clients on how they perceive themselves, following Gendlin's model of focusing and experiencing.

Kernberg's view is that the client shows and works through their object relations in the session with the therapist. The therapeutic relationship resolves the client's issues. Through the transference, the therapist notices how the client uses splitting; how the client represents themselves, the therapist, and the environment in negative and positive ways; and how the client tolerates the good and bad in the therapist and others. He calls his approach transference-focused psychotherapy because it applies object relations to the transference in the room.

Thus, along with Klein, Kernberg transformed psychodynamic theory from a theory of the individual person to a theory of the relational: from a one-person psychology to a two-person psychology. Freud and Klein emphasised early relationships in the development of the personality. But Klein established the idea that internal representations of people, parts of people, things, needs, and events are preserved via social interactions. That is, internal representations are preserved by repeated relationship patterns – by confirming and reconfirming objects.

With our aforementioned client, this means that low expectations of caregivers are maintained when they invite people into their life who embody low expectations. Kernberg asks us to view the relationship as the primary mechanism of change. Object relations theory is one of the first relationship-focused therapies.

Basic Fault and Primary Love

Object relations therapy focuses on primary love in childhood. It uses empathy and support to help people internalise the self more vividly and congruently. Equally, the environment, through support and empathy, is internalised in more complex ways, with the client more able to tolerate conflictual feelings in relationships.

Michael Balint was a Hungarian psychoanalyst who recognised the importance of primary love in his work. As an object relations theorist, he understood primary love as the mechanism for how people internalise themselves as good or bad objects. He noticed that children who lack attentive caregivers tend to become more depressed and anxious as they grow up. He called this 'the basic fault', meaning that inadequate caregiving leads to more destructive personalities. The 'fault' of a person's mental health lies in their early absence of love.

Missing love in early life leads some people to fixate on ideal objects. For example, the client might use substances as a way to experience soothing. Or the person may fixate on sexual relationships as a way to achieve temporary unconditional love. Being unable to tolerate the depressive position, the good and bad in ideal objects means the person is likely to "turn the world bad," in Klein's words. The client splits someone into a bad object and induces them to become bad. This is similar to the gaslighting situation, where a person convinces another person they are crazy or angry, or something they are not. With enough bad-object energy, the person turns others into the pre-perceived bad object. That is, the ideal romantic partner is then experienced as a painful bad object, criticised, or even abused. The relationship pattern recreates itself over time unless the basic fault is addressed, and the client internalises different self-and-other images.

Early psychodynamic theory modelled the mind as growing out of conflict. The different needs of the id, ego, and superego lead individuals to repress and defend against certain experiences. Object relations, as we have shown in this chapter, deviates from this line of thinking. Instead, it places the parent–infant relationship, usually the mother–child relationship, as the primary influence on mental health. They are not contradictory views, but just different models of the same psychological landscape.

William Fairbairn, a Scottish psychiatrist and psychoanalyst, pushed object relations further to consider the importance of security in the early relationship. Therapists started to criticise some of Melanie Klein's early work, particularly where it led to rather stoic analytical treatments of children. Fairbairn is someone who, like Carl Rogers, began to see the healing significance of the relationship.

Fairbairn studied interactions between children and their caregivers, as well as how children depict their relationships. He found some astonishing results. Well, astonishing to those from a time where attachments and relationships were not common concepts (see Chapter 6). Children with deprivation of care tended to internalise themselves as bad objects. Even in the face of serious health issues, children with early deprivation saw themselves as bad and the depriving parent as good. This splitting caused children to grow up with a basic sense of being a fault, as Balint said earlier.

Fairbairn's interpretation was that children repress bad objects when they rely on the object's goodness. That is, the child repressed the bad parent to survive a hostile environment – to be clothed and fed. This may account for why people in adulthood fail to recognise abusers. It can take many caring people to convince a victim that they are a victim of abuse. In my experience working with domestic violence, for example, many people cannot even say the word victim. They identify so little with that label, and yet they can hold the needs and wants of the abuser in mind without effort, and they repress their own victimhood. I say this confidently because after therapy many clients begin to use words like abuse and victim much more congruently. When the self-representation is more vivid and more cared for, abuse is easier to identify.

The False Self

After Klein, Balint, Kernberg, and Fairbairn developed object relations theory, Donald Winnicott, who coined the phrase "good enough parenting," took object relations into the field of paediatrics. There he extended object relations theory and created many of his own concepts. Winnicott's work focused on helping children and adults to tolerate difficult emotions. He saw this as a primary task of childhood. Good-enough parenting instils in the child a sense of acceptance of life's forceful contradictions and terrifying emotions.

But in early life, the child doesn't perceive a difference between themselves and their parent. Infants experience their caregiver as part of themselves. The baby doesn't understand that their mother has her own emotions, needs, and responsibilities. If the parent survives the child's emotional demands, the child achieves the capacity for self-tolerance. Once this happens the child starts to attune to others.

An overwhelming environment causes children to override their needs. They don't learn to self-regulate; rather they shut down feelings in fear of bad objects. We know this already from Freud, that defence mechanisms remove feelings from awareness. Children without an experience of their emotions, who try and please others or avoid contact, struggle to become coherent people. Winnicott calls this "the false self" because the self is built from incongruent strands of experience and is hidden behind defences.

Let's take an example of a fourteen-year-old boy who suffered physical abuse from his mother. Assigned to his foster placement, my role was to lower his anxiety in the community. Our mental health team would accompany the more traumatised young people as they rode buses and walked to appointments, to build relationships.

The boy panicked when travelling on buses. Claustrophobia caused him to re-experience the sensation of being trapped in an abusive household. We agreed to some exposure work (see Chapter 9), on route to our appointment. He sat far away from me. And, out of nowhere, I turned towards him and threw him an imaginary ball. In the moment, he pretended to catch it, and then he threw it back to me. I did some pretend juggling, then threw it to him – I know, quite a weird thing to do in public!

But, with a devious look in his eye, he paused the game, and popped the ball. When he threw the ball back, it was deflated and lifeless. The adventure circus I had in mind was callously burst.

Being resilient, I sliced the ball back to him, as though it was now a frisbee. But he was cunning and dodged the frisbee as though it was a boomerang. Again, it came back my way. For a few minutes, we played out a scene of offerings and rejections.

From an object relations perspective, the boy is exploring bad objects. My playfulness was rejected safely in the spirit of play. That is, the play allowed the boy to explore his rejection of the ball and frisbee in a symbolic way. Winnicott suggests that if a child has been traumatised, they are likely to minimise their needs. The false self might show itself in our fourteen-year-old boy as a rejection of a need for relationship. That is, deep down he wants to play and connect but presents himself as unconnectable.

In the context of the safe relationship, our play dealt with real anxieties without the pressure of conversation, or even of sitting close together. The client's difficulties could quite literally be played out, understood, and contained.

A more direct example happened when a female client asked me if I was thinking of ending the therapy. I said I wasn't, but was curious to understand where this message came from. She said she is fine if I 'really' want to end the therapy, and that I could just tell her. My feelings were the opposite, that we were forming a strong therapeutic relationship. I asked if this is an experience she has, that she feels others want to end relationships with her. She became aware of feeling abandoned by her mother, of never having 'serious' friendships, and was scared to depend on me. The false self was presenting reality as though it wanted to end the relationship. The real self, the vulnerable self, wanted a deep unconditional connection.

The object relations concept of the false self guides integrative person-centred work. It helps understand why a person in therapy denies needs or pretends not to care if you are late for the appointment, or when the client holds back or is measured in their responses. Noticing the characteristics of the false self helps people connect with their true self. For me the concept brings my attention to supporting the spontaneous and real feelings of the client, giving space for their authentic emotions and needs.

Summary

Object relations theory was developed by Melanie Klein. She deviated from Freud's model of the mind, with its emphasis on mental conflict as the explanation for mental ill health. Instead, she saw the relationship as foundational to why people become emotionally unwell. Through early experience, the child internalises the world into objects. These are representations of experience that have good or bad emotional associations. In early life, children cannot comprehend good and bad in all things, and they split off mental representations into positive and negative. The goal of object relations therapy is to help people have realistic internal representations and to tolerate the imperfect good and bad in people, places, events, and life.

Integrative person-centred therapy uses object relations' concepts to work in a humanistic way. We looked at Gendlin's work with focusing and experiencing, in which bad objects and good objects are named. The experience of these internal representations is amplified, faced, and tolerated. Inevitably, the client works through splitting towards a more congruent and self-affirming view. Reminding ourselves of the research that people who use the defence of splitting have a higher tendency to see themselves negatively, we integrated the ideas into one. That is, the experiencing process is a way to achieve change in object relations. And the client naturally creates hope against the negative self-image and the pessimistic view of the world.

Further Reading

Calverley, R.M., Fischer, K.W., and Ayoub, C. (1994). Complex splitting of self-representations in sexually abused adolescent girls. *Development and Psychopathology* 6 (1): 195–213. https://doi.org/10.1017/S0954579400005952.

Gendlin, E.T. (1961). Experiencing: a variable in the process of therapeutic change. *American Journal of Psychotherapy* 1961 (15): 233–245.

Gomez, L. (1997). *An Introduction to Object Relations*. London: Free Association Books.

Korkmaz, B. (20112011). Theory of mind and neurodevelopmental disorders of childhood. *Pediatric Research* 69: 101–108 (2011). https//doi.org/10.1203/PDR.0b013e318212c177.

Mason, B. (1993). Towards positions of safe uncertainty. *Human Systems* 4 (3–4): 189–200.

Rogers, C.R. (1951). *Client-Centered Therapy*. London: Constable.

Rogers, C.R. (1957). The necessary and sufficient conditions of therapeutic personality change. *Journal of Consulting Psychology* 21: 95–103.

Rogers, C. (1959). A theory of therapy. In: *A Study of Science: Study 1* (ed. S. In Koch). New York: McGraw Hill.

Taylor, J., Lauder, W., Moy, M., and Corlett, J. (2009). Practitioner assessments of 'good enough' parenting: factorial survey. *Journal of Clinical Nursing* 18: 1180–1189.

Winnicott, D.W. (1971). *Playing and Reality*. London: Routledge.

6

Attachment

Matt Schofield

Person-centred therapy puts counselling in a phenomenological frame. The three core conditions, embodied by the therapist, offer the client an alternative *experience*, an emotionally transformative one that enables the client to see themselves, others, and the world in a new light. It understands the importance of the therapeutic relationship in terms of process and outcomes. Given the centrality of this relationship, it is surprising that person-centred theory tells us little about how clients respond to unconditional positive regard, congruence, and empathy. Most clinicians experience clients who attend therapy ready to make use of the therapist, while other clients cannot tolerate, hear, or internalise the therapeutic qualities that Rogers stressed as crucial to change. It is a truism within psychotherapy that those who most benefit from the healing effects of the therapeutic relationship are those who find it most problematic. Consider, for example, the following interaction between Alex, a middle-aged male client, and his female therapist. The client began individual therapy at his partner's request, prompted by growing estrangement in their relationship and is returning for a second session:

Client: (*long silence*) "I can't even remember what we did in last week's session."

Therapist: "It's hard to recall … Well, we talked about how you've been feeling disconnected from your partner. I'm curious how things have been for you since then."

Client: *(shrugs, avoids eye contact)* "It's fine. I think I was just making a big deal out of nothing."

Integrative Person-Centred Counselling: The Combined Model of Counselling and Psychotherapy, First Edition. Rick Murphy.

Therapist: *(gently)* "It seemed like it was weighing on you last time. You left looking sad."

Client: *(leaning back, crossing arms)* "No, not really. I don't see the point in going over this stuff again and again. We've talked about it. I nearly didn't come today as I thought there was no point."

Therapist: *(pausing)* "Perhaps this feels repetitive or frustrating for you. Can we explore what's coming up for you right now as we talk about this?"

Client: *(shaking head)* "Honestly, I just don't think talking about this is helpful. I'd rather focus on just getting on with things."

Therapist: *(leaning in)* "I hear you wanting to focus on moving on, and I also wonder if it feels uncomfortable to sit with the emotions that come up when we talk about connection or disconnection."

Client: *(visibly irritated)* "I'm not uncomfortable. I just think it's a waste of time."

Therapist: *(gently but firmly)* "I wonder if part of what's happening is that it's hard to let someone else in when things feel vulnerable."

Client: *(standing firm)* "No, that's not it. Like I said, I'm fine."

Clearly the therapist and client have reached an impasse. But how do we make sense of the client's resistance to the therapist's efforts to connect and understand? After all, the therapist offers qualities that Rogers identified as fundamental to his person-centred approach. Influenced by an object relations perspective, attachment theory provides a lens through which to understand the difficulties and ruptures that occur in the therapeutic relationship. Centring on the evolutionary drive for survival, attachment explains how individuals like Alex adapt to their caregiving environment and, when entering therapy, act on unconscious expectations about helping relationships. In this chapter, we explore the groundbreaking attachment research of Bowlby, Ainsworth, Main, and beyond, demonstrating how attachment-thinking can be integrated with person-centred counselling.

A Person-Centred Attachment Theory

Attachment theory and person-centred therapy share a common thread that an individual's experience of relationship is fundamental to development. Humanism proposes that people lean towards growth, given the right conditions. In Chapter 1, we named this the 'actualising tendency'.

We discussed Rogers' view that the therapeutic relationship leads to self-actualisation. Maslow, being an academic psychologist, conceived of self-actualisation as a hierarchy of needs, which is shown in its pyramidic form in Figure 6.1. When human needs are met at the pyramid's lower levels, motivation for the upper levels is activated.

Working at the Tavistock Clinic in London, John Bowlby, a British psychiatrist, developed an alternative view of development. Informed by evolution and object relations theory, Bowlby's attachment theory studies biological motivations in relationships. It acknowledges that humans are wired for connection. Safe relationships reduce danger and aid survival, procreation, and ultimately the transmission of genes. Although attachment theorists don't use the language of self-actualisation, the idea that environmental conditions are necessary for growth is fundamental to Bowlby's work.

All children show a preference for familiar caregivers. Bowlby termed this 'an attachment figure'. When a child experiences, recalling Winnicott's words, a 'good enough' attachment figure, the relationship acts as a secure base. The secure base is a source of safety from which the child explores the world and takes risks. Think of a child learning to crawl. As they explore their newfound freedom, they need a safe relationship to look back to for reassurance. Similarly, when the child encounters stress or distress while exploring, the good-enough caregiver acts as a safe haven, which the child

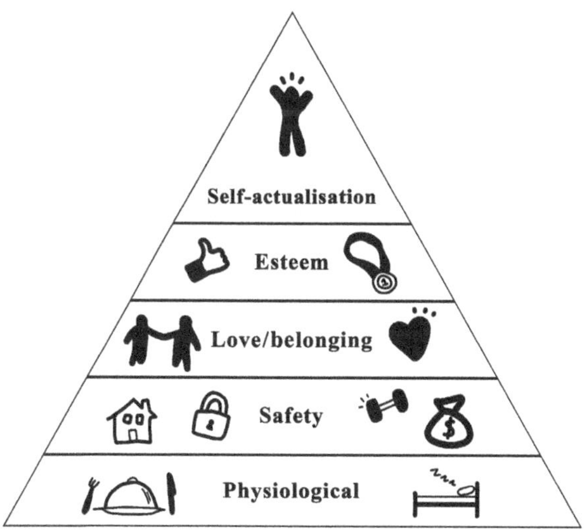

Figure 6.1 Attachment and Maslow's Hierarchy of Needs

can return to. The conditions for the development of secure attachment are summarised by a set of caregiving qualities. These are:

- Attunement,
- Availability,
- Consistency,
- Predictability,
- Sensitivity, and
- Warmth.

Rogers' core conditions, which are empathy, acceptance, and authenticity, are implicit in attachment qualities. One cannot be sensitive without empathy, available without acceptance, or warm without authenticity. When the child experiences caregiving as insensitive, inconsistent, and unavailable, the child cannot use the attachment figure as a safe haven. Insecure environments lead to insecure attachments. The quality of attachment between a caregiver and child has a cascading effect, impacting all levels of Maslow's hierarchy of needs. In Table 6.1, the hierarchy is reconceptualised in terms of attachment experiences and needs.

Table 6.1 Attachment and Self-actualisation

Psychological Need	Impact of Attachment Figure
Physiological	A responsive caregiver accepts a child's communication of physiological needs. The child integrates bodily information, becoming aware of physical signals for hunger, thirst, tiredness, and temperature control.
Safety	When a caregiver protects a child from danger, whilst encouraging exploration, the child learns to take risks and tolerate separation.
Belonging and love	When a caregiver responds to a child's stress and distress with availability, sensitivity, and consistency, the child is able to develop physical and emotional intimacy in relationships.
Esteem	When a caregiver attends to and celebrates a child's achievements, he learns that he is loved, valued, and worthy of esteem.
Self-actualisation	Secure attachment is predictive of higher levels of self-actualisation.

Relationship and Rupture

The caregiver exerts significant influence on the infant, but attachment is an interpersonal process in which both partners impact the relationship's quality. A child's characteristics such as temperament, sensitivity, health, neurodivergence, and disability play a crucial role in the quality of attachment. Goldsmith compares attachment to an 'emotional dance' in which each partner attunes and responds to the other's emotional cues. Missteps or ruptures are common, even in good-enough relationships. From time to time, all parents miss emotional communications, and this is tolerable and essential for the child's socio-emotional development.

The founder of self-psychology, Heinz Kohut, saw that children develop a healthy sense of self from minor misattunements and ruptures, something he termed 'optimal' frustrations. When rupture is coupled with repair, it strengthens the attachment relationship and fosters resilience. The child learns that the environment cannot provide exactly what they need when they need it, and that frustration is survivable. Research shows that when ruptures are not repaired or caregiving is consistently misattuned, insecurity develops and a child becomes less resilient.

One form of relational rupture is separation. Bowlby noted that when an infant is separated from an attachment figure, they exhibit a set of unique behaviours that change as the separation is prolonged. The first stage is marked by the child's anxiety about the separation. Anxiety manifests in protests like crying, calling out, and efforts to gain physical proximity to the caregiver. The child attempts to re-establish contact with the caregiver. Where no reunion is possible, the child moves into a secondary phase marked by despair and withdrawal. The child stops calling out and presents in a listless, sad, and passive manner. The child has given up on the parent returning. In the face of sustained separation, the child moves into a state of detachment, withdrawing their emotional dependence on the caregiver, even when the parent returns.

Attachment Behaviours and Experiences

Person-centred therapy emphasises experience both as route to understanding the client and facilitating change. Alternatively, attachment theory helps understand the significance of behaviour, an aspect not typically a focus of this modality. Bowlby proposed that attachment is principally a behavioural system activated as a means of addressing insecurity. When faced with danger, a child seeks safety; when faced with distress, they seek comfort; when faced with isolation, the child seeks closeness; and when faced with perceived chaos, the child seeks predictability. Infants display a range of attachment behaviours aimed at achieving reunion or sustaining contact with a caregiver. These can be seen in Table 6.2.

When considering person-centred theory and attachment together, it is possible to think about the relationship between behaviour and experience (Figure 6.2). As stress or threat activates the child's attachment behaviours, they experience greater or lesser ability to affect desired caregiver responses. Secure and insecure experiences shape the child's attachment strategies for resolving future incidents of stress or threat. Underlying this feedback loop is the adaptive nature of attachment. The child's behaviour shapes and is shaped by experiences of caregiving.

While infancy is a key period during which attachment bonds are formed, contemporaries of Bowlby such as Hazan, Shaver, and Main have

Table 6.2 Attachment Behaviours and Their Aims

Behaviour Type	Child's Actions	Aim of Behaviour
Signalling behaviour	Looking at, smiling at, waving to, or calling attachment figure	Establishing contact
Aversive behaviour	Crying, shouting, screaming	Eliciting comfort and/or protection
Active behaviour	Moving towards (e.g. crawling, reaching, following) or clinging to attachment figure	Maintaining physical closeness

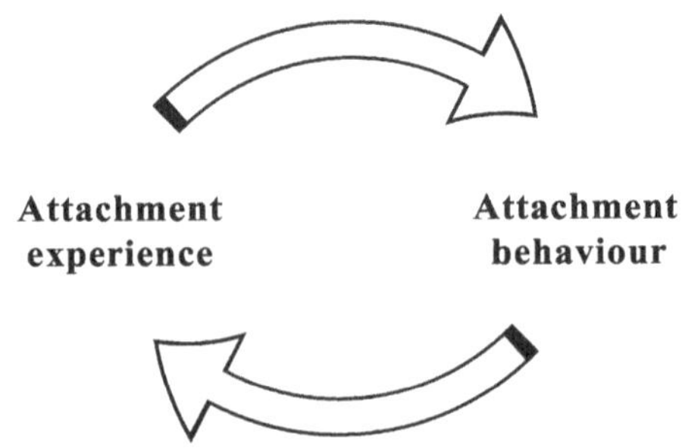

Figure 6.2 A Feedback Loop Between Attachment Behaviours and Experiences

demonstrated that attachment is a lifelong need that evolves across the lifespan. Patterns of behaviour in relationship, or attachment styles, develop into adolescence and across adulthood as new experiences confirm or disconfirm past caregiving experiences. Primary attachment figures change throughout the person's lifecycle, as they form romantic partners, for example, or during old-age when they rely on adult children or carers for support.

Attachment Styles

Person-centred counsellors traditionally resist categorising difficulties that bring clients to therapy, avoiding pathologising language and a medicalised view of mental health. Therapists see the client as a unique individual, not just a collection of symptoms. However, reluctance to use pre-existing frameworks overlooks recurring patterns in human relationships, which can make sense of challenges in the counselling room. Attachment research proposes that individuals respond to stress and distress in largely predictable and coherent ways. Noticing these strategies gives important insights into how clients experience the therapist.

Mary Ainsworth, a contemporary of John Bowlby, was the first researcher to discover different attachment types. These became known as 'attachment styles'. Her now-famous Strange Situation test captured infant behaviours when presented with a series of progressively challenging attachment-based encounters, paying particular attention to the caregiver–child reunion. Ainsworth noticed that infants' behaviours could be grouped into four distinct patterns, which she called secure, avoidant, ambivalent, and unclassifiable. While secure attachment is linked to better mental health outcomes, Bowlby and Ainsworth emphasised that attachment styles are adaptive and help infants survive their environment. For instance, in hostile and abusive environments, insecure attachment reduces danger and maintains connections with caregivers.

Around 60–65% of infants observed in the Strange Situation displayed secure attachment. These children explored with confidence, displayed distress when separated, and were quickly comforted upon reunion with their caregiver. Secure attachment correlates with a trusting relationship, where the caregiver is available, responsive, and capable of regulating distress. A smaller proportion of infants (roughly 14%) exhibited ambivalent attachment, showing wariness of strangers, distress during separation, and conflicted behaviour upon reunion. These children oscillated between clingy and angry behaviours, reflecting unpredictability in caregiver responses. Anxiously attached children often have caregivers who are inconsistent and less responsive, attuning to signals of fear or vulnerability but not to their exploratory efforts. As adults, these children fear abandonment and experience greater anxiety.

Around 20% of children displayed avoidant attachment. These infants showed minimal distress during separation and little interest in or anger at their caregiver during reunions. Ainsworth hypothesised that avoidant children learned to suppress their needs due to repeated experiences of insensitivity or rejection. Later studies revealed that their fewer signs of distress were covering a deeper anxiety, as evidenced by physiological stress markers.

The fourth attachment style, initially labelled unclassifiable, was renamed 'disorganised attachment' by Mary Main and Jerome Solomon. Children in this category exhibited contradictory and confusing behaviours, such as simultaneously approaching and avoiding the caregiver. These children appeared disoriented and fearful, indicating a dilemma where the caregiver is a source of both safety and threat. Disorganised attachment often arises when caregivers are frightening or frightened, creating a conflict between the child's need for connection and fear of harm.

Recent studies explored how social factors, such as poverty and culture, affect attachment development. Van Ijzendoorn and Kroonenberg found that insecure attachment is more common in children from lower socioeconomic backgrounds. Cultural differences also play a significant role in attachment styles. In studies conducted across multiple countries, most children were securely attached, but patterns of insecure attachment varied widely. In Germany, avoidant attachment was highly prevalent, while in Japan it was far less common. These findings underscore Bowlby's theory that children adapt their attachment style to their environment, influenced by cultural norms and parenting practices.

Internal Working Models

Bowlby modelled attachment-based feedback loops, between behaviour and experience, from infancy into adulthood. His research pointed to an internal representation of attachment, used to predict future relating, which he termed an 'internal working model'. This model is action orientated because it initiates a set of behaviours (the attachment style) aimed at resolving stress or distress. Attachment behaviours originate from the internal working model, which is a set of beliefs about self, others, and the world. Unconscious beliefs colour how the person comes to experience and respond to the internal and external world.

The internal working model shares features with other counselling concepts, including schemas, scripts, and core beliefs. In the person-centred model, there is significant crossover between internal working models and Rogers' idea of conditions of worth. Conditions of worth contribute to the individual's self-concept, discussed in Chapter 1. We can think of conditions of worth as being what the individual learns they can and cannot do, be, think, or feel to experience love from a caregiver. Stern and colleagues' work on intersubjectivity reveals that attachment experiences teach individuals about the consequences of sharing and not sharing feelings. Therefore, the internal working model is a blueprint for what feelings can and can't be shared or experienced.

By adulthood, attachment patterns tend to crystalise and remain stable. The conditions of worth attached to internal working models can be self-confirming, leading to old patterns of behaviour being re-enacted in new relationships. There is hope, though, because attachment styles are adaptable. New experiences change attachment styles. Such 'earned security' comes from romantic or helping relationships that confound insecure childhood experiences of love and care. We will now explore how the person-centred relationship contributes to securer ways of relating.

Integrating Attachment Theory and Person-Centred Therapy

An integration of attachment theory and person-centred practice proposes that client growth stems from developing a secure attachment with the therapist. Many clients enter therapy with insecure attachment histories, and security is earned through the therapist's embodiment of the core conditions – qualities of availability, responsiveness, attunement, consistency, and containment. As the client feels secure, they trust previously excluded aspects of self. By accepting the client's experience, the therapist provides a safe space for experimenting with new ways of being, aligning the client more closely with their true self, a change which Rogers named the 'organismic valuing process'. In attachment terms, this means integrating salient information about the relationship between self and the environment.

Attachment experiences signal to clients what information can and can't be integrated to maintain a safe relationship with the caregiver and meet conditions of worth. Avoidant clients exclude negative emotions from experience to prevent rejection. Ambivalent clients exclude factual details that are less effective than emotion at eliciting caregiver attention. For disorganised clients, elements of emotional and cognitive information remain unintegrated in the face of unresolvable fear. The goal for integrative person-centred therapy is to facilitate the re-integration of missing information. This takes place when clients can access emotional *and* cognitive information within the safety of an accepting relationship, where this information can be experienced as trustworthy, informative, and authentic to the self.

In person-centred therapy, a focus on here-and-now experiences overwrites old internal working models. Avoidant clients need to feel their disowned emotions and safety in dependence; ambivalent clients need to experience consistency and resilience; disorganised clients need coherence and safety. The client's internal working model distorts predictions of how the therapist will respond to them, but safe, authentic experiences override these insecurities. Feedback loops that originate in infancy perpetuate relational difficulties in the client's present (Figure 6.3). The here-and-now, moment-by-moment relating with the therapist therefore always contains the past. By utilising the now of the therapeutic relationship, the therapist helps the client work through old relational ruptures and traumas.

Working with Avoidant Attachment

Clients with avoidant attachment are often the least likely to frequent the therapy room due to the nature of their relational adaptations. They have learnt to deactivate attachment behaviours because of persistent experiences of rejection, intrusion, or dismissal. Conditions of worth are centred around being self-sufficient and self-controlled, sacrificing needs within relationships to attend to those of the other. The avoidant client believes, from their internal working model, that it is safer to look after themself than to seek help.

There are significant hurdles for avoidant clients when making use of therapy. Therapy invites them to express thoughts and feelings attached to

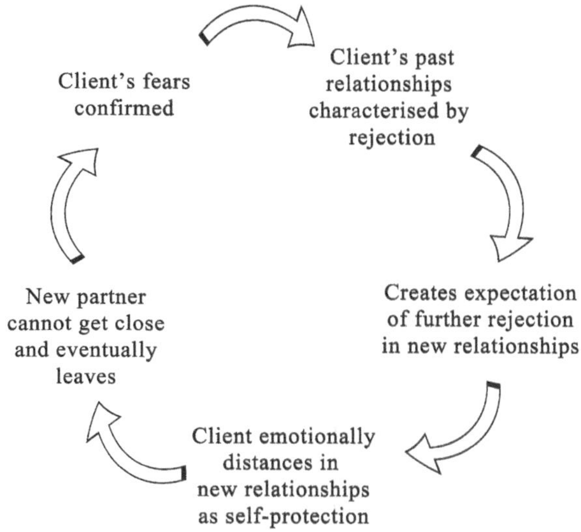

Figure 6.3 Relational Difficulties as an Attachment Feedback Loop

vulnerable aspects of self. By its non-reciprocal nature, therapy prevents the client from gaining false self-esteem by attending to the other at the expense of themselves. A trusted intimate relationship is the main catalyst for change. These are the very elements of attachment avoidant clients have learned so painfully to avoid!

When working with avoidant clients, it helps the person-centred therapist to consider two common difficulties: (1) tolerating and internalising empathy and (2) identifying and communicating experience. We will now explore how these issues create ruptures and impasses in the therapeutic relationship and how the therapist might respond.

Tolerating and Internalising Empathy

In person-centred therapy, empathy is central to the change process. A client feeling deeply understood and attuned to is often a healing experience. However, avoidant clients struggle to tolerate empathy, perceiving it as disingenuous, disorienting, or even threatening. For individuals whose vulnerability has been met with rejection or hostility, empathy activates long-established defence mechanisms constructed to maintain emotional safety and a façade of invulnerability.

It might be obvious by now that Alex, our client who resisted empathy at the opening of this chapter, is showing signs of avoidant attachment. Consider another similar scenario in which a therapist empathises with a client after a relationship break-up:

Therapist: "It must have really hurt hearing Ava say that she no longer loved you after so many years together."

For an avoidant client, this acknowledgment of pain might feel intrusive or uncomfortable, leading them to minimise their feelings:

Client: "Not really, I wasn't surprised. I've always known things would end eventually. It was just a matter of time."

The client's response reflects their discomfort with vulnerability. Wachtel argues that empathy must be titrated for avoidant clients, with the therapist supporting them to gradually build tolerance. For example, the therapist acknowledges the client's immediate reaction to empathy:

Therapist: "You don't like to be told you're in pain."

This respects the client's defensive adaptations whilst opening space to explore their resistance to vulnerability. Over time, the therapist gently introduces reflections that bring disowned feelings into awareness, such as:

Therapist: "You feel uncomfortable with the idea of pain."

Wachtel stresses that the therapist is not saying the client *is* in pain here but names their aversion to being a person that *might* feel pain. This gives room for exploring relational patterns in which the client hides emotional information from self and others. As greater tolerance for empathy is built, the therapist names disowned feelings more openly:

Therapist: "Letting me see your pain is scary for you. You've worked hard to make sure others don't notice it and letting me see it feels risky."

This acknowledges the client's need for safety while slowly opening the door to deeper emotional work. Attachment theory helps person-centred therapists recognise that empathy-attempts trigger clients' defensive strategies, allowing therapists to respond in a more attuned and effective way.

Identifying and Communicating Experience

Attachment theory sheds light on how avoidant clients struggle to identify and express emotions. Person-centred therapists are familiar with clients who respond to feeling-questions with 'I don't know' responses. Attachment theory frames protective responses as strategies learned in environments where emotions were unsafe to express. In early childhood, a caregiver's sensitive attunement helps a child understand and label experiences. When a caregiver consistently dismisses, ignores, or disapproves of a child's emotions, the child becomes alienated from their feelings. As adults, their emotional awareness is limited, and they lack the language to communicate them. Wallin points out that feeling questions are 'unanswerable' for clients with avoidant attachment when they "involve experiences of the sort that the first relationships excluded."

Immediacy is an invaluable person-centred intervention that brings avoidant clients closer to experiences by drawing attention to physical manifestations. Small shifts in body language – yawning, averting gaze, changes in posture or breathing – provide subtle cues of unexpressed emotion. Noticing differences between what is said and *how* it is said points clients to disowned feelings. For avoidant clients, body language is less threatening than talking about feelings.

For example, a young man I worked with excluded unacceptable feelings from awareness and had great difficulty in putting his feelings into words. Sleepiness, changing the subject, taking sips of water, and biting his lip were some of the indications that our talk had provoked an emotion, and I used immediacy to draw the client's attention to this:

Therapist: "I noticed just now, as we began to talk about the way your brother treated you, you started to look sleepy and more distant. I wonder what is going on for you right now?"

Therapists must respect the client's unreadiness to feel disowned affect. Insisting on denied emotions is counterproductive. Instead, immediacy fosters a safe environment where clients can begin trusting bodily cues and emotions, learning they no longer need to exclude feelings as they did in the original caregiving environment.

Therapist self-disclosure can also help avoidant clients who struggle to identify emotions. Instead of naming the client's feeling directly, therapists share their emotional experience to gently prompt awareness. For example, rather than saying, "Your teary eyes suggest sadness," the therapist reframes this, reflecting, "As you talked about your brother walking out, I felt a real sadness and some tears came to my eyes. I wonder if that resonates with you?"

Self-disclosure non-threateningly invites the client to explore feelings. It demonstrates that emotional openness and vulnerability within a relationship are survivable and meaningful. The client can decline the invitation without shame, fostering trust and safety.

Working with Ambivalent Attachment

Adults with ambivalent attachment are typically more familiar with eliciting help than avoidant clients. They have learnt to hyper-activate attachment behaviours in response to inconsistent and under-responsive caregiving. Their conditions of worth are centred around heightened emotional expression, seeking reassurance, and maintaining closeness to others at all costs. The ambivalent client believes that their safety and self-worth depend on constantly monitoring and managing the emotional availability of others.

When working with ambivalent clients, it is helpful for person-centred therapists to understand challenges in three areas: (1) managing therapist congruence and attunement, (2) maintaining unconditional positive regard, and (3) fostering exploratory behaviours. We will now explore how these issues can lead to ruptures and impasses in the therapeutic relationship and how the therapist might respond.

Therapist Congruence and Attunement

Congruence and transparency from the therapist must be approached with caution when working with ambivalent clients. While self-disclosure can help avoidant clients connect with disowned feelings, for anxiously attached clients, it may reinforce fears of abandonment or emotional unavailability.

A therapist might self-disclose, like below, as an invitation for the avoidant client to connect with disowned feelings:

Therapist: "As you talked about your brother walking out on you, I felt sadness come up in me and some tears. I wonder whether you make any sense of that?"

For the ambivalently attached client, transparency may provoke responses that indicate anxiety about self and the relationship. This could look like:

Guilt about burdening the therapist:

Client: "I'm sorry for making you feel that way. I'm often demanding of people and now I'm doing the same with you. You must think I'm too much."

Efforts to please the therapist:

Client: "It must be horrible for you to feel all your clients' emotions. Are you ok? I'm fine really, it's not a big deal."

Preoccupation with vulnerability:

Client: "If I'm making you feel sad, things must be bad. What's wrong with me?"

At the heart of these anxieties is the client's belief that open expression of their needs and emotions results in abandonment by the therapist. Therapists should be mindful that ambivalent clients are hypervigilant to signs of misattunement and that instances of distraction or inattention can lead to ruptures requiring repair. To counter the client's experience of inconsistent caregiver attention and availability, Brown suggests that therapists maintain a 'positive opposite' stance, focusing consistently on the client's state of mind. Limiting self-disclosure and paying close attention to moment-by-moment fluctuations in the client's emotional communication reduces the client's pull towards the therapist's mind at the expense of their own.

Unconditional Positive Regard

Acceptance is essential for all clients in person-centred therapy but requires special attention when working with ambivalent attachment, those stuck in early caregiving patterns where behaviours aimed at eliciting closeness push attachment figures away (Figure 6.4). Client fears of being judged or abandoned have often been reinforced by past instances where their emotions were labelled as excessive or dramatic. The therapist counters these experiences by providing unconditional positive regard in the face of sometimes intense feeling states. This acceptance must not depend on the client's ability to regulate feelings or appear resilient.

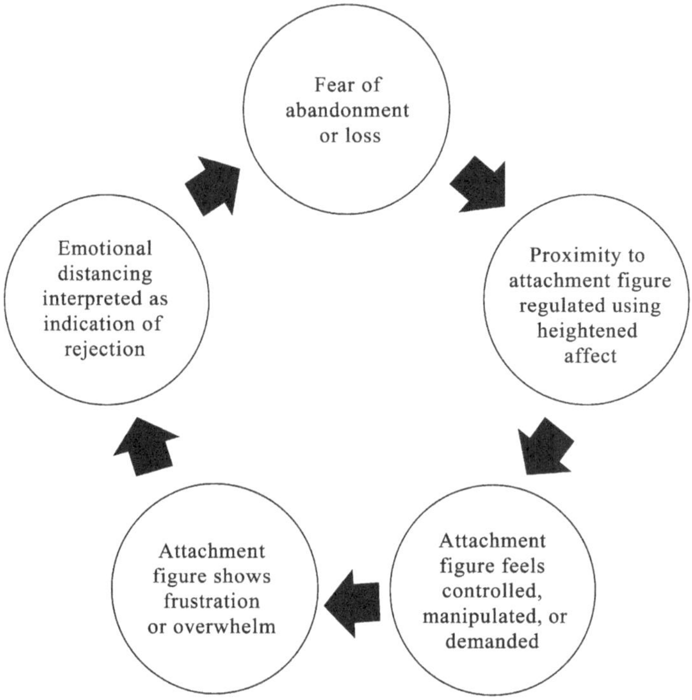

Figure 6.4 Cycle of Ambivalence

Brown highlights calmness as an essential feature of acceptance. Calmness reassures the client that their emotions are not overwhelming and are not likely to push the therapist away. It avoids reinforcing the client's beliefs that heightened emotion is necessary to keep the attachment figures close. This is undoubtedly a challenge for the therapist, requiring them to self-regulate with very distressed clients who are unaware of how they contribute to their predicament. Attachment theory helps therapists develop empathy by holding in mind the child in the room and the role of separation in the development of their fears.

Fostering Exploratory Behaviours

Research on ambivalent attachment shows that caregivers tend to ignore or disrupt a child's exploratory behaviours while reinforcing communications of fear or vulnerability. In adulthood, this dynamic leads to heightened anxiety about the world and the client's ability to navigate it safely. Challenging or dismissing these anxieties is unlikely to be productive, given these clients' sensitivity to misattunement. At the same time, client-centred therapists may find themselves unintentionally reinforcing learned helplessness when interactions simply mirror the client's fears and vulnerabilities.

What the therapist focuses on is crucial here, maintaining a keen awareness of any signs of exploratory behaviours in the client, like moments of self-reflection, interest in the external world, or risk taking. Thinking, rather than feeling, is significant for ambivalent clients, who often struggle with reflective function due to their preoccupation with others' minds. A therapist draws attention to their developing capacity in the following way:

Client: "I realised that during the argument, my anger was pushing him away. This is the pattern I always fall into – pushing others away before they leave."

Therapist: "You really noticed something about yourself there – not just the anger driving the argument, but that it's part of a bigger pattern in your life. What was it like to notice that?"

By reflecting these behaviours, the therapist helps the client see that new ways of functioning are possible. As a result, clients may begin to verbalise insights like the following:

Internal reflection: "When I focus on myself instead of others, I understand my emotions better and they feel more manageable. My fear that other people will forget me or get fed up with me doesn't happen. I feel safer and more secure."

External exploration: "Taking risks in the world helps me see myself as more capable and resilient. I can do lots of things I never thought I could cope with."

By emphasising these shifts, the therapist fosters a secure base for the client to explore new ways of relating and being.

Working with Disorganised Attachment

Theorists vary in how they conceptualise disorganised attachment, which mirrors the confusing and contradictory presentation of these clients. Unable to resolve experiences of fear within attachment relationships, disorganised individuals display incoherent behaviours when faced with stress or distress. Therapists observe oscillations between hyperactivating and deactivating behaviours, expressing the need to simultaneously connect and defend. These strategies reduce danger with psychological distance from, and control of, the attachment figure.

Clients' experience of trauma is central to attachment counselling and establishing safety a key task in the therapeutic relationship. Clients enter therapy with a dilemma: attachment figures, including the therapist, are both a source of fear and safety. While conflicting wishes are common in the therapeutic process for all clients, disorganised individuals find developing a relationship with the therapist particularly challenging because they have not resolved the contradictory belief that they can neither live with nor without attachment figures. For person-centred therapists, the formation of the therapeutic relationship is inseparable from trauma work. As Wallin suggests, "The incremental achievement of a sense of safety in relation to the therapist does resolve trauma, while the incremental resolution of trauma gradually obviates the necessity in the [client] to reexperience the therapeutic relationship (and others) as a rendezvous with old threats."

When working with disorganised clients, it is helpful for the person-centred therapist to understand three important issues: (1) dissociation (2) the role of the body, and (3) noticing positive emotion.

Dissociation

Clients with disorganised attachment often dissociate as an adaptation to dangerous relationships. When a child experiences overwhelming fear without resolution from a source of safety (i.e. the caregiver), the brain rejects this information. Dissociation fragments contradictory and unthinkable memories into what Liotti calls "simultaneous multiple representations of reality." By compartmentalising experience, dissociation preserves even the most dysfunctional relationships, suppressing negative emotions towards abusive or unavailable caregivers. Although adaptive, dissociation brings debilitating effects including depersonalisation, derealisation, amnesia, and a fragmented self.

Therapists promote safety and emotional regulation with dissociative clients by using sensory experience to ground or anchor them. While grounding techniques are common to directive modalities like cognitive behavioural therapy, integrative therapists may need to use proactive interventions in response to dissociation to prevent re-enacting experiences of caregiver absence, neglect, or indifference. Counsellors offer simple invitations for clients to take notice of their senses:

Therapist: "Take a look around the room and notice some details – the colours, shapes, or textures around you. What do you see?"
Therapist: "Let's notice the sounds inside or outside the room. What do you hear?"

The therapist connects the client with smells, tactile sensations, and taste, until the client feels present in the room. Therapists help clients understand the function of their dissociation. Using immediacy, therapists draw attention to patterns in the therapy session:

Therapist: "I've noticed you disappear when we talk about feelings around your brother. What do you make of that?"
Therapist: "Dissociation seems to keep feelings and memories at a distance. I wonder what you think dissociation protects you from?"

The Role of the Body

Trauma is rooted in the nervous system and physiological responses, making bodywork highly relevant for disorganised clients. Peter Levine explains that natural responses to trauma – such as fight or flight – are interrupted when individuals cannot escape the source of danger, as is often the case in attachment trauma. When survival energy cannot be discharged, it becomes 'frozen' in the body, leaving the person stuck in dysregulation. Therapists reconnect clients with their bodies to release this trapped energy gradually.

Levine's process of 'titration', which involves oscillating between safety and discomfort, can be adapted for person-centred therapy. The therapist is guided by verbal and non-verbal cues to keep the client within their tolerance zone. Imagine a client who begins to talk about his violent father:

Client: "I guess I was just ..." [Therapist notices signs of dysregulation (e.g. leg shaking, zoning out)].
Therapist: "I can see it's hard to stay with this. Can you find a part of your body that feels safe or at ease right now?"
Client: "My legs feel okay."

Therapist: "Let's focus on that feeling for a moment. Notice how it feels to have your legs grounded on the floor."

Once grounded, the therapist gently guides the client to explore the source of dysregulation in a controlled manner:

Therapist: "Now that you feel more grounded, let's notice the difficult feeling for a moment. Where do you feel it in your body? If it feels overwhelming, let me know, and we can return to your legs."

Moving between physical sensations of safety and danger, the client releases trapped trauma energy, expressed in movements such as shaking, twitches, changes in breathing or bodily temperature, and emotion.

Noticing Positive Emotion

For disorganised clients, expressing positive emotions is challenging, as their world is coloured by trauma. Brown suggests that therapists attune to subtle indications of positive affect, inviting the client to expand on these experiences. The person-centred therapist is not creating positive emotions but facilitating expression of hidden parts of the self, such as joy or pleasure, that have previously been overshadowed. This might look like:

Therapist: "When you talked about playing with your child, I sensed some enjoyment there. What was that like for you?"

Therapist: "I noticed your face light up just now. What word might describe that feeling—free, excited, or something else?"

Therapists can also use bodily cues to facilitate self-expression:

Therapist: "When you mentioned walking in the park, it seemed like something shifted in your body. What was that like for you?"

Providing space for positive feelings creates an opportunity to integrate disowned parts, fostering a richer and more cohesive sense of self.

Conclusion

Attachment theory provides a powerful lens for understanding relational dynamics within person-centred therapy. Integrating the insights of attachment science with the core conditions of empathy, acceptance, and authenticity, therapists can better respond to ruptures and impasses within the therapy room, promoting safety and trust. This model helps clients address unresolved attachment dilemmas whilst developing a more authentic sense of self. Whether working with avoidant, ambivalent, or disorganised attachment styles, therapists tailor interventions to foster security, develop congruence, and encourage new patterns of relating. An attachment-informed therapeutic relationship is an opportunity for clients to challenge old ways of being, develop a more accurate self-concept, and experience greater relational trust, ultimately supporting their journey toward self-actualisation and wholeness.

Further Reading

Ainsworth, M.D. and Wittig, B.A. (1969). Attachment and exploratory behaviour of one-year-olds in a strange situation. In: *Determinants of Infant Behaviour*, vol. 4 (ed. B.M. Foss), 113–136. London: Methuen.

Ainsworth, M.D.S., Blehar, M., Waters, E., and Wall, S. (1978). *Patterns of Attachment: A Psychological Study of the Strange Situation*. Hillsdale, NJ: Erlbaum Associates.

Bowlby, J. (1969). *Attachment: Attachment and Loss: Vol. 1: Loss*. New York, NY: Basic Books.

Bowlby, J. (1988). *A Secure Base: Clinical Applications of Attachment Theory*. Hove: Brunner-Routledge.

Brown, D.P. and Elliott, D.S. (2016). *Attachment Disturbances in Adults: Treatment for Comprehensive Repair*. WW Norton & Co.

Cornelius-White, J.H., Motschnig-Pitrik, R., and Lux, M. (2013). *Interdisciplinary Applications of the Person-Centred Approach*. New York: Springer.

Crittenden, P.M. (2006). A dynamic-maturational model of attachment. *Australian and New Zealand Journal of Family Therapy* 27 (2): 105–115.

Crittenden, P. (2013). *Raising Parents: Attachment, Parenting and Child Safety*. Routledge.

Goldsmith, D.F. (2010). The emotional dance of attachment. *Clinical Social Work Journal* 38 (1): 4–7.

Hazan, C. and Shaver, P.R. (1987). Romantic love conceptualized as an attachment process. *Journal of Personality and Social Psychology* 52: 511–524.

Kohut, H. (2009). *The Restoration of the Self*. University of Chicago Press.

Levine, P.A. (2010). *In an Unspoken Voice: How the Body Releases Trauma and Restores Goodness*. North Atlantic Books.

Liotti, G. (2006). A model of dissociation based on attachment theory and research. *Journal of Trauma & Dissociation* 7 (4): 55–73.

Main, M. and Solomon, J. (1986). Discovery of a new, insecure-disorganized/disoriented attachment pattern. In: *Affective Development in Infancy* (ed. M. Yogman and T.B. Brazelton), 95–124. Norwood, NJ: Ablex.

Maslow, A.H. (1943). A theory of human motivation. *Psychological Review* 50 (4): 370–396.

Otway, L. and Carnelley, K. (2013). Exploring the associations between adult attachment security and self-actualisation and self-transcendence. *Self and Identity* 12: 217–230. https://doi.org/10.1080/15298868.2012.667570.

Rogers, C.R. (1951). *Client-Centred Therapy*. London: Constable.

Stern, D.N. (2018). *The Interpersonal World of the Infant: A View from Psychoanalysis and Developmental Psychology*. Routledge.

Van Ijzendoorn, M.H. and Kroonberg, P.M. (1988). Cross-cultural patterns of attachment: a meta-analysis of the strange situation. *Child Development* 59 (1): 147–156.

Wallin, D.J. (2007). *Attachment in Psychotherapy*. The Guilford Press.

Wachtel, P.L. (2011). *Therapeutic Communication: Knowing What to Say When*. Guilford Press.

White, M. (2020). An exploration of 'earned-secure' attachment and the role of attachment-informed psychotherapy. [Higher diploma thesis, Dublin Business School]. Dublin. https://esource.dbs.ie/server/api/core/bitstreams/5a219e4a-327f-4c33-bae0-9ce51f1126f0/content (accessed 21 April 2025).

Winnicott, D.W. (1971). *Playing and Reality*. London: Routledge.

7

Existential

Dr. Lisa Dvorjetz

On the weekend I went to the East Coast of England to witness the annual birthing of grey seals. Each year, thousands of seal pups are born amidst crowds of awe-inspired human onlookers. It's a privilege to see new life breathing and playing for the first time (Figure 7.1).

But this incredible spectacle of nature has a darker side. A local news outlet reported, "Seal Pup Chased to Its Death". Tragically, a seal pup died as the result of being surrounded by humans trying to take selfies. Its mother, unable to get milk to her pup, abandoned it. The vulnerable pup, chased by two unsupervised children, escaped from the humans into the unforgiving sea, weeks before it grew its waterproof fur, and so it drowned.

This event captured the horror and beauty of nature, themes which are discussed in this chapter. In existentialism, we focus on issues of life and death. The theme of human mortality is found lurking behind all client issues. From anxiety to depression, meaning and death are the ultimate concerns.

I argue in this chapter for existentialist ideas to be integrated into the person-centred model of counselling. Through life experience, media, and self-awareness, people become conscious of death between two and five years old. At that age, we understand that being dead is different from being alive. But it's not until around age 10 where people grasp the true finality of death. As Shakespeare writes in *Richard II*, "Woe, destruction, ruin and decay; The worst is death, and death will have his day."

The inevitability of death, and how to live life knowing this fact, lies at the heart of existential therapy. Here we demonstrate the usefulness and inevitability of existential themes in integrative counselling.

Integrative Person-Centred Counselling: The Combined Model of Counselling and Psychotherapy, First Edition. Rick Murphy.

Figure 7.1 Pup Season, Winterton-on-Sea

The Pillars of Existentialism

Existentialism focuses on each person's unique experience of what it is to be human. It's not just about death but also the meaning of living. While there are numerous branches of existential philosophy, the three fundamental pillars are that humans have choice, responsibility, and freedom to create purpose. This is like the humanistic belief that people have a sense of agency. People change and self-actualise. But above Maslow's pyramid is a cloud of realisation – the fact that none of us can grow forever.

One of the main critiques that the existentialists had with earlier psychotherapies, such as Freud's psychoanalysis, was that in the subjective thoughts, emotions, and bodily sensations that people experience was an absence of the fact that subjective experience connects with a person's ultimate existence.

If a client walks into the therapy room and says to the therapist "I'm feeling depressed," the Freudian therapist analyses the client's depression and provides interpretations about conflicts between needs, reality, and value judgements. The person-centred therapist provides safety to sit with the experience in the here-and-now. But the existentially trained therapist explores both – how their present experience, needs, reality, and value judgements are linked with death, meaning, isolation, and freedom.

Underscoring all psychotherapies, including those discussed in this book, are existential issues.

The German philosopher Martin Heidegger and French philosophers Jean-Paul Sartre and Maurice Merleau-Ponty rejected the mind–body split that humans have a physical body and a non-physical mind. This has consequences for psychological issues since the mortal body is therefore part of our psychology. For example, if you were to ask two people standing in the woods what they experience, you are likely to get two different responses. One notices the wind rustling through the leaves, feeling a chill across their face. The other feels the warmth of the sunlight on their hands, feeling their shoes crunch on the autumnal leaves. If you hadn't asked the same question twice, you wouldn't know how differently people experience the same environment. It is therefore the therapist's task to help the client become aware of how they uniquely experience the world via their own existence.

In this chapter, I will help you become familiar with working from an existential and person-centred lens, providing you with techniques to work from this integrated approach. Existential psychotherapy consists of multiple strands that overlap in their fundamental beliefs but differ in how they are practiced. We will start by looking at Viktor Frankl's logotherapy followed by Irvin Yalom's four basic existential givens, concluding with Emmy Van Deurzen's four dimensions of existence.

Logotherapy: Finding Meaning Through Suffering and Choice

A new therapy referral has just entered your inbox from a man, Stephen, in his 60s, who has recently been diagnosed with cancer. Stephen is unsure whether his cancer is curable. The referral states that he wants therapy to help him sleep. He has tried sleeping tablets, herbal remedies, and mindfulness, but to no avail. How could you provide therapy to Stephen?

One approach is to utilise Viktor Frankl's logotherapy. 'Logos' translated from Greek means 'reason' or 'meaning', so 'logotherapy' involves helping the client find meaning or a reason to be alive. Frankl's autobiographical book, *Man's Search For Meaning*, depicts his experience of being sent to multiple Nazi concentration camps, including Auschwitz, and his reflections on what helped him survive against the odds.

Frankl stresses that each person strives for meaning in life, which is unique to them. When first meeting Stephen, he says he has been married to Hannah for over 40 years and they have a daughter, Ellie, in her 30s. Stephen's parents are still alive and before he started chemotherapy he cared for them. Stephen described feeling guilty that he can no longer look after his parents.

Using logotherapy, we attend to Stephen's experience of guilt. Feelings of guilt imply that Stephen feels he has contradicted his meaningful set of values. Part of his purpose in life has been caring for his parents. Chemotherapy has taken that ability and role away from him. Although his wife has taken on the practical care of his parents, his feelings of guilt remain because it's his responsibility to care for them.

Frankl confronted death and suffering daily in the concentration camps. This highlighted to him the finiteness of life. He describes coming close to being sent to a gas chamber, beaten for no apparent reason, and rationing food, all of which emphasised how close he was to death. Despite this, he speaks of each person finding purpose and meaning. With the example of food, he said that every day he received a small ration of bread and a bowl of watery soup. He had a choice of eating the bread all in one go, which would satisfy his hunger pangs, but the satiation would be temporary. Or he could break off small pieces to spread the consumption throughout the day but risk losing the bread or having it stolen. Even the piece of bread has finiteness, and he had the responsibility of choosing what he makes of it.

Going back to Stephen, he loses sight of meaning when he speaks about his fears. Given the uncertainty of whether his cancer is curable or not, Stephen describes feelings of panic. This panic is in knowing how long he has left to live and how his wife and daughter will cope with their grief after his death. He fears going to sleep as he is unsure whether he will wake up again. Equally he dreads the morning as his frail body brutally reminds him of the cancer and the gradual descent to death.

Frankl claims that psychological distress is less existential in terms of death itself, but more often connected to a lack of meaning. How could we test this out using logotherapy with Stephen?

Existential Socratic Dialogue

One of the techniques to understand Stephen's thoughts, feelings, and values around meaning is Socratic dialogue. Socratic dialogue was created by Plato to deconstruct knowledge. It is a question-based technique that explores a subject matter to the point that the original premise has been broken down into how the client reached conclusions about a subject. The therapist takes a 'not knowing' position to find alternative ways of viewing the client's assumptions. With Stephen, Socratic dialogue helps him reflect on meaning (Table 7.1).

Table 7.1 Existential Dialogue

Dialogue	**Existential & Humanistic Reflections**
Lisa: When you mention that you feel 'panic', are there particular times of the day when this feeling occurs?	I actively listen to Stephen by repeating the word 'panic'. We demonstrate unconditional positive regard by taking a genuine interest in his difficulties. We are alongside him in his experience, getting him to provide details about his lived experience. Strictly person-centred therapists may see this question as leading the client because the therapist asks about the times of day when panic occurs. I argue that to reflect on the existential meaning of Stephen's experience, the therapist needs to alternate between the micro and macro levels of his life.
Stephen: Um, yes, probably first thing in the morning, and when I'm about to go to sleep. I keep thinking what's the point of continuing with the chemotherapy treatment if I'm going to die anyway? Perhaps I should stop the treatment now so it can hasten my death?	
Lisa: What I'm hearing you question is why postpone your death when you know that it is inevitable?	Here, I paraphrase Stephen's question to show empathy and summarise what is important to him. I introduce Socratic questioning to understand the significance of the treatment.
Stephen: Yes. I'm so fatigued, I keep falling as I have low blood pressure and I'm constantly in pain so must get my wife to do the cooking and cleaning.	
Lisa: It sounds like the chemotherapy is having an impact on your physical ability to live your life how it used to be. I'm wondering, Why continue with the chemotherapy at all?	For Stephen it was a given that he had to have chemotherapy, yet he has a choice and responsibility to proceed with the treatment or to stop it. I use a Socratic question to find out what Stephen's driving forces are for continuing to endure the physical and psychological consequences of the treatment. I'm trying to elicit what Stephen's assumptions are around having the treatment and not having it.

(*Continued*)

Table 7.1 (Continued)

Dialogue	**Existential & Humanistic Reflections**
Stephen: Well, I just have to!	
Lisa: It feels like it's a given.	Picking up on a sense of powerlessness from Stephen's response, I reiterate his feeling of not having any choice.
Stephen: My wife, daughter, and parents would think I've given up on them if I don't continue with the treatment, so I have to keep going with it.	Stephen has introduced the people that are important to him in his life and part of his decision-making process. I enquire further about that as there may be meaningfulness in his relationships.
Lisa: As challenging as it is for you to continue with the treatment because of the physical side effects, you're choosing to attend the chemotherapy sessions because you don't want to let your family down?	I introduce the idea of choice to remind Stephen that he has choice in each decision he makes but I recognise that the decision is not straightforward and without consequence. There is suffering if he chooses to continue with treatment and equally if he chooses to stop.
Stephen: Well, how will they cope when I'm not here? I have to stay alive for as long as possible so I can prepare them for after I'm gone.	Stephen begins to express the meaning for him of having the treatment. He sees it is a way of extending his life so that he can prepare his family for the emotional and physical pain following his death. He places a high value on being a father, husband, and son. It is important for him to remain within those roles for as long as he is alive. This, it sounds like, is part of his meaning of life.

Through active listening, paraphrasing, empathy, and Socratic questioning, Stephen recognises that his panic is about questioning whether he should continue with treatment. He wants to fulfil his roles of father, husband, and son as he gains a sense of meaning from being in those relationships. This correlates with Frankl's two premises that people find meaning in life through being in relation to someone else and people even find meaning when suffering. If we were to continue the session with Stephen in this existential way, how could we support him in making decisions that empower him to maintain his role of carer, husband, father, and son? We might explore emotional connections to family members, even when he is physically ill. For example, how can he connect more to his daughter that lives far away given he can't travel to see her? How can he care for his parents despite not being physically able to like how he used to?

Yalom's Approach – The Existential Givens

Irvin Yalom, the American psychiatrist, is one of the most recognisable existential psychotherapists in the field due to his literary contributions of both fictional and non-fictional works. If you've ever picked up one of his books, you might notice his style of writing to be one of trying to relate to, rather than didactically teach, the reader. He calls it "the teaching novel." His approach to storytelling allows the reader to see each client as an individual and a unique person rather than a case study exhibiting psychiatric symptoms.

Yalom's fundamental belief is that emotional distress occurs when we experience existential conflict. Psychological tension surfaces when we are confronted by the inescapable parts of being human. These life unavoidables, or existential givens, are death, freedom, isolation, and meaninglessness. Although we experience all facets of existence, Yalom believes that some are prominent for clients at different points in therapy. He is not suggesting that, as therapists, we enter each session with an intention to force existential theory onto clients. Rather we attune to moments when existential ideas arise. We will go through each of the existential givens, using client examples to illustrate Yalom's existential approach.

Death

Coming from a 'stiff upper lip' British culture, the words 'death', 'dying', and 'dead' are taboo. In a recent Marie Curie survey on attitudes towards death and dying, 59% of participants said there is a lack of talking about death in society. However, on a personal level, 66% said they feel comfortable talking about end-of-life themes. Only 14% said they had death-themed discussions with friends or family. These figures imply that unless therapists proactively bring death into the conversation, the topic won't arise. We can take this as our cue to invite clients into a conversation about death.

Yalom saw death as life's ultimate terror-inducing consequence. It makes sense that we create avoidance strategies like denial, protecting ourselves from experiencing the terror. We saw in Chapter 3 that psychopathology occurs when someone's coping strategies prevent them from growing and, as the humanistic theory showed, reaching self-actualisation. Working within the field of oncology and palliative care, death anxiety is prevalent because patients make treatment decisions based on life and death. But what would working with death look like in a non-cancer-based setting? Are death-themes relevant to psychotherapy more broadly?

I am thinking of a client named Susan. She is a middle-aged woman, married with young children, working as a banker. She came for therapy because she was feeling low in mood, struggling to concentrate, and lacking in energy. She disclosed feeling suicidal although had not attempted to hurt herself. After a few sessions, Susan linked her low mood to her disappointment about where she was in her life. She grew up in a divorced household where her role was being the high achiever amongst her siblings. She believed that a well-paid job, marriage, children, and home ownership would bring her happiness. As the sessions progressed, she became aware that her life ambitions turned to feelings of loneliness. In that loneliness came a want to numb the feeling, and so she started increasing her alcohol consumption.

Susan's life vision, from childhood, was that once she had achieved all that she wanted in life she would be happy until death; however, this hadn't happened. She thought, 'Is this all there is to life?' Her self-image of being a successful person became a barrier to expressing emotions to friends and family, fearing they'd think she was weak.

Yalom would say that Susan's focus on achieving is a defence against acknowledging the finiteness of life. The more Susan moves forward and achieves, the smaller her future gets. Bringing Susan back to the present, we explored the areas in her life she wanted to feel more connected to. She spoke fondly of her close group of friends yet none of whom knew of her emotional struggles. Susan experienced incongruence between how others saw her, "the person who has her life together," and how she viewed herself, "achieving in personal and professional life but feeling unsatisfied and lonely." Susan wanted to feel more congruent between how others viewed her and how she viewed herself, so we explored how it would be for her to be more open with her friends about her struggles. At the next session, she informed me that she had told the entire friendship group of her low mood and suicidal thoughts, which understandably surprised them, being the first time they heard Susan express her feelings. This conversation paved the way for further conversations with her friends who, in turn, opened up more about their struggles, strengthening the emotional connection between them. Susan gave less energy to achieving at work and more time to emotionally connecting with her friends.

Although our work is person centred, because we use Rogers' core conditions to support the client, it is existential in that we work with the underlying dread and meaninglessness that comes with human existence.

Freedom

As I sit here typing, I'm noticing that my upper back is hunched over the keyboard and is starting to ache. I could take a break by going for a walk in the nearby forest, but I tell myself that I can't because it's pouring with rain – which is to be expected with the British weather!

Yalom would say that in this situation, I have the choice or freedom to decide what to do, and therefore I must bear the weight of my decision not to go outside for a walk and continue experiencing back ache. To take responsibility for my decision, he encourages me to change the sentence, "I can't because it's pouring with rain" to, "I choose not to because it's pouring with rain." Going from 'I can't' to 'I choose' means I am the sole person responsible for my pain and cannot blame the rain for causing it.

Autonomy links to the seven stages of process in the person-centred approach, specifically to stage three, where we support the client to take responsibility. The role of the existential therapist is to encourage clients to notice the areas in their life where they may or may not be taking responsibility for their actions. This can connect them to how they create their lives.

One way to create awareness of clients' responsibility is by noticing the language and vocabulary used when describing experience. The statement, "My voice won't make a difference," could be viewed as, "I'm choosing not to speak up because I think it won't make a difference." Speaking up requires taking a stand, having an opinion, and therefore communicating to yourself and others that you exist. In drawing attention to the client's difficulty for taking responsibility, the client can continue to choose not to speak up or can choose to respond differently. But the choice to exist is reflected to the client.

Another way of highlighting choice and freedom to clients is to suggest alternative options to them. A common issue in the therapy room is clients burning out from work, social commitments, or family care duties. Clients say things like, "I feel stressed because I've got so much going on at work.

I've got to stay until 11 pm in the office to finish it all" or "I had to check my work emails whilst I was away on holiday because my boss needed information from me regarding a project I'm working on." Whilst the person-centred approach focuses on the feelings of stress, empathising with the situation, Yalom's existential lens offers alternative choices to the client. He might say,

> I'm hearing that you're feeling stressed because you've got so much work on at the moment, but I'm wondering what it would be like for you to leave the office at 6 pm?

We are not telling the client our opinion or suggesting what to do. We introduce the dilemma to the client to see how they respond. The client often responds like "Oh, I can't leave at 6 pm! I'll come back to the office in the morning to a mountain of work." The client communicates that it's important for them to feel like they're on top of their workload, which is a priority for them. The therapist enquires about what else is important in the client's life in working until 11 pm or leaving earlier. For example:

> What are the consequences of you staying in the office until 11 pm aside from reducing the mountain of work?

Let's imagine the client replies, "Well, I feel physically and mentally exhausted when I get home so don't have time to exercise, I grab something quick and usually unhealthy to eat, then go to sleep before waking up early to do it all again the next day."

The decision to stay in the office until 11 pm comes with a series of subsequent decisions around eating unhealthily, not doing exercise, and not allowing enough time to decompress at the end of the day. When the therapist encourages the client to reflect on the negative consequences of leaving the office at 11 pm, the client may still decide that this is the best course of action for them. But now they are more aware that they could be eating healthier, exercising more, and sleeping better if they left the office earlier. Our job isn't to tell the client what is right or wrong but rather reflect the responsibility for decisions back to them and highlight they are the agents of their own lives.

Existential therapists sit in a place of unconditional regard towards the client by not judging their decisions. We consider a client making an unwise decision, but we don't dictate how the client lives their life. We can raise a client's awareness of their decision-making but only they can take responsibility for why they're deciding to act or not act. Hence existentialist therapy fits in with the humanistic view that clients are in control of their destiny.

Isolation

Yalom believed that when humans confront death and responsibility, we inevitably experience isolation. Like feeling isolated from friends or family or feeling separated from parts of oneself. Yalom refers to existential isolation as the acknowledgement that we all die alone and only we can take responsibility for our lives. We might die with people surrounding us, but we cannot die with anyone else, nor can we trade our death for someone else's. Similarly, we can take onboard other people's suggestions on correct decisions, but, ultimately, we are self-reliant beings and are responsible for our choices. To defend against this conflict, we might try and fuse with another. If we fuse with another then we lose our sense of self to become a 'we' rather than an 'I' and 'you'.

Yalom states that a therapist's role in working with existential isolation is bringing awareness to how the client relates to others when confronted by isolation. As with Carl Rogers, he emphasised the importance of the therapeutic relationship in helping clients to self-actualise. Yalom similarly views the client–therapist interaction as vital information about how clients experience themselves in relation to others. Some of the questions the therapist can ask themself about the client's experience of relating are:

- To what extent is the client able to hold another person in mind?
- To what extent does the client get stuck into fixed roles when relating to others? For example, are they always the carer or the one receiving care?
- To what extent does the client share their vulnerabilities with others?
- To what extent does the client get 'engulfed' by the other(s)? Do they take on the other's values, language, and mannerisms?
- How does the client position or see you? Do they depend on you to make the decisions in therapy? Do they take on your thinking or phrases? Do they challenge what you say?

Once a client experiences an awareness of existential isolation, the therapist sits with the client in full exploration. We cannot fix the situation. This isn't to say that clients can't have intimate relationships, but existential isolation is about recognising that relationships temporarily provide comfort from feeling lonely but can never take away the fact that the client must live their life and die on their own.

A client came to therapy because he wanted to explore his anxiety, linked to his relationship with his sister's mental health. Anytime his sister's mental health deteriorated, where she self-harmed and contemplated suicide, the client's anxiety levels increased. He was unable to function at university, constantly checking his phone for messages from his sister, and was mentally consumed by trying to support her.

The client only recently started university and had moved countries, away from his family for the first time. The therapy sessions focused on supporting him to transition into adulthood which meant having to make decisions that had previously been done by his mother. The client described feelings of sadness, loss, unfairness, anger, resentment, and reluctance in recognising that he was an adult and not a child anymore, bearing the heavy weight of life's responsibility. The therapy focused on bringing awareness to the client that his want to find solutions for his sister's mental health was pushing her away and resulting in her communicating less. It became extremely challenging for the client to sit with feeling that he cannot rescue his sister from her mental health difficulties or take them on himself. It was hard for the client to sit in his feelings of existential loneliness. Our integrative existential work was about helping him to tolerate his separateness from his sister and both of their existential isolation.

Meaninglessness

Meaning refers to a sense of purpose in one's life. It is a combination of what we do in life and why we do it. Meaning is linked with values, creativity, spirituality, relationships, legacy, and career. How can we get to a place of personal development and what could that end goal look like?

Meaning changes as society and culture evolves. Today's Western society encourages questioning one's purpose in life and we have more available choices for how and why to live, that is, assuming the fundamentals of human needs are met, like shelter, food, and safety. I acknowledge this is coming from a privileged perspective as, referring to Maslow's hierarchy of needs, there are overwhelming amounts of people struggling to feed themselves and their children, as well as many having no adequate shelter or heat. But part of their meaning in life will be to find a way to put food on the table, secure shelter, or resources for heating. This is what keeps people going. Thus, all humans find meaning, irrespective of their place in the social hierarchy.

Meaninglessness manifests itself in many ways in the therapy room – through boredom, feeling lost, indifference, or dedicating oneself to important causes regardless of what the cause is. Part of the therapist's role is to elicit what the client attaches meaning to through their system of values. What, on the surface to a non-therapist, might seem like a conversation about the client's enjoyable activities is a profound way to get to know a client's purpose for living. A 14-year-old client was talking about how upset she felt when her parents took away her iPad, as a punishment for her anger outbursts. Her tone and voice changed when she mentioned the iPad. Upon further enquiry, she informed me that she loved to do graphic design on it, and she stated, in an extremely confident manner, how good she was. The iPad was a conduit for her creative expression, something she valued and found meaning from. Removing the device was removing her meaningfulness (this is not an advocacy of giving children iPads!)

If meaninglessness is a feeling of being separated from a sense of connection to things, people, and values, then Yalom suggests that the therapist's role is to help clients engage in life again. The aim is to help clients towards personal growth by identifying the blocks towards that growth. We use the person-centred techniques to uncover meaning in the client's life, paying attention to ways they respond to meaninglessness. Our role is not to decide whether meaning or meaningless is the correct thing to explore but only to notice via the client's language what meaning (or lack thereof) is implied by their experiences. Person-centred therapy tends to miss this important and universal theme.

Van Deurzen's Approach – The Possibilities and Limitations of the Everyday

The third and final existential approach we attend to is based on the work of Emmy Van Deurzen, a Dutch-born philosopher, counselling psychologist, and existential therapist. She is one of the leading contemporary existential theorists and practitioners based in the United Kingdom who has brought a surge of life into the existential field.

Like Frankl and Yalom, Van Deurzen works from a non-diagnostic perspective, focusing on how the client experiences the world. She calls counselling a 'philosophical investigation' where the client is encouraged, through phenomenological enquiry, to describe the challenges they experience in everyday life. She says that working existentially with someone isn't necessarily thinking about the bigger philosophical questions, but rather helping clients to work with everyday struggles. Her approach also draws on the client's resilience and confidence to face life's challenges.

Van Deurzen developed a framework to help the therapist explore the client's lived experiences: physical dimension (Umwelt), social dimension (Mitwelt), personal dimension (Eigenwelt), and spiritual dimension (Uberwelt). Don't worry so much about trying to remember the German names for the dimensions! The concepts have roughly been translated into English but inevitably we will miss some subtle nuances in the original German words. What Van Deurzen is proposing with these four dimensions is that clients come to therapy because of an imbalance, struggle, or lack of awareness in how they are living their lives. By the therapist asking questions to clarify the dichotomies that exist in these dimensions, the client takes responsibility for their action and inaction. The dimensions should not be viewed separately but rather intertwined, having numerous crossovers (Figure 7.2).

Let's use a client example to illustrate the dimensions of existence. Rachel is a woman in her 50s who came for therapy following her husband's cancer treatment. She felt confused and guilty that she hadn't re-evaluated and changed her life after he was given the all-clear. She believed her lack of an

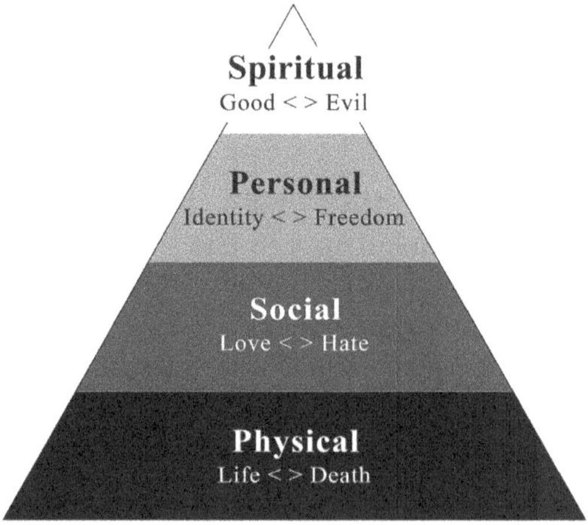

Figure 7.2 Dimensions of Existence Diagram

emotional response was because of her upbringing. She wanted to explore childhood experiences to understand who she has become today.

In Rachel's physical dimension, we try to get a sense of how Rachel, as a human being with a body, connects to the world. How does she make sense of how her body is experiencing themes such as illness, food, and physical activity? She says that she cycles from her office to her therapy sessions, so what is she aware of, in her body, as she cycles from the office? Are there patterns of comforts or discomforts? What is her relationship with her body?

On one occasion, Rachel couldn't leave work on time to go to a separate space for her therapy, so she stayed at work. She described feeling unsettled in her stomach, mentally distracted, and unable to physically relax. Upon further exploration she explained that she found it challenging to be in her workspace where she takes on a professional role. Talking about her personal life within the workspace felt jarring.

She decided that therapy from her office in future would mean going to a different room within the building, to disconnect from her work-self. This led to an exploration of her social dimension, which is how we relate to the society, culture, and the political climate.

Rachel articulated her struggle with being vulnerable. In therapy she expresses her emotions but recognises that if she were to express her emotions in front of her subordinates, she may face rejection and exclusion. By exploring her social world, we want to hear how she experiences themes of appreciation and resentment, acceptance and rejection, inclusion and exclusion, dominance and submission. We cannot escape the fact that we interact with other human beings daily. As therapists, we enquire into how a client experiences the multitude of interactions.

A major theme that arises from Rachel's sessions is around how she struggles with being the manager of her company whilst wanting to befriend her employees. One day she came into therapy furious that a department within her organisation, that she has significant involvements with, didn't invite her to a team lunch. She felt hurt, upset, and offended. Rather than voice her upset to the organiser of the lunch, Rachel decided to offload to a different colleague because she didn't want to be seen as weak. Rachel had learnt that, as a businesswoman, living in a Western society, expressing her feelings can be viewed as a sign of weakness. She'd rather not be seen that way by others. But by not expressing her feelings, Rachel feels unheard, furious, and alone.

The third dimension that Van Deurzen includes in her framework is the personal world that the client experiences. This includes what the client thinks, feels, aspires for, and her intimate relationships. We explore how the client describes themselves. How do they express who they are? How do they describe themselves to you and others?

Some clients, when asked that question, say, "others would describe me as introverted." But what we want to know is how they describe themselves, not how others describe them. By getting the client to take accountability for who they are as a person, they are responsible for their challenges and gain agency. Existential integrative therapy empathises with and accepts the client, but we work on responsibility and meaning. Van Deurzen states that providing people with acceptance and unconditional positive regard, one of the core conditions in person-centred therapy, is unhelpful because it doesn't deal with the conflicts of life that need to be dealt with directly. I disagree with her views as I think she is referring to two different processes. The purpose of the therapist using unconditional positive regard is to help foster a trusting and supportive therapeutic relationship. Van Deurzen claims that unconditional positive regard in the existential approach doesn't confront the paradoxes of life. In my experience, unconditional positive regard helps the client feel safe enough to explore those challenges. The fact that therapists are humans who experience similar difficulties means that we can be accepting of what the client chooses to do or not but still highlight the choice.

The final aspect to worldly living that Van Deurzen mentions is the spiritual dimension. For those readers that are atheist or agnostic, don't be put off by the world 'spiritual'. It doesn't only refer to religion. Exploring a client's religious beliefs is one aspect to the spiritual dimension but it can also be seen from the broader umbrella of exploring clients' values: making the implicit values in their actions explicit. What beliefs and principles are important in how a client chooses to live? For some clients it's living a life based on altruism, and for others it's spontaneity or justice. Quite often when clients are asked whether they think they are living according to their values, many say they aren't. This is partly what causes them distress. While there is not enough scope in this chapter to delve into Acceptance and Commitment Therapy (ACT), I want to signpost the reader to this approach as it focuses specifically on helping clients recognise what they are feeling and support clients in accepting those feelings rather than avoiding or minimising them to live a meaningful life.

For Rachel, she mentioned several times about feeling 'Catholic guilt', having been raised in a Catholic household, being a 'good' Catholic girl. When she was younger, she described showing her parents a piece of art-work. She was proud of it but then was shut down by her parents because showing off was perceived as arrogance, something viewed as sinful in their faith. Rachel struggled with being proud of the work she had done in setting up her company, as creativity is a strong value of hers, but simultaneously feeling guilty and shameful in showing her work to others. In this way, Van Deurzen's framework is helpful in breaking down the different dimensions that we, as humans, exist in the world and experience it. It allows clients to focus on universal themes of existence, giving the person-centred counsellor some concrete areas to explore in therapy.

Summary

We have seen in this chapter that there are different ways of integrating an existential approach into person-centred therapy, from Frankl's logotherapy to Yalom's existential-givens and Van Deurzen's four-dimensional worldview. The existential approach integrates with the person-centred approach because they share similarities in believing in the self-actualisation and agency that clients have. Both approaches take a non-interpretative and diagnostic view of client issues and maintain a curious, non-judgemental stance to understand how a client experiences their life in an embodied way.

Clara Hill, from the University of Maryland, surveyed therapists about whether they worked with existential themes. Her results showed that clients didn't attend therapy with the intention of specifically talking about the meaning of life but rather the therapists introduced the theme into the work. Her promising research showed that when therapists introduced existential themes, this led to clients engaging more in life, having more meaning and purpose. Therapists noticed that clients had a reduction in symptoms, stronger interpersonal connections, and more engagement in therapy. From this she suggests that taking an existential lens with presenting problems can reduce psychological distress.

Further Reading

Cooper, M. (2017). *Existential Therapies*, 2e. London: Sage Publications.

Frankl, V. (1959). *Man's Search For Meaning*. London: Penguin Random House UK.

Harris, R. (2019). *ACT Made Simple*, 2e. Oakland, CA: New Harbinger.

Hill, C. (2017). Therapists' perspectives about working with meaning in life in psychotherapy: a survey. *Counselling Psychology Quarterly* 30 (4): 373–391.

Marie Curie. (2024). Public attitudes to death, dying and bereavement in the UK re-visited: 2023 survey Summary report. Available online: https://www.

mariecurie.org.uk/globalassets/media/documents/policy/policy-publications/2024/n401_padd_report_final.pdf (accessed 21 April 2025)

Maslow, A.H. (1943). A theory of human motivation. *Psychological Review* 50 (4): 370–396.

Rogers, C. (1961). *On Becoming a Person*. London: Constable & Robinson LTD.

Rogers, C. (2003). *Client-Centered Therapy*, 70th Anniversarye. Robinson Publishing.

Van Deurzen, E. (2012). *Existential Counselling & Psychotherapy in Practice*, 3e. London: Sage Publications.

Van Deurzen, E. and Adams, M. (2016). *Skills in Existential Counselling & Psychotherapy*, 2e. London: Sage Publications.

Yalom, I. (1980). *Existential Psychotherapy*. New York: Basic Books.

Yalom, I. (2008). *Staring at the sun. Overcoming the Dread of Death*. London: Piatkus.

Yalom, I. (2017). *Becoming Myself. A Psychiatrist's Memoir*. New York: Basic Books.

8

Gestalt

Psychotherapy emphasises the importance of present awareness. Can clients experience the whole of their self and their environment? Can they sit in their experience and tolerate it, without anxiously pushing it underground?

Experience gets buried beneath low self-worth, childhood trauma, defence mechanisms, a shielding persona, a lack of secure attachments, and a paralysis from the terror of death. Therapies like integrative person-centred counselling harness safe therapeutic environments for the client to genuinely experience what it's like to be themselves. But what does this mean?

On the popular psychology bookshelves are techniques like mindfulness that focus people on their present experience without judgement or interpretation. The science behind this fairly new meditation approach – though its roots span centuries – is quite intriguing. Firstly, mindfulness trains the attention on being in the moment, bringing about calm and positive mental states. Neuroscience reveals that the brain's stress pathways relax and change for the better during long periods of mindfulness. When over 12,000 people were studied, mindfulness-based therapies proved to reduce mental health issues like depression, anxiety, and chronic stress, and at similar rates as other therapies. It's clear that people who learn to focus on their awareness are more able to think positively, feel energised, and tolerate life.

Meditation is a profound and deeply human activity. But some psychotherapists have referred to mindfulness-like approaches as structured avoidance. That is, meditation can avoid complex emotional experiences.

Integrative Person-Centred Counselling: The Combined Model of Counselling and Psychotherapy, First Edition. Rick Murphy.

Our question above, what does it mean to be in touch with experience, is not necessarily answered via meditation.

The issue boils down to this. Some meditation practices are caught up in the self-help quick-fix literature. They don't support people to tolerate the inevitable upsets that come their way. Instead, like alcohol in the bloodstream, they alleviate emotional pain by turning off perceptive parts of the brain. This metaphorical plaster over the wound might prevent the more traumatised clients from healing. Although the mindfulness research combats this, because it says that guided mindfulness with a real therapist is as good as other therapies, it's important we explore deeper awareness-raising approaches, and we'll do so in this chapter.

Feeling in the Moment

In person-centred therapy, we encourage the client's experience to come through transparently. We do not try to lead the client towards a nirvana state of mind. Instead, we help them accept their feelings, to raise awareness, and grow. The core conditions of empathy, congruence, and unconditional positive regard bring us in touch with the client's genuine experience. When we feel what they feel, it amplifies their mental state and awareness.

Once the client is comfortable experiencing their true emotions, their natural state is to self-actualise, to reach towards higher states of being. This doesn't always lead to tranquillity, and many times it is rather upsetting. But in the upset the client goes from dimmer one-dimensional experiences to brighter multidimensional experiences. They feel more alive.

The person-centred tradition always said that feeling the actual feelings, sensing the real emotions, and deepening the awareness were the cornerstones of a healthy mind. One form of therapy that specialises in this is gestalt therapy. Here, working with experience is like a special interest, and its core theory is about using experience and awareness for psychological growth. In fact, the founder of gestalt therapy, Fritz Perls, subtitled his most famous book "Excitement and Growth." That is, when therapy excites and stimulates awareness then personal growth is inevitable (Figure 8.1).

Carl Rogers said that a person does not experience themselves fully when their ideal self is misaligned with their real self. In this situation, a person is in a state of incongruence. Gestalt therapy takes incongruence to a deeper level, showing how people disown parts of themselves. Perls said that the gestalt therapist attempts to "turn paper people into real people." By being

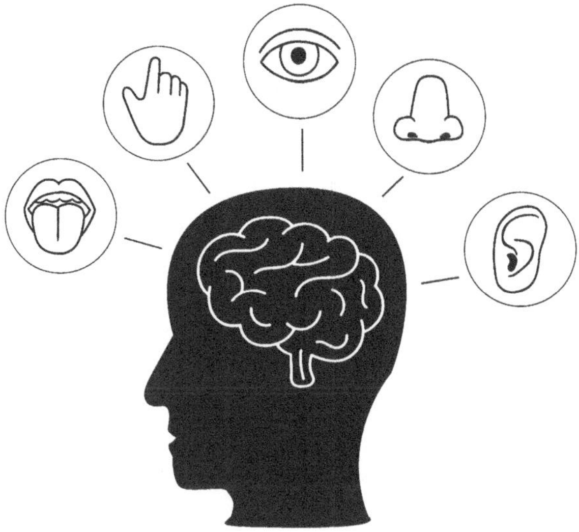

Figure 8.1 Awareness Diagram

self-aware the person is more genuine and able to reclaim hidden or rejected experiences.

Let's look at an example of Perls working with a psychotherapy student. The student, having just turned 21, wants to become independent from her mother. She starts by describing a dream in which she and her mother are in a department store. Perls asks her to take on the identity of the department store and speak from its point of view. In a flat and detached voice, she says:

Student: I am the department store. I am big. I have many things inside my stomach. I hold everything, everything in the world. It's all there. Anything you want you can find inside me. There are books, records, and furniture.
Perls: Now, can you listen to your voice? Can you play your voice?
Student: Like an instrument (melodically) la, la, la, la, la.
Perls: That's not how I hear your voice. It's more like (monotonously) "uh, uh, uh, uh."
Student: I can't hear it.
Perls: That's right, you don't hear your disappearing voice.

Gestalt therapy encourages us to forget the interpretative side of therapy and notice what is obvious. To notice the obvious ways the client is incongruent, by looking at what they say and how they say it. Someone whose ideal self is assertive will not experience their real self as anxious, and their voice tone discloses this. The therapist attunes to the fact that the student does not experience her 'little' voice, bringing her awareness to it. We use our eyes and ears rather than our thoughts and theories.

Gestalt therapy calls this phenomenological inquiry. This means to draw attention to any obvious phenomenon in the room – like a voice tone, a tear in the eye, a scrunching up of paper. Using the experience of the therapist – their congruence – helps the client notice obvious behaviours and emotions outside of their normal awareness. The client becomes aware of contradictions between their perceived self and their real self, between their conscious and unconscious processes. Gestalt therapy refers to the conscious part as their 'life script', and therapy rewrites the life script.

Phenomenological inquiry means to ask about the client's experience using 'what' and 'how' questions, such as, "What is it like to hear your voice?" or "How do you experience being in conversation with your mother?" By observing and describing what's happening in the room, the client discovers their deeper experience. With the aforementioned student, her deeper experience is that she shuts down her voice and elevates her mother's voice. To help the client gain independence from her mother, we support her to reclaim the power she has disowned. If she unknowingly backs off from being independent, she is likely to remain incongruent and not reach her higher potential – which is greater independence and self-reliance. Hence Perls asks her to play both roles and to integrate each voice into her sense of self.

Integrating Awareness into the Self

The word 'gestalt' means something like 'organised whole'. Like being congruent, the organised whole means that people experience all parts of themselves, rather than only the parts they are used to or comfortable with. It's like the picture of the elephant and the blindfolded group. A blindfolded person who touches the tail would describe something completely different from a blindfolded person who touches the side, tusks, ears, legs, or head (Figure 8.2).

If a person is like the blindfolded group and the elephant, they do not integrate the different parts of their experience. They are not an organised whole but are incongruent and disconnected from parts of themselves. The person may feel happy in relationships, but secretly harbour hatred. The person may

Figure 8.2 Blindfolded Scientists and the Elephant

Table 8.1 Types of Incongruence

Type of Incongruence	Definition	Example
Retroflection	Withholding emotions about people and the environment, then turning the emotion onto the self	Self harming when a person has feelings of wanting to harm another.
Introjection	Taking on conflicting values and voices from the family and culture as though they were their own	Boys don't cry. Girls don't get angry. I am a bad person.
Projection	The unconscious transfer of emotions or desires to another person	A man, insecure about masculinity, mocks other men for being weak.

be familiar with their anxiety but ignorant of their confidence. Developing the concept of incongruence further, gestalt therapy separates incongruence into three key areas. Fritz Perls described them as ways the client manipulates themselves to avoid experiencing. These are shown in Table 8.1.

The goal of gestalt therapy is like the goal of the blindfolded elephant scientists, to combine awareness of the self (or elephant) into an organised whole. We call the process 'assimilation'. In person-centred words, this means that the transition from being incongruent to congruent requires a person to assimilate hidden experiences.

Thinking back to the flat-voiced student, she was blindfolded to her voice, and many aspects of her experience. Thus, the integrative person-centred model takes from gestalt therapy an emphasis on assimilating present awareness into the person's sense of self. We don't have to be as direct as Perls – he is known for being unapologetically crass – but we empathically support the client with fitting the parts of experience into a meaningful self-image – like noticing trunks and tails that form an elephant picture.

The student's dream is interesting for other reasons. When she pretends to be the department store, she says she is "big", "holds everything in the world", and knows that "anything you want you can find inside me". This illustrates person-centred theory. The client has the resources for growth if given the safety to find them.

On a symbolic level, the client is aware they have what they need, they hold everything in the world, but they have not assimilated that into their self-image. Otherwise, their voice would match their sense of self. They would speak more confidently. Hence, they project their resources into the department store. In the next part of the session, Perls invites the student to imagine she is speaking with her mother, talking to an imaginary version of her in an empty chair. We see the client reclaim some of her projected resources. She says:

Student (to imagined mother): Uh, I have to be myself … I want to tell you because you never listen. But … I have to live my own life. I'm not you.

Perls: Does she hear you? (implying the student should take up her mother's position in the conversation).

Mother (played by student): I don't think you're me. I don't expect you to be like me. I have my own life. You know that.

Student (as self): But … You're there. You won't go away.

Perls: Let your mother go into the department store. Let's see what she experiences there.

Mother: Look Julie, here's a nice dress. Don't you think it'll look nice on you?

Student: But I don't like the colour.

Mother: But, what colour do you want?

Student: I want red.

Mother: But you don't look good in red! You know you don't look good in red!

...

Perls: Are you aware how much more alive you are when you play your mother?

Student: (Smiles in acknowledgement)

Here the student disowned her power and her confidence. She gave her mother's voice a self-assured and authoritative timbre that hers lacked. By having the client act out the conversation, she became aware of her internalised mother. She became aware of her role in accepting her mother's authority. She assimilated her (pretend) mother's voice, by taking the energy from her mother and experiencing it in herself. That is, her incongruence dissipated by noticing her anger ("I don't like the colour"), apathy ("you never listen"), and self-manipulation (quietening her voice), while validating her mother's control over her ("I want red"). She discovered how she created her dependence.

In a pure gestalt model, the therapist's technique looks more like a stage director than an emotional and accepting presence. This is because gestalt therapy has been enormously influenced by psychodrama – a model based on performing emotional roles as a route to experimenting with new self-images. In drama, the person has more licence to explore deeper parts of the self and to play out unacceptable fantasies. Gestalt theory says that psychological health comes from one's ability to be present in experience. Person-centred skills like empathic noticing, probing questions, and paraphrasing integrate well into the gestalt theory of change. Integrative person-centred counselling acknowledges the importance of self-acceptance, responsibility, and awareness in creating a sense of mental stability.

As well as a person naturally growing from a therapeutic relationship, we integrate the view that the person grows from active engagement and psychodrama. That is, embodiment work brings an extra dimension to therapy that is missed from purist person-centred approaches.

The Hollow Man

Fritz Perls was an interesting and dramatic person. Though he was influenced by humanistic principles like self-actualisation, he didn't directly engage with the work of Carl Rogers or Abraham Maslow. He was shunned by the psychoanalytic community for having been a trainer outside of the orthodox psychotherapy circles in Europe – having set up his practice in South Africa after the persecution of the Jewish people during the war. Some scholars interpret his criticism of psychoanalysis as a compensation for his rejection from it. But Perls saw interpretations like this as the issue in psychotherapy. Psychoanalysis promotes itself as the almighty judge. Its role is self-serving, using interpretation to garner social status. It's possible that both theories are true, that Perls's rejection and his moral critiques of psychoanalysis played a part in him developing gestalt therapy.

Perls also criticised non-directive therapies for their lack of active engagement with the body. Two gestalt authors, Petruska Clarkson and Jennifer Mackewn, tell a story of Perls being true to his word. When meeting Abraham Maslow at a conference, apparently bored by his overly theoretical presentation, Perls mockingly rolled around the floor on his stomach. Maslow, we learn, believed Perls was crazy.

In the famous Gloria tapes, Perls and Rogers, in separate sessions, work with the same client. Their therapeutic approaches seem to come from different universes – one is alien to the other. Rogers actively listens to Gloria, accepting her, being reflective. Perls is confrontational yet observant, challenging Gloria to notice her behaviour in the moment. At the end, Gloria is asked by the film crew for her perspective on the different approaches. When asked to choose the approach she preferred, alas, Gloria chose Perls, not Rogers.

Gloria's choice shocked many. One professor, Howard Rosenthal, said:

> Personally, I thought it was the strangest response (from a client who was not psychotic) I had come across in the entire field of psychotherapy, and that's saying a lot!

When I first saw the film, I found Rogers to be genuine and present. But personally, I didn't see many moments where Gloria came alive in the room. Perls was aggressive and overpowering, but he responded to Gloria in an observant way – noticing her unresolved conflict around wanting but rejecting other people's care. From this perspective, it seemed clear she preferred Perls's style. With more time, we cannot know how Gloria's experience might have developed.

Like existentialism, which Lisa discussed in the previous chapter, Perls emphasised responsibility. He wanted to support clients away from manipulating the environment for support towards developing greater self-support. Once Gloria stands on her own two feet emotionally, her need for therapy collapses. She acknowledges this when saying to Perls that she wanted to hug her friend and at the same time she felt uncomfortable about the hug – a conflict of interests. He noticed Gloria's disgust at the idea of being hugged, but her look of care when imagining giving someone a hug.

His approach was too harsh, I would say, and arrogant, according to the many students and colleagues I have witnessed reviewing the tape. But the idea that trusting the client to take responsibility, and highlighting ways in which they abandon responsibility, awakens their potential to be responsible and more in control. I would suggest that Gloria with Rogers feels accepted and understood, and Gloria with Perls experiments with how she projects her power onto the therapist while disowning her own. In role-play, when pretending to be Perls, Gloria is more self-assured than when she is being herself. When she pretended that Perls was 30 years younger, she related to him with greater self-assurance and care. In fact, she re-perceived him from an untouchable high-status doctor to a vulnerable and self-protective fragile man.

I don't think we need to decide, like Gloria, on a preference for the style of each of these great contributors to the psychotherapy field. We can learn from and integrate their messages into a coherent approach for ourselves. Both attempt to support the client's resources via different routes.

Fritz Perls brings to the conversation that empathy and acceptance are important but so too are approaches that draw out unresolved conflict. As Perls puts it, "the idea of gestalt therapy is to change paper people into real people."

Perls explains the above quote using the metaphor of the hollow man – a person who is spiritually and experientially dead. He doubtlessly was influenced by the poet T. S. Elliot. His 1925 poem *The Hollow Men* referred to 'empty men' and 'lost souls', people without the feeling of being alive. Interestingly, Elliot refers to these people as 'sightless', unable to experience good, evil, or real human emotions. Interpretations of the poem tend to be biblical. Its emphasis on good and evil, and on the soul, direct attention towards the Bible. But there is a humanistic interpretation too, which is that being alive means having the awareness (the sight) to see and experience the world as it is, the good and the evil.

Perls connects the hollow man to society and culture. By being civilised, a person represses many feelings. If people live for being good or for being entertained, for example, for moralism or hedonism, then this is a 'serious setback'. That is, people avoid their immoral sides or they become phobic towards pain and suffering. This is the hollow man, the person who cannot face themselves.

Traditional person-centred therapy focuses on experience to encourage the person's natural potential. This fits well into the gestalt outlook. But what's different is an emphasis on helping the client 'use' their inborn potential, moment to moment.

For Rogers, human potential is like a discovery when one accepts themselves, improves their sense of belonging and self-esteem, and reaches higher states of mind. For Perls, human potential is something to use and experiment with in the moment; it is a skill and an action of the client. Hence, psychodrama is used more than, for example, questions and other curiosities. The person is encouraged to self-actualise live in the room. Through dramatic techniques the person becomes more aware of themselves and uses their potential for emotion, frustration, gratitude, regret, and confidence.

Perls draws on a metaphorical description of change, which is the idea of being "a leader without a rebel," as in somebody who becomes self-aware and behaves less rebelliously towards themselves, less self-destructively – the idea that even on our own we refuse to respect and obey ourselves. We rebel against the self.

Both metaphors allude to the defence mechanism, the self-mutiny, the self-sabotage as a thing that prevents progress. Gestalt therapy offers a fire escape from self-mutiny. It says that instead of sitting on the analyst's couch, interpreting experience for many years, the person has the option of changing here and now. By using awareness, ideally by dramatic and physical techniques (by action), the person integrates their desire for self-destruction. They notice where in the body the feeling of tension comes from, which leads to the tightening of the chest, the tensing of the fists, the silencing of the voice, and the frantic scratching of the leg.

Completing the Gestalt

Recently my daughter Nora and I completed a jigsaw puzzle of a cute cat wearing a funny hat. As we came to the end, alas, one of the pieces was missing! We looked under the table, in the box, traced our steps back to the game cupboard, but no – the piece was nowhere to be found.

Gestalt psychologists tell me that the missing jigsaw piece frustrates me because my brain is wired to complete things. Completing the 'gestalt' or the 'whole' puzzle takes me from a state of focus and tension to one of satisfaction. Gestalt therapy invites us to see the person's issues like my jigsaw puzzle scenario. If a person loses a piece of their guilt or their shame, their self-image is unfinished. Gestalt therapy assists in getting hold of the real in-the-moment parts of the self, helping piece themselves together into an organised, aware person.

In gestalt psychology, a complete gestalt is a finished interaction or experience that satisfies a person. The theory is that perception is based on seeing whole pictures. Sight, for example, can feel unsatisfying when only part images can be seen, as is the case with the British game show, Catchphrase. In that game show, contestants decipher an image to extract a commonly used expression or catchphrase. For example, an image of the word 'IT' containing a foot would be, "putting your foot in it." Or, the funniest one I have seen, is the catchphrase "holding down a job," which many contestants got horribly wrong (Figure 8.3).

Completing a picture (a gestalt) is the basis of many professions. Science completes the gestalt by solving the puzzle of reality. The satisfaction from finishing a math's problem or writing a paper comes from taking fragments of things and putting them into an organised whole.

Psychologists tell us that people process information holistically. The meaning or perception of a thing is found in its whole image, not in its parts. Only having parts creates tension in the body – it is an 'unfinished situation'. As an example, I could ask you to complete a riddle, say something like, "What is greater than God, more evil than the Devil, and if you eat it you die?" Think for a moment about the resolution. What is greater than God, more evil than the Devil, and if you eat it you die?

. . .

Figure 8.3 Funny Catchphrase Image for Holding Down a Job

Gestalt psychology tells us that your brain begins to process the parts of the puzzle. The human brain naturally wants to fill in the parts that are missing, in this case the solution. If it cannot achieve this, the tension remains. If you don't have the answer yet (and you haven't Googled it), it'll likely sit inside your muscles, jaw bones, and forehead until it's resolved. Until the puzzle is complete, and the organised whole is revealed, the brain struggles to relax.

Withholding the solution to a puzzle is frustrating but imagine never completing a more emotional gestalt, for example, a need for fighting back against an abuser or for accepting love from a caregiver. Thousands of these kinds of unfinished gestalts create the tension we experience in our bodies, beyond conscious awareness. Hence people clench their jaw all day without realising that, unless they bite back at their boss, their father, or their sibling, they'll continue to turn the tension onto themselves. Finishing the gestalt means putting an end to the puzzle or resolving an emotional situation.

The answer to the riddle by the way is 'nothing'. Nothing is greater than God, nothing is more evil than the Devil, and if you eat nothing ... you die. Ah, tension resolved.

Gestalt brings to the integrative person-centred model an important idea. Bodily insight and awareness help people resolve situations from the past. When the client sorts out a personal issue, such as a hidden need for revenge, the gestalt is complete. Ah, tension resolved. Through these unfinished situations, people organise things (like cars, squirrels, and insults) into things they are interested in (called figures) and things they are not interested in (called ground). They become interested in the things that are unfinished in their perception, especially something like an insult that carries a negative emotion with it.

Psychologists call this scanning. If I lose a jigsaw piece, I am suddenly interested in small wooden shapes, and I scan my environment until I find them. Without finding the pieces, and finishing the puzzle, tension is stored in my body. The same is true if we have been undermined at work or physically hurt by a caregiver; we look for the piece to end that suffering. If it doesn't come, such as by allowing ourselves to be angry or by accepting our own weakness, we show heightened interest in things that are undermining and abusive.

To make this clear, what we mean is that the fragmented need for revenge or for love – seen via the person's behaviour in the session – becomes integrated into the whole person and resolved. The person shows an interest in revenge or love because this gestalt was not completed, was unfinished. That is, people experience themselves truly when they wake up to their needs or when their needs are met.

We can see this in therapy when a client has a serious argument and gets frustrated with someone. Their need to get angry bothers them until they hide the need or get angry with the person. Or if someone has been bullied, they replay the name-calling and abuse over and over, often falsely resolving it with a fantasy about hurting the bullies.

In the case of someone who is powerless, this serious argument happens repeatedly and the need to get angry is routinely evoked. Like not knowing the answer to a puzzle, but in a more troubling way, the need to complete the gestalt – to get angry – creates a stronger impulse that develops into chronic anger problems or the opposite, into a person who represses anger and cuts off from experience, turning the anger inwardly. The first person might need to connect with their powerlessness to organise that into themselves, while the second person might need to connect with their anger. Hence therapy for some is about learning to be angry, while for others it is about learning to be vulnerable.

Therapy gets hold of the unfinished situations in motion, by looking at the surface behaviours in the room. If a client holds their throat while discussing a conversation with their partner, or if a client makes their voice smaller when they speak as themselves and louder when they speak as their mother, the unfinished situation is shown. The most important unfinished situations come to the surface first because they take up most of the client's energy. Working in the here and now brings the client's awareness to needs that want to be resolved.

Madeline's Dream

In the spirit of working in the here and now, Fritz Perls' method for working with dreams was to re-enact the dream in the present moment. The client describes their dream as if experiencing it now, connecting with various gestalts and unfinished situations.

One emphasis in gestalt therapy is on the word 'how'. Throughout the last few centuries, philosophers and scientists have focused on 'why' questions. They want to know why the universe came into existence. Why the body develops diseases. Or why people act morally even when no one is looking. Perls noticed that 'why' questions end up fixating on causes, rationalisations, intellectualisations, and move from experience to cognitions. 'How' questions, on the other hand, attempt to understand structure. How did the universe begin? How does a body develop a disease? How does a person act morally when nobody is looking?

The 'how' question figures out the way something works so it can be changed. If we want to understand a person's experience, knowing *why* somebody feels depressed might be less helpful than knowing *how* they experience depression. This 'how' question brings the person into contact with experience rather than abstract thinking. Hence, in dreamwork, like in any other gestalt method, we emphasise how and what the person experiences in the present.

To give an example from a group run by Perls, Madeline is asked to retell a dream. For interested readers, the video clip from this transcript can be found for free online (Perls 2015).

Telling the dream, Madeline takes on the role of a statue inside her dream:

Madeline: I'm grey, and I'm pretty classical looking. I'm looking like most little statues of a boy you would see. And I hold a vase, which has a small neck and is big in the bottom. And I hold it. Though I'm immobile I pour it. And water … I pour this water in the lake. I don't know where it comes from. But this water is extremely pure. And you would really benefit from drinking this water. It feels all good all over because you had water on the outside of your body. From the lake, I am sitting in the middle. And the water is really good outside your body. But I really want you to drink the water I'm giving from my vessel because it will really make you feel good inside. I don't know why, but sometimes you can't drink it. You come to drink, you're all happy, and you're swimming, you want to drink it and then you can't drink it. I cannot bend for you. I can just keep on pouring my water and I'm hoping that you come and drink it.

Perls: Say this again, the last sentence.

Madeline: I can't come down and give the water to you. I just can keep on pouring it and hoping that you'll come and drink it. I just can keep on pouring it.

Perls: Okay. Now play this. Play the water. You're now the water.

Madeline: In the vessel?

Perls: Yes, the water in the vessel. What's your script? What's your story water?

The dream is building into a revelation for Madeline. In the here and now, she takes on the role of parts of her dream. Perls follows the obvious things that stand out. They stand out because Madeline repeats them. For example, she repeats that the water is so pure, out of reach, and she just wishes someone would drink it.

Perls was clear that interpretation is very often unhelpful for the client. At this stage, he says that interpretation is a therapeutic mistake. It interrupts the client's active process. Instead, he encourages the client to take on different roles, projections, or personas, invented by the client via the dream (via the imagination).

The dream starts to put Madeline in touch with something deeper:

Perls: Okay. Now play this. Play the water. You're now the water.
Madeline: In the vessel?
Perls: Yes, the water in the vessel. What's your script? What's your story water?
Madeline: I don't know much about myself (begins to cry)
Perls: Say this again.
Madeline: I don't know much about myself.
Perls: And again.
Madeline: I don't know much about myself. (Pause, begins to cry). I don't know much … I come. (Pause). I don't know why I come. But I know I'm good (breaks down crying). That's all I know. I know … I would like you to drink me because I know I'm good.
Perls: Now get up and tell each one of us.
Madeline: I'm water in a vase and I don't know where I come from. But I know I'm good to drink.
Perls: Use your own words now.
Madeline: I look like water and they call me water. I'm just there in the vase. I'm just there all the time, and I'm just pouring out and I'd like you to drink me.

What is Madeline discovering about herself? How is she experiencing being a vessel of pure water, desperate for others to drink her goodness, but is unreachable to others?

Gestalt and person-centred approaches suggest that the client knows best. They know everything. Any interpretation from the therapist would mislead the client. To me, Madeline is realising she has a goodness inside her. She is a good person who struggles to show this, which is a painful experience. But my interpretation is not relevant, and probably says something more about me than Madeline.

And here is the point. By encouraging the client to experience in the here and now, via a dream or by reliving a moment from the week, the client's unfinished business emerges.

The Cycle of Experience

Gestalt therapy has modelled experience into a cycle. The process is not necessarily linear, though tends to involve seven stages. Using the cycle of experience encourages emotional and needy parts of the client to show themselves.

First, a client like Madeline has a sensation, which might be a feeling in the stomach. Then they have awareness of the sensation, which might mean realising they want to eat or feeling socially awkward. The person is mobilised to walk to the fridge or think of excuses to leave. Then they act, by eating a sandwich, or leaving the gathering. Afterwards the person connects with the experience, such as by feeling pleasure from the sandwich or relief from walking out of the room. The person assimilates that experience into themselves – they affirm that sandwich-eating relieves hunger or that exiting social situations reduces anxiety. And finally, they withdraw from the experience, by moving onto a new cycle of experience and pushing that into the background (Figure 8.4).

In Madeline's dream, the importance of running through the full cycle of experience is clear. Often the cycle is interrupted by defences, self-sabotage, discomfort, or, in a dream, waking up. Madeline had the dream multiple times but couldn't quite understand it. By noticing the sensations in the dream, by becoming aware of them, by mobilising herself during the experiment, she had more access to the fuller experience. She began to assimilate something deeply personal, "I know I'm good and I want you to drink me."

On the symbolic level, the client creates a dream about her existence. Something like, she knows she is good but that other people cannot access that. By giving space for the cycle of experience, the client integrates thoughts, feelings, and fantasises into their fuller self. Other practices can interrupt this, such as asking questions and making interpretations, and so when the integrative person-centred counsellor sees a window onto experience, the advice is to support the client to run through the cycle of

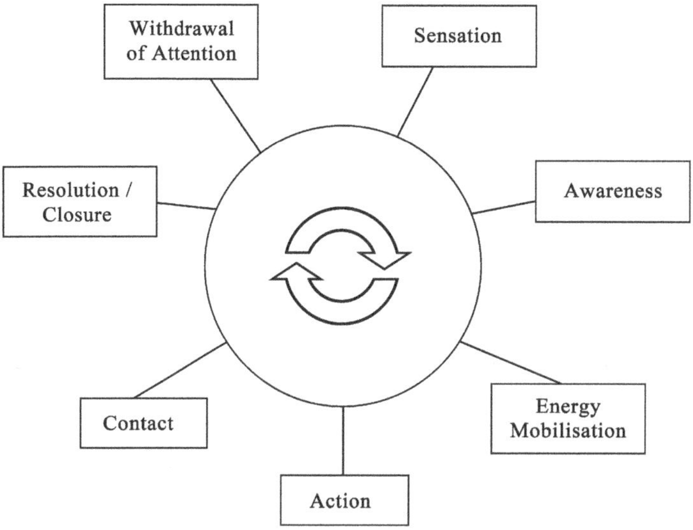

Figure 8.4 The Cycle of Experience

experience – taking time on each step. This might mean asking specific questions or encouraging drama and experimentation in the room.

The client often responds differently to the experience. They create new perspectives or integrations. In a sense, this is the creation of a new gestalt. That is, while previously Madeline might have held back her goodness, now she might perceive and share her goodness. This is called a 'creative adjustment' in gestalt theory because the client adjusts to the new information by perceiving more positively (forming more positive gestalts), as in, the client self-actualises and has more impulses to show their goodness. In this case, 'completing a gestalt' means the person feels compelled to do good, be confident, and speak their mind.

Summary

Gestalt therapy brings several ideas and concepts to the integrative person-centred model. First is the idea that present awareness is all that is required to develop the self. People are cut off from how they feel and what they experience, and the gestalt process focuses the attention on the here and now. Organically, the most important concerns emerge if the therapist is open to them. Its purpose is seeing and inquiring into the surface-level behaviours of the client and supporting them to work them through, tolerate the emotions, and grow from the experience. This, we said, was in line with the humanistic model of therapy. Both use experience as the route to personal growth. We discussed the concept of 'phenomenological inquiry' as a model for how to get hold of the visible, audible, and perceivable things in the client's behaviour.

From gestalt psychology, we integrated the idea that people are compelled to organise their experience into whole structures. Unable to do so, a person fixates on satisfying associated but unmet needs. If someone is fixated on revenge against an abusive person, for example, the gestalt will not complete until either they verbally or physically attack the abuser or they accept their helplessness to the abuser as part of themselves. We used the metaphor of the blindfolded scientists and the elephant. If a person only perceives parts of who they are, they form an unreliable self-image.

Unlike psychodynamic therapies, which make links from the present to the past, and which offer interpretations, we took from gestalt therapy an emphasis on trusting the client to make the interpretation. This does not mean our psychoanalytic thinking needs to be discarded, but only that when working on the here and now we remove the practice of link-making, trusting the client to embody the knowledge they discover. By feeling on an emotional level what unfinished situations need resolving, in the safety of the therapeutic relationship, the client improves their autonomy and mental wellbeing.

Further Reading

Farias, M. and Wikholm, C. (2015). *The Buddha Pill: Can Meditation Change You?* London: Watkins.

Goldberg, S.B., Tucker, R.P., Greene, P.A. et al. (2018). Mindfulness-based interventions for psychiatric disorders: a systematic review and meta-analysis. *Clinical Psychology Review* 59: 52–60. https://doi.org/10.1016/j.cpr.2017.10.011m.

Husserl, E. (1989). *Ideas Pertaining to a Pure Phenomenology and to a Phenomenological Philosophy*. Boston, MA: Springer.

Moodley, R., Sutherland, P., and Oulanova, O. (2008). Traditional healing, the body and mind in psychotherapy. *Counseling Psychology Quarterly* 21 (2): 153–165. https://doi.org/10.1080/09515070802066870.

Moreno, J. (1994). *Psychodrama Since Moreno* (ed. M. Karp and M. Watson). New York: Routledge.

Perls, F. (1969). *Ego, Hunger, and Aggression; The Beginning of Gestalt Therapy*. New York: Random House.

Perls, F. (1973). *The Gestalt Approach & Eye Witness to Therapy*. Mountain View, CA: Science and Behavior Books.

Perls, F. (2015). Madeline's Dream. (Video file). https://www.youtube.com/watch?v=TFqhPe5DR98&list=PLcEd0IYai8aSoVldXdUbUKPjvtN_OJUjZ&index=5 (accessed 06 December 2015).

Perls, F. (2016). Fritz Perls explains Gestalt Therapy. (Video file). https://www.youtube.com/watch?v=2hhtNjjBAhA&list=PLcEd0IYai8aSoVldXdUbUKPjvtN_OJUjZ (accessed 18 February 2016).

Perls, F., Hefferline, R., and Goodman, P. (1951). *Gestalt Therapy: Excitement and Growth in the Human Personality*. New York: Dell.

Rosenthal, H. (2016). The Gloria Films. Psychotherapy.Net. https://www.psychotherapy.net/blog/title/the-gloria-films-candid-answers-to-questions-therapists-ask-most#:~:text=In%20the%20movie%2C%20Rogers%20comes, Perls (accessed 21 April 2025)

Williams, M., Teasdale, J., Segal, Z., and Kabat-Zinn, J. (2007). *The Mindful Way Through Depression: Freeing Yourself from Chronic Unhappiness*. New York: Guilford.

9

Cognitive Behavioural Therapy

In the very first psychology textbook, *The Principles of Psychology*, William James said that a person's greatest weapon against stress is their ability to choose one thought over another. This assumption was vigorously studied in the following century. The findings were clear: people change how they experience by shifting how they think and behave.

Chapter 9 merges into the integrated person-centred model the idea that thoughts unravel feelings and sculpt behaviour. We remodel self-actualisation into a cognitive and behavioural perspective. And we promote the view that using a thought–feeling–behaviour model enhances integrative therapy, especially how cognitive behavioural therapy (CBT) provides a clear focus for the client and therapist.

A Word on Integration

This book is making quite a big claim. I am saying that all psychotherapies are models of reality. None of them is superior, though some are easier to understand. If psychotherapy is really a model for mental wellbeing, then – in theory – all psychotherapies can be integrated, and each one can be redescribed in the language of the other. It's like translating French into English.

This does not mean that all psychotherapies talk about the same things – and neither do French and English people. Psychoanalysis models the client's unconscious motivations. Person-centred therapy models the client's capacity to experience. When we combine these ideas into one model, we

Integrative Person-Centred Counselling: The Combined Model of Counselling and Psychotherapy, First Edition. Rick Murphy.

discover where one is lacking. It's like the word 'snack' in English that has no parallel in French. Or Le Goûter in French, which roughly translates as "a light piece of food specifically for the afternoon," which has no English version. This has nothing to do with language, but with 'concept'. There are no concepts for Le Goûter in English, whereas the Swedes have 'Fika', which translates roughly as coffee and cake in the afternoon (one of my favourite things about Sweden!).

That is, psychoanalysis cannot understand self-actualisation as an organic thing, something that happens on its own because it has no concept for it. And person-centred therapy cannot understand countertransference, or why the therapist acts like the client's neglectful caregiver – it has no concept for it. Integration helps us mine each model for its unique concepts and combine them into a greater whole. In the integrative person-centred model, we expect the client to grow naturally within the relationship (self-actualisation) while we monitor and share our personal reactions with the client (countertransference). In traditional person-centred therapy, there is no room for countertransference. Rogers said we are "only playing at the real world of relationships" when we talk about the client's experience "in terms of transference and countertransference." He feels quite deeply about that. While we can put the therapeutic interaction into a "highly intellectualised framework," for Rogers, "it completely misses the point."

My argument here is that any idea – even the idea of empathy or congruence – can lead to practices that 'miss the point' of the relationship. Try being empathic yet congruent with somebody who annoys you (as we said a few chapters back, the therapeutic skill helps us find the empathy needed to be *therapeutically* congruent). For those who have not read Carl Roger's paper on the encounter group, called "My Way of Facilitating a Group," let me give you an example of this contradiction from the man himself.

Carl is facilitating an encounter group for counselling students. He aims to explore relationships, resonances with the course material, and personal development. Noticing one group discussing superficial topics, he became bored and annoyed. Finding it difficult to be empathic and congruent, this is what happened next. He writes:

> I was in a quandary. In order to allay a considerable early anxiety in the group, I had stressed in the first session that they could make of this group exactly what they wished, and operationally they seemed to be saying very loudly, "we wish to spend expensive, hard-won, weekend time talking of

> trivia." Consequently, to express my annoyance seemed contradictory to the permission I had given them. After wrestling in myself for a few moments, I decided that they had a perfect right to talk trivia, and I decided I had a perfect right not to endure that trivia. So I simply walked quietly out of the room, and I went to bed.

Here, congruence and empathy self-destruct. My point is that the idea is not the issue; there probably was a way to be empathic and congruent, instead of going to bed. The issue is how we apply the idea in therapy. In this case, Carl's annoyance may have instigated change in the group dynamics, as he implies later in the paper – but he could have used the ideas in other ways too. Respecting the need to protect psychotherapy from intellectual game playing, as Rogers argues for, I suggest we take on any idea that supports the therapeutic relationship. If the idea doesn't support the relationship, we review if it's a problem-idea or a problematic way of using it. Hence countertransference could have been a more effective idea than congruence for Carl during that group encounter.

I think all models are intellectual frames for the client's unique experience. They describe the complex world to the psychotherapist in a way that supports clients. As Barry Mason said, it's about 'accessible complexity'. Thus, therapy models can be used to describe and re-describe a counselling session.

To put my money where my mouth is, I want to try and describe the Gloria tapes, discussed in the previous chapter, from the perspective of a cognitive behavioural therapist. If psychotherapies are just models, or French- and English-like languages, which concept-ualise the world in certain ways, then – like someone who is French who can understand Gloria via subtitles – any therapist should be able to translate the Gloria session into their therapy language. When a therapy model reaches its limits, having no words for what it sees, an integration (or a development of theory) is possible.

The Gloria Tapes

We know what Carl Rogers thought about his session with Gloria because he told us at the end of the video tape. He said:

> I felt that Gloria and I really encountered each other and that in some small but I believe lasting way we were, each of us, enriched by the experience ... Gloria showed what I've come to feel are characteristics of therapeutic movement.

> In the first part of the interview, she was talking about her feelings, and they were past feelings. She was talking about aspects of her behaviour and of herself, as if she didn't quite own them. She was looking outside herself for a centre or locus of evaluation, some source of authority. She saw some of the things she was talking about in a fairly "black-and-white fashion". By the end of the interview, she was experiencing her feelings in the immediate moment. Not only as evidenced by her tears but by her ability to express very directly and with immediacy her feelings toward me. She was also much more aware of her ability to make her own judgments and choices.

Although Rogers is careful not to intellectualise, his statement does have a theory of change, a theory of therapeutic process, and a theory of technique. We know the intellectual history of these ideas, from Husserl and Heidegger, in terms of the immediacy of experience, and from Maslow and humanistic psychologists, in terms of using the therapeutic relationship for the client's self-authority. His description is valid but has clear implications for the way he is with Gloria. Those impacts are undoubtedly beneficial, but how else could we model the session? How would changing the model impact the therapist's behaviour?

In this section, we visit the part of the session that Carl Rogers refers to earlier. He encourages Gloria's emotional presence and self-reliance.

Gloria: I mentioned this word a lot in therapy and most therapists grin at me or giggle or something when I say 'utopia', but when I do follow a feeling and I feel this good feeling inside of me, that's sort of utopia. That's what I mean. That's the way I like to feel whether it's a bad thing or a good thing. But I feel right about me. This is what I want to …

Carl: I sense that in those utopian moments, you really feel kind of whole. You feel all in one piece.

Gloria: Yes. It gives me a choked-up feeling when you say that because I don't get that as often as I'd like. I like that whole feeling. That's real precious to me.

Carl used the skill of paraphrasing. He listened to Gloria's words, "this good feeling inside of me" and "I feel right about me." He experienced those words genuinely and congruently. And he changed them empathically into "you feel all in one piece." In his own words, he was not intending to paraphrase like a detached robot. He responded spontaneously because of what he authentically felt.

But we shouldn't overlook the fact that the session is mostly, at the response or skill level, Carl restating and paraphrasing Gloria's words. This is because the underlying theory shows itself in the counselling process. It is easy to identify this therapist, compared with another therapist, and to model his therapeutic approach based on his actions.

To prove this, what follow are four real extracts from the Gloria tapes. See if you can tell which two are Fritz Perls and which two are Carl Rogers:

Therapist 1: You really do miss the fact that you couldn't be open with your own dad.
Therapist 2: You say you're scared, but you are smiling. I don't understand how one can be scared and smile at the same time.
Therapist 3: Are you aware of your facial expression, the kind of disgust on it?
Therapist 4: Mhm. (pause) But you feel, really, that at times you're acting in ways that are not in accord with your own inner standards.

In these extracts, therapist one and therapist four restate and paraphrase the client's words. The 'Mhm' shows the therapist is listening and verbally acknowledging the client, naming and tolerating their difficult experience.

Therapist two and therapist three act differently. Their statements draw attention to body language. They use phenomenological inquiry by highlighting facial expressions and contradictions in feeling fear when smiling.

From this short analysis, we can be confident that one and four are humanistic, and two and three are gestalt. Hence, Rogers is one and four and Perls is two and three.

We are not saying that the integrative person-centred therapist can look either like Perls or Rogers. We are saying that one needs to practice the principles of humanism as the foundation to the approach, which Perls isn't. In our model, like Rogers, we privilege empathy and the relationship.

The integrative therapist might vary Perls's comments by putting themself non-judgementally in relation to the client. From, "You say you're scared, but you are smiling. I don't understand how one can be scared and smile at the same time," to something like, "I hear you say you're scared, and I see you are smiling. Could you say a bit more about what happens when you express your fear to me?"

Here we used phenomenological inquiry as a skill but attached it to empathy rather than observation alone. In the content that follows, like combining gestalt with person centred, we demonstrate how to remodel the encounter, showing that CBT concepts can integrate into the work with Gloria.

Thought–Feeling–Behaviour Cycles

The idea of regulating people's feelings by changing their thoughts and actions was a great example of integrating two major theories in psychology, behaviourism and cognitive psychology. The 1920s saw the first behaviourist experiment on humans. It set to prove that behaviour is a reflex to environmental conditions, something that is reinforced by positive and negative associations. We must note that this is an awful experiment that shouldn't be tried at home!

The psychologist John Watson and research student Rosalie Rayner carried out the experiment. They named it 'Little Albert', after the 9-month-old boy who unconsentingly took part. Watson and Rayner introduced Albert to a harmless white rat. At first, Albert was curious about the rat and showed no signs of fear. Then, out of nowhere, Rayner made loud bangs behind Albert's head – an attempt to associate the rat with scary loud bangs.

The loud noise distressed Albert. After repeating the pairing several times, banging equipment when Albert played with the rat, Albert grew fearful of the rat. Even the sight of the rat made Albert cry, where before he was comfortable with it. In fact, the fear became more abstract, and Albert showed fear around other fluffy white things. These included dogs, coats, and even, around Christmas time, Father Christmas' beard.

Behaviourism found two concepts: associative learning and classical conditioning. These mean that people associate threat, safety, risk, and pleasure with paired things in their environment, and they become conditioned to feel paired emotions – such as comfort with safe associations and fear with threatening associations. Behaviour is the result of a reflex to feelings that have been conditioned. Similar experiments replicated the little Albert study with humans and animals, confirming the result.

Forty years later, the cognitive psychologists added a final piece to the conditioning puzzle. They found that it's not only the feeling that associates with the behaviour, but the cognitive system – a person's thoughts and ideas. That is, cognitive change (such as thinking a rat is harmful) aids behavioural conditioning. Hence, CBT is fundamentally about supporting change in thoughts and behaviour as a route to positive feelings.

Research by B. F. Skinner in the 1940s showed that focusing on behaviour reduced depression and anxiety. In the 1950s, psychiatrist Aaron T. Beck showed that working on the cognitive thought process of anxious and depressed patients made each condition better. And, since the 1990s, CBT has become one of the most common interventions for anxiety and depression, alongside a range of other mental health diagnoses, recommended by the National Health Service (NHS). There are many schools of CBT, including mindfulness-based and acceptance-based CBT, and the CBT literature is growing exponentially.

Person-Centred CBT

In 2005, Nina Josefowitz and Joseph Myran, from the University of Toronto, wrote a paper called "Towards a Person-Centred Cognitive Behaviour Therapy." They essentially wrote the chapter we are now reading but in reverse, showing how CBT can accommodate person-centred principles, particularly empathy and congruence. Their conclusion was that CBT and person-centred values are "highly consistent."

Let's examine this using the Gloria transcript. If you recall, Gloria is connecting with 'utopian moments' and Carl is feeding back that Gloria seems like a whole person, like herself. The dialogue continues:

Carl: I sense that in those utopian moments, you really feel kind of whole. You feel all in one piece.

Gloria: Yes. Yeah, it gives me a choked-up feeling when you say that because I don't get that as often as I'd like. I like that whole feeling. That's real precious to me.

Carl: I expect none of us get it as often as we'd like, but I really do understand it. (Gloria starts to cry.) Mhm, that really does touch you, doesn't it?

Gloria: Yeah, and you know what else I was just thinking? I feel dumb saying it – that all of a sudden while I was talking to you I thought, "Gee, how nice I can talk to you and I want you to approve of me and I respect you, but I miss that my father couldn't talk to me like you are."
I mean, I'd like to say,
"Gee, I'd like you for my father."
...

There are several person-centred features in this dialogue. Carl remains present with Gloria's experience, using himself and his feelings to reflect back her words. Gloria is in a later stage of process, which we described in Chapter 3 because she moves from being shut off emotionally towards naming, intensifying, and taking some ownership for her feelings.

A CBT therapist models the situation differently, using the same facts. First, what are Gloria's thoughts, feelings, and behaviours? Second, how do we model why she is feeling this way? Third, what can Gloria do behaviourally to gain more autonomy?

The therapy intervention can be mapped into the CBT model, called a 'cognitive triangle', as shown in Figure 9.1.

The cognitive behavioural theory alone cannot explain all the observations from the counselling session. One way this lens changes the picture, if you notice, is to completely cut the therapist out. Josefowitz and Myran argue that this needn't lead to a lack of reflection on the role of the therapist. Nor should it lead to a lower priority for the relationship. It serves an important function, to isolate the components of the client's issue. Focusing on the issues clarifies the therapy in an overflowing forest of complex experiences.

An interesting observation comes out of Gloria's Cognitive Triangle (see Figure 9.1). After Gloria <u>thinks</u> she doesn't get the utopian feeling as much as she needs it, she <u>thinks</u> she is dumb, and she <u>thinks</u> she needs Carl's

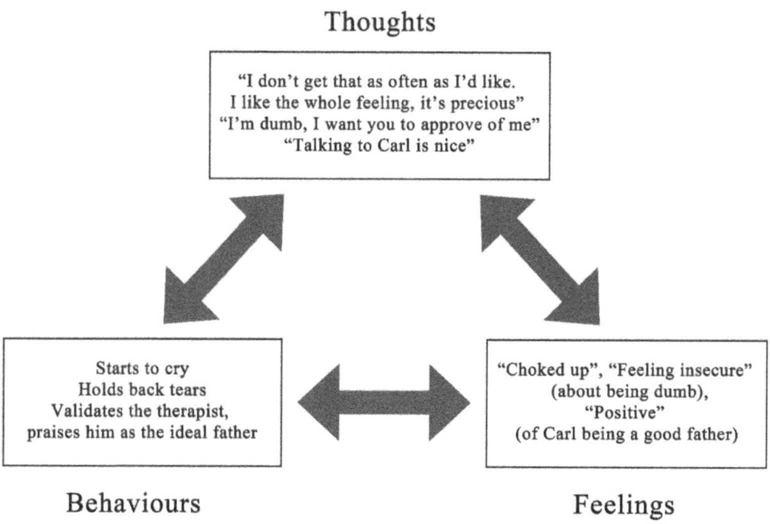

Figure 9.1 Gloria's Cognitive Triangle

approval. At the same time, she goes from feeling choked up and teary to feeling insecure and then feeling positive. In parallel, Gloria behaves by starting to cry, then by holding back tears, and then by validating the therapist. A CBT lens changes the model of the interaction. It's more akin to describing a defence mechanism, in which the client's behaviour serves to hide painful feelings – in this case by praising the therapist.

Carl's response to Gloria is to express congruence with how he is feeling.

Gloria: I mean, I'd like to say, "Gee, I'd like you for my father." I don't even know why that came to me.

Carl: You look to me like a pretty nice daughter … But you really do miss the fact that you couldn't be open with your own dad.

Carl feels that Gloria would be a nice daughter, and he expresses that to her. Although he does not approve of the intellectual label of countertransference, it is possible that here the description fits well. Gloria transfers a helplessness that a therapist wants to rescue her from. Hence, validating her as the daughter could invalidate her father. Maybe it is helpful to her autonomy for this to happen. Or maybe it confirms in her a need of validation from others, and this prevents her from showing the emotion that was beginning to surface. After all, behaviourally, she started to cry, then called herself 'dumb', and then validated the goodness in Carl. The integrative lens unpacks counselling interactions in detail and comes up with extra ideas and options.

An orthodox CBT response would, instead of validation, highlight thinking, behaviour, and feeling, encouraging Gloria to explore links between them, something like what follows:

Gloria: I mean, I'd like to say, "Gee, I'd like you for my father." I don't even know why that came to me.

CBT Therapist: Ah, you're not sure where that came from … When you think about wanting a different father, what feelings come up?

Or

Gloria: I mean, I'd like to say, "Gee, I'd like you for my father." I don't even know why that came to me.

CBT Therapist: Ah, you're not sure where that came from … Could you break that down a bit more. What thoughts are linked with this?

By connecting feelings, thoughts, and actions, Gloria gains more self-awareness. Growth happens when she becomes aware of how thinking of a different dad leads her to feel and behave in ways that seek reassurance, rather than in ways that generate self-assurance. That is, probably people feel a sense of wanting to rescue her, but you cannot rescue someone from an entrenched self-image.

With Gloria, the CBT therapist will have intervened in the transcript earlier, whenever thoughts, feelings, and actions surfaced. And this may have had more emotional impact, depending on how the therapist related to her. For example, in the following section:

Carl: I sense that in those utopian moments, you really feel kind of whole. You feel all in one piece.

Gloria: Yeah, it gives me a choked-up feeling when you say that because I don't get that as often as I'd like. I like that whole feeling. That's real precious to me.

Carl: <u>I expect none of us get it as often as we'd like</u>, but I really do understand it. (Gloria begins to cry.) Mhm, that really does touch you, doesn't it?

In this conversation, the underlined section is where I think Gloria starts to shut down her emotion. The statement generalises Gloria's concern, as though "none of us" get that need met – and hence it's not a big concern or it's at least common. Then Carl slightly protests "But I really do understand it." In the bigger picture of the relationship, this is a minor event. But what kinds of responses might have stuck with Gloria's emotion here? Bearing in mind, after this, Gloria starts to validate Carl instead of experiencing her "choked-up feeling" (hence countertransference happened again).

CBT gives us the following options:

Stick with the Feeling

Gloria: Yes. Yeah, it gives me a choked-up feeling when you say that because I don't get that as often as I'd like. I like that whole feeling. That's real precious to me.

Carl Rogers (CBT Version): Can you describe the feeling?

Stick with the Thought

Gloria: Yes. Yeah, it gives me a choked-up feeling when you say that because I don't get that as often as I'd like. I like that whole feeling. That's real precious to me.

Carl Rogers (CBT Version): What thoughts come to mind when you get this choked-up feeling?

Stick with the Behaviour

Gloria: Yes. Yeah, it gives me a choked-up feeling when you say that because I don't get that as often as I'd like. I like that whole feeling. That's real precious to me.

Carl Rogers (CBT Version): When you feel choked up or upset, how do you tend to respond?

It is true that we start to become a little more directive, at least in the sense of intentionally inquiring about thoughts, feelings, and behaviours. The humanistic integration is in accepting what the client brings non-judgementally, validating it, restating it, probing into it, but with a view to stick around in the three themes and to explore their connections. Here's an example of where this might lead:

Gloria: Yes. Yeah, it gives me a choked-up feeling when you say that because I don't get that as often as I'd like. I like that whole feeling. That's real precious to me.

Carl Rogers (CBT Version): When you feel choked up or upset, how do you tend to respond?

Gloria: I don't know. You know, when I feel it, I almost want to get rid of the feeling. I just move on or talk about something else.

Carl Rogers (CBT Version): When you feel upset ... you try and move on somehow. To do something else.

Gloria: Yeah. But do you know what I want? To just feel it, and to just trust that someone will care about it.

In this fictitious example, person-centred CBT gets to understand Gloria using empathy, unconditional positive regard, and congruence. But it notices the importance of sticking with a person's cognitive and behavioural process – noticing what they do next, how they think, and how they feel.

Every question needn't be straightjacketed into the CBT frame, but the therapist highlights those themes in their questions, balancing this with their spontaneous responses.

The stereotypical CBT therapist teaches the client that their thinking is dysfunctional and to combat the so-called 'cognitive distortions'. In fact, for those who have not seen the Gloria tapes, she does visit a third therapist. He is called Albert Ellis, and he pioneered a CBT-like approach called rational emotive therapy. Gloria is subjected to a full 30 minutes of rationalising her worry, with very little curiosity or relationship to hang on to. The Ellis 'lecture' highlights the risk of thinking like a behaviourist or a cognitive psychologist. As with Little Albert and the White Rat, trying to condition someone often takes away their humanity.

Some people contend that Ellis' session was empowering, that he was showing Gloria a way out of a difficult existence. But this type of quote-on-quote "therapy" appears to be more about rationalising emotions – a very masculine trope in relationships, and often signals a person who struggles to tolerate emotions. As a couple's therapist, I see this fail miserably. One person wants to *think* about the relationship and the other wants to *feel* it. Probably much of couple's therapy is the balancing act between emotion and rationalising, but we need both.

I don't think CBT has to be like this. The framework doesn't dictate a sort of teacher-like persona. In my CBT training, I have been trained to think like a teacher, at times, not a therapist, and so it does happen. But taking the thought–feeling–behaviour idea into a person-centred world is perfectly possible. I hope this has already been demonstrated at the technique level with our imagined session with Gloria.

Core Beliefs

When I teach CBT, many students latch onto it quickly because it offers a safety net unlike any other model. The techniques are like IKEA flat-pack furniture; they come with a manual and a clear end product. Even if the instructions feel difficult to follow, they're much more reassuring than a box full of wood and nails. But where they struggle (or where I struggle to teach?) is when communicating the concept of core beliefs.

Students say the idea of core beliefs is easy to grasp. It's the application where they struggle. It stems from a puzzle about why people painstakingly think themselves to high blood pressure. If negative thoughts lead to negative feelings, why not just change the thoughts? Why mentally torture yourself? Just think about something else!

The concept of core beliefs answered this puzzle. It's not like people choose to dislike themselves or ruminate over what someone called them last week. Instead, the person develops behaviours and cognitions linked with an underlying set of values. That is, a core belief is a belief that someone holds about themselves, about other people, and about the world. They exist at the core of a person's thoughts and act like a set of colouring pens that colour – or give feeling to – experience. Thoughts and behaviours that arise out of these core beliefs take on the colour or emotion they evoke.

Most people are unaware of their core beliefs, and so, like many psychotherapies, CBT has some concept of the unconscious. While the thinking is at the conscious level, it can be, if examined, a window onto an underlying unconscious world of values. The cognitive scientist relates this to neuroscience. Core beliefs are created from neural processes linked with how a person perceives the external world and forms a personal meaning. The core belief, on a neurological level, underlies a person's emotions, choices, and goals.

The struggle I have seen when teaching this concept is how to get to a core belief. To find out what the core of a belief is, we probe deeper into a thought, feeling, or behaviour. The clinical psychologist Russell Grieger writes about three steps in what he calls a 'core construct'.

First we explore the thoughts or 'self-talk' of the client. Then we explore the beliefs about the self-talk. Finally, we explore the belief about the belief. This third step is usually a core belief (or, in Grieger's language, a core 'paradigm').

Let's push our luck with fictionalising Gloria's session a bit further. Imagine we wanted to encourage Gloria to figure out her paradigm, her underlying perspective, her core belief. We might pick up where we left off:

Integrative Therapist: When you feel upset … you try and move on somehow. To do something else.

Gloria: Yeah. But do you know what I want? To just feel it, and to just trust that someone will care about it.

Integrative Therapist: It's like a wish for someone to care about you …. I'm trying to imagine what thoughts come to mind here?

Gloria: With my father …. I think he would never listen to me talk like you are. He wouldn't care about my feelings.

Integrative Therapist: And what stands out to you about that?

Gloria: (pause) That fathers should care about their daughters, you know. He should, I think … care about me.

Integrative Therapist: You think your father doesn't care about you, but that he should. Where does that lead you? In terms of, what conclusions are you making here?

Gloria: If I just sit still a minute, it feels like a great big hurt down there. I guess I sometimes wonder if people just can't care about me.

Obviously, this situation is now fictionalised – and my script-writing skills will not win an Oscar anytime soon! The point is to comprehend how we integrate CBT and core beliefs into the person-centred model. We highlight the self-talk, probe the surface belief, and go into the core belief. That is, the imagined Gloria thinks her father doesn't care about her. She believes that he should care about her. And when she doesn't experience care from him, the core belief that people don't care about her forms (Figure 9.2). The core belief of the real Gloria was probably less "People don't care about me" and more "I make things worse."

A core belief is a cognitive bias for how someone views the world. When a client thinks, they do so through the lens of an unwritten yet embodied value. If my core belief is that I make things worse, I rarely accept positive change. I constantly worry about messing things up. Hence CBT brings to person-centred therapy a framework for getting to the client's innermost self.

Clients interpret the world through their core beliefs. Like a photo that gets edited with a filter, the photo can be made more horrific, more beautiful, darker, or brighter. So too can the belief filter of the client. The conscious aspect is the client's self-talk, but underneath is a conditioned view of the self.

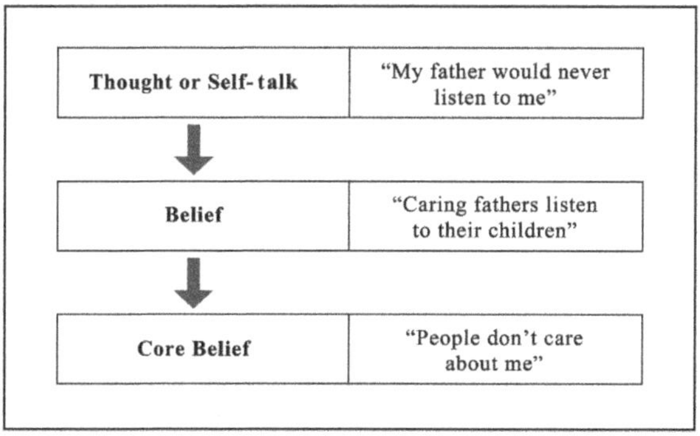

Figure 9.2 Gloria's (Imagined) Core Belief

Imagine a client with the core belief 'I am unlikeable'. How do they experience meeting a new group of people? How do they respond when others try to make friends with them? CBT says that when the client rethinks these situations, they alter their core beliefs with the therapist.

A person-centred therapist wouldn't see it that way, but there would still be (invisible) cognitive change during the process. Again, we return to model-dependent realism from Chapter 3. The reality we see is based on how we model it. The truth is that thousands of changes occur every second – the eye movement, the voice tone, the posture. Each psychotherapy model highlights the portion of change that appeals to its theory. Hence, my view that integrating multiple theories offers the therapist more descriptions of reality, not contradictory descriptions.

Like humanistic therapies and phenomenological therapies, CBT focuses on the here and now. Sometimes it can be future oriented, but its theory is based on the influence of the past on the present. Childhood is not discussed in much of the literature, but the idea is that through childhood and environmental events, a person wires their brain to certain perspectives. For therapy clients, the core perspectives often get stuck in pessimism. By processing, exploring, and challenging the surface thinking, feeling, and behaving, the core self – in CBT language – is restructured. In fact, cognitive restructuring is a fundamental theory of change in CBT with clinical depression and anxiety.

In this way, CBT has observed a similar concept to person-centred counselling. This is that experience is filtered through psychological constructs. CBT emphasises the 'belief' aspect of this where person-centred emphasises the 'worth' aspect. Hence core beliefs are close to conditions of worth but are not the same thing. Someone who has the core belief that money equals success has the condition of worth that they must have money to be valuable. Hence what we integrate into our person-centred model is two things. One is the three-level structure of a core belief, discussed earlier. The other is how to support change in a condition of worth by probing into thoughts, feelings, and behaviours.

Cognitive Distortions

The person-centred view of mental health is that healthy people tolerate experience and use it for personal growth. The CBT view of mental health is that the cognitive behavioural features produce negative perspectives and unhealthy reflexes – and these lead to adverse emotional states. I have suggested that we layer the cognitive and behavioural concepts onto our experience-based model. Integrative person-centred therapy continues to intensify, tolerate, and process experience, but pauses to explore thought–feeling–behaviour links, when they arise organically in the session.

There are practical benefits to the cognitive way of describing therapy. For example, our skill attunes to many kinds of thinking that are unseen or unconceptualised in person-centred theory. One such thinking type is a 'cognitive distortion'. This describes the situation where a client thinks in a biased and exaggerated way. A person-centred view rightly accepts the client's experience as reality, albeit with the goal to support clients in shifting how they experience reality. Thus, cognitive distortions reduce when the client accepts their experience and their autonomy. The reason I think it's worth adopting this concept in the integrative approach is the simplicity of the idea. It's accessible at times when clients are profoundly pessimistic.

The Gloria transcript reveals many cognitive distortions. One example follows, where she discusses if her child would accept her. At the point of a cognitive distortion, where she says that her daughter could really think she's a 'devil', notice how Carl Rogers implicitly picks up on the distortion. But, having no concept for 'cognitive distortion', his idea is implied rather than made transparent. And as a result, Gloria contradicts his paraphrase:

Gloria (about daughter): I feel that in time she will distrust me, yes. And also I thought well, gee, what about when she gets a little older and she finds herself in touchy situations. She probably wouldn't want to admit it to me because she thinks I'm so good and so sweet. **And yet I'm afraid she could think I'm really a – a devil.** And I want so bad for her to accept me. And I don't know how much a nine-year-old can take.

Carl: And really both alternatives concern you. That she may think you're too good or better than you really are.

Gloria: Yes.

Carl: **And she may think you are worse than you are.**

Gloria: **Not worse than I am.** I don't know if she can accept me the way I am. I think I paint a picture that I'm all sweet and motherly. And – I'm a little ashamed of my shady side too.

Carl Rogers is working hard to empathise with Gloria. He notices the word 'devil' presents Gloria as 'worse' than she really is – her thinking misrepresents the magnitude of her daughter's feelings. Without the concept of cognitive distortion, he subtly implies it and momentarily loses touch with her experience. Carl works through the incongruence therapeutically, rolling with Gloria's correction, accepting the thoughts that surface. My contention is that the concept 'cognitive distortion' would have helped him to identify this common pattern in the way Gloria thinks. On the technique level, this might create more empathy for the experience underlying emotive words. For instance, Carl could explore the 'devil' in her thoughts and what impact this devil has on her behaviour. Instead, he expresses his judgement subtly, and Gloria rejects it.

Integrative counselling is not trying to cover over all the cracks in therapy. This, of course, is impossible. It's easy for me to sit in my office and pull out moments where therapists could have done better (actually I am sat eating cake in a farmhouse café, just for full disclosure). My intention is more to show where integration into a person-centred model can aid the therapist in different scenarios. I understand purist therapists who say they don't need integrative ideas to do their therapy. And the scientific evidence supports them. But, remaining in our way of thinking, we miss out on knowledge from other therapy models.

To integrate the concept of a cognitive distortion into our model, we could probe into the client's thinking. For those therapists who prefer not to ask questions, another route is to restate and paraphrase the distortion to intensify the client's awareness of it, such as:

Gloria (about daughter): She probably wouldn't want to admit it to me because she thinks I'm so good and so sweet. And yet I'm afraid she could think I'm really a – a devil. And I want so bad for her to accept me. And I don't know how much a nine-year-old can take.

Carl (integrative version): And really both alternatives concern you. That she may think you're too good or better than you really are.

Gloria: Yes.

Carl: And she may think you really are a devil.

Gloria: Yes. (now Gloria is aware of her cognitive distortion, we can intensify it.)

I think many outside observers would miss the CBT in this interaction. Integrative therapy doesn't have to mean looking like a CBT therapist, someone who might be more prone to psychoeducation – to drawing and diagramming this via a worksheet. The invisibility of CBT is because, at the skill level, we do exactly what Carl does. The difference is, instead of drawing from our therapeutic intuition, we draw knowledge from other psychotherapy models to create empathic responses. The CBT concept sharpened the awareness around the catastrophising thought, "If I'm not good and sweet, people might see me as the devil." Hence, the cognitive distortion was not picked up within this session but may have been in an integrative scenario.

CBT refers to cognitive distortions as 'mood congruent'. That is, the mood the person feels filters the facts of life emotionally. If the person has the core belief that they always get things wrong, then they experience themselves, even as a parent, through negative emotion. People tend to confirm and reconfirm their reality in their behaviour (by being a bad person, for example). By perceiving information through this filter, clients distort their self-image, like a funhouse mirror. The purpose of CBT sounds different from person-centred therapy, but the outcome is the same. By overcoming negative representations of the world – by feeling more accepted and by nurturing self-esteem – clients perceive more of reality and grow from it.

Summary

In this chapter we have integrated cognitive behavioural therapy into our counselling model. With the Gloria tapes, we showed how pausing on a feeling or a behaviour aids the therapist in helping the client escape from detrimental thinking. Not thinking like a CBT therapist meant we underprivileged cognitive and behavioural components of the client's issue.

We did not discuss the enormous storehouse of techniques that CBT offers. We didn't consider the books on graded exposure, thought diaries, hot-cross-bun worksheets, putting the thought on trial, or cognitive restructuring. This is because we stressed the importance of being present with the client and not overtly technique focused. This does not mean we cannot take on those helpful ways of working with clients. Interested readers are encouraged to find their own way to adopt the techniques from the wider literature into integrative person-centred counselling.

Instead, we focused on the CBT idea that client-presenting problems are shown in thoughts, feelings, and behaviours. These characteristics are influenced by values and judgements held deep inside the brain. Through environmental conditioning, through 'experience', people create core beliefs that colour how they think and feel about the world.

In person-centred CBT we identify specific problems by listening out for thoughts, feelings, and behaviours. We support the client to intensify and become aware of how they think and feel – exploring the impact this has on their actions. We focus on situations where cognitive distortions happen, using the therapeutic relationship to support the client in reshaping negative thinking. This already happens in person-centred therapy – people organically "find hope against the negative experience," in Carl Rogers' words – but CBT gives us new concepts to help achieve this goal with clients.

Further Reading

Baker, R., Owens, M., Thomas, S. et al. (2012). Does CBT facilitate emotional processing? *Behavioural and Cognitive Psychotherapy* 40 (1): 19–37.

Beck, J. (1995). *Cognitive Therapy: Basics and Beyond*. New York: Guilford.

Beck, J.S. and Fleming, S. (2021). A brief history of Aaron T. Beck, MD, and cognitive behavior therapy. *Clinical Psychology in Europe* 3 (2): 1–7.

Dryden, W. (2012). *The Therapeutic Relationship in CBT. The CBT Handbook*, 83–100. London: Sage.

Ellis, A. (2003). Early theories and practices of rational emotive behavior theory and how they have been augmented and revised during the last three decades. *Journal of Rational-Emotive & Cognitive-Behavior Therapy* 21 (3/4): 219–243.

Fordham, B., Sugavanam, T., Edwards, K. et al. (2021). The evidence for cognitive behavioural therapy in any condition, population or context: a meta-review of systematic reviews and panoramic meta-analysis. *Psychological Medicine* 51 (1): 21–29. https://doi.org/10.1017/S0033291720005292.

Greiger, R. (2018). *On Becoming a Cognitive Behavioural Therapist*. London: Routledge.

James, W. (1890). *The Principles of Psychology*, vol. 1. Henry Holt and Co. https://doi.org/10.1037/10538-000.

Josefowitz, N. and Myran, D. (2005). Towards a person-centred cognitive behaviour therapy. *Counselling Psychology Quarterly* 18 (4): 329–336. https://doi.org/10.1080/09515070500473600.

Morgan, D. (2003). Mindfulness-based cognitive therapy for depression: a new approach to preventing relapse. *Psychotherapy Research* 13 (1): 123–125. https://doi.org/10.1080/713869628.

Rogers, C. (1971). My way of facilitating a group. *American Journal of Nursing* 71 (2): 275–279.

Shostrom, E. L. (1965). Three approaches to psychotherapy (Part I) [Film]. Orange, CA: Psychological Films. Adapted from the Transcripts of Carl Rogers' Therapy Sessions, Edited by Barbara T. Brodley and Germain Lietaer [online]. https://anamartinspsicoterapiaacp.files.wordpress.com/2016/04/brodley-transcripts-of-carl-rogers-therapy-sessions.pdf

Skinner, B.F. (1988). *About Behaviourism*. New York: Random House.

10

Systemic

Person-centred therapy sees counselling problems like a gardener sees a wilting flowerbed. A gardener does not try and convince a plant how it should grow, neither do they shield the plant from the rain. Rather, they enrich the environment for it to grow in its own way, supporting it to become resilient within its natural surroundings.

Because a person-centred therapist is like a gardener, at least in this respect, we hold back from attitudes towards clients that try to convince them how they should be. In this respect, psychiatry has been questioned regarding how labelling the client 'disordered' leads to coercive treatment. Language is shown to have powerful effects on people's wellbeing.

It is not surprising that the first psychoanalysts were psychiatrists. They are expert fields in which a doctor describes reality to the client in words they accept as true. The anti-psychiatry movement, started in the 1960s by the psychiatrist R. D. Laing, argued that words like 'disorder', 'anorectic', 'psychotic', and 'depressive', were anti-humanistic. That is, psychiatric labels are obstacles to empathy, curiosity, and positive regard. If we think, talk, and act like the 'patient' is disordered, we use authority as a treatment in place of a relationship.

Stephen Joseph from the University of Nottingham compiled a book arguing for a person-centred psychiatry in the United Kingdom. He created a two-way street between relationship-based therapies and mainstream mental health treatment. Although this is clearly humane, Carl Rogers spoke out against including mental health labels in therapy. To him, psychological problems are humanistic. A psychiatric eye sees chronic

Integrative Person-Centred Counselling: The Combined Model of Counselling and Psychotherapy, First Edition. Rick Murphy.

anxiety as a disorder, but the person-centred eye sees anxiety like a map to the client's inner world. We do not try to delete the person's internal vocabulary and replace it with a psychiatric phrasebook, like the *Diagnostic and Statistical Manual of Mental Disorders*. Instead, we compile a unique and deeply personal dictionary with each client and one that evolves as their experience does by our empathy and acceptance.

How then do we fit psychiatry with a person-centred approach? Can we just ignore it?

My view is we cannot ignore psychiatric labels in therapy any more than we can ignore labels put onto the client by parents, siblings, neighbours, bullies, friends, teachers, ex-partners, or employers. There is a bigger picture to grasp. This is that the way a person experiences is clearly linked with, if not completely fused with, their social world. Psychiatry is one of a variety of social contexts that describe the client and their problem, and these descriptions, as philosopher Michel Foucault points out, have power over experience.

In this chapter, we model the client's experience through their family and social context, showing the importance of attending to social-emotional-political systems in integrative therapy.

The Politics of Experience

By seeing experience as the individual's responsibility, we unintentionally miss the relationship between the client's problem and the social context. The social norms, national government, political climate, education system, culture, local community, and family dominate the possible ways of experiencing. In R. D. Laing's most famous book, he refers to this as *The Politics of Experience*. We can't experience things independently from society; everything we think and feel has hidden political features.

To illustrate this, I'd like to draw on an example. I was lecturing on the person-centred theory of experience. A bright and conscientious student, Salma Mohamed, felt some discomfort and courageously questioned me. In trying to apply the theory to her life, she found a tension between the model of personal responsibility and her experience of social injustice. I have invited her in this chapter to discuss.

Rick: "Could you talk about what happened in the lecture, when you were learning about the idea that change comes from perspective and experience?"

Salma: On Wednesday evening I went to the university's hotel lobby to work on my dissertation proposal. My chronic illness made it too painful to sit in my room. I was immersed in my work, wearing noise-cancelling headphones, when a security officer approached me.

Her tone was cold, her posture was defensive, and her presence felt invasive. 'Why are you sitting here?' she said, standing over me.

I panicked. She had walked past a white man in the same lobby without questioning him and came straight to me. I knew this encounter wasn't going to be fair. Experiences like this trigger an overwhelming sense of fear and shame. Smiling, over-explaining myself, and trying to appear non-threatening, I explained to her that I was doing an assignment.

She asked for my room key. But when I showed her the key and explained that my health condition prevented me from sitting in the room, she wasn't satisfied and said, 'This doesn't explain why you're here at this time. I still find it odd. I'm trying to understand the need.'

The questions came until I mentioned the security manager and explained I had a support package set up, and she finally backed off. She walked away with a cold response as I was still talking, clutching her security vest as if to reinforce her authority.

The interaction lasted about ten minutes but felt like an eternity. I was left shaken and embarrassed, while a white man nearby asked if I was okay and suggested I reported her. I did, focusing on what I could control. I called the security office, and their response felt equally dismissive. They claimed she was 'just checking if I was safe', which felt blatantly untrue. It felt like my experience didn't matter, and I was left to carry the emotional burden alone.

When I came into class the next day, I felt physically inflamed from my condition due to the stress, and I was emotionally drained. Sitting in a room full of white people, I felt small, invisible, and insignificant. Trauma teaches you to shrink yourself, and that's exactly how I felt.

The discussion in class about how change comes from perspective and experience didn't sit right with me, so I had to share my experience. How could I change my perspective when the system itself is broken? Person-centred therapy felt inadequate in that moment. It seemed to place responsibility for change on the individual while ignoring the systemic forces shaping their reality. It may unintentionally strengthen unjust mechanisms by failing to recognise the larger systemic reality.

> In my experience, the person-centred approach validated my emotions, but it didn't offer much support to deal with the bigger systemic issues that were affecting my life. Institutional racism, microaggressions, unequal power dynamics, and Islamophobia, these are realities I face frequently. While emotional validation is important, it doesn't address the external forces that cause so much harm.

I think Salma has poked an enormous hole in our psychotherapy model. By avoiding labels and seeing experience as the determiner of the person, we ignored society's grip on the individual's experience. Racism, sexism, ableism, classism, Islamophobia: how are each of these obvious hindrances to safe and trustful experience accounted for in the person-centred model? In some sense, is this not an example of colonialism in therapy and academia? That is, adding to the white male dominance of psychotherapy literature, doesn't a model of personality ignore the social injustices embedded in people's thoughts and behaviours? On some level, I think it legitimises the injustices in our culture.

In this book, we have talked about the environment in vague terms. The challenge this chapter takes up is how to model influences from the family and society in the world of experience. What does the integrative person-centred model need to add to acknowledge the politics of Salma's experience?

Interpersonal Patterns

To answer these important questions, systemic psychotherapy enters the conversation with a few helpful suggestions. The first is that experience serves a social purpose. Instead of probing into the experience, it probes into the role the experience leads a person to take in a relationship.

Consider the situation where a person experiences jealousy. What purpose does jealousy have?

Evolutionary psychologists say that jealousy serves the purpose of motivating partners to protect sexual interests and offspring. Negative experience motivates the person to keep the relationship and ensure the survival of their children. Humans without jealousy would be less likely to procreate.

Does this mean that jealousy is a good thing? Not quite. There are other, systemic, interpretations of jealousy, such as an outcome of male dominance in relationships, insecure attachments, and emotional control. It may be that all humans have the possibility of jealousy, but how they show jealousy is determined by previous relationships. Hence, jealousy is one of the scariest emotions domestically, where partners – usually women – are horrifically murdered in fits of jealous rage.

Here's how systemic psychotherapy models the situation. Two people interact. Let's say one person hides their smartphone screen from another – the female, let's say – in a heterosexual relationship. This behaviour is a social communication that is received by her boyfriend; he notices her hiding the phone. He interprets the situation as, "She is hiding promiscuity from me." What does he do? Again, this depends on how his experience motivates him to act. Some men give space, some men confront, some men become angry, and some become self-doubting. Hence, in systemic psychotherapy, experience is not the sole focus. The interaction sequence, the interpretation, and the experience are explored together (Figure 10.1).

The above interaction is a real one that ended with my client's boyfriend grabbing her phone and throwing it across the room. She comes from a background of domestic violence, and she is 15 years old. She hid her phone screen because her boyfriend was controlling, and she feared triggering him by scrolling on her social media feed. This was a self-fulfilling prophecy. By trying to stop the controlling behaviour, the behaviour became more controlling.

A model of experience can reach the same conclusion – we aren't claiming that the models are incompatible. For example, we could work with her or him to sit with the experience, becoming more aware of their responsibility in the moment. Maybe he learns to tolerate jealousy without aggression. Maybe she learns to trust her fear about some males and block the aggressive ones from her life. But the individual lens misses how each person's experience becomes a relationship dynamic (Figure 10.2).

To help my client, it was important for her to reflect on how she lets down her boundaries for aggressive people. We do not mean to imply that she is responsible for his aggression. Only that the reason people have repeated abusive relationships is often sadly about learned communication patterns. Figure 10.2 shows the dynamic, that the more she withdraws and defends herself, the more her partner acts attackingly. A systemic view sees this pattern as important to her experience.

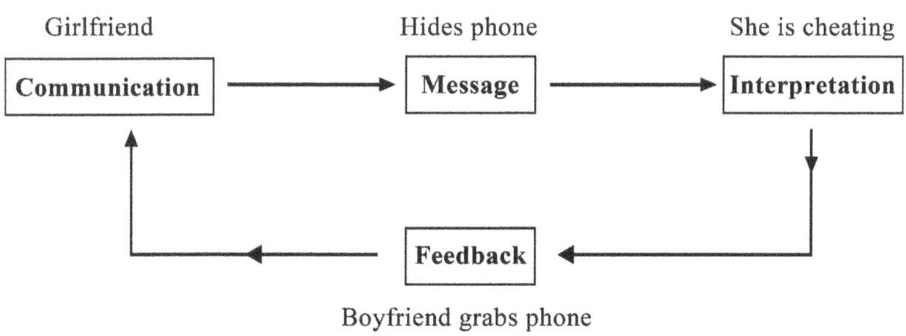

Figure 10.1 Jealousy Interaction Pattern

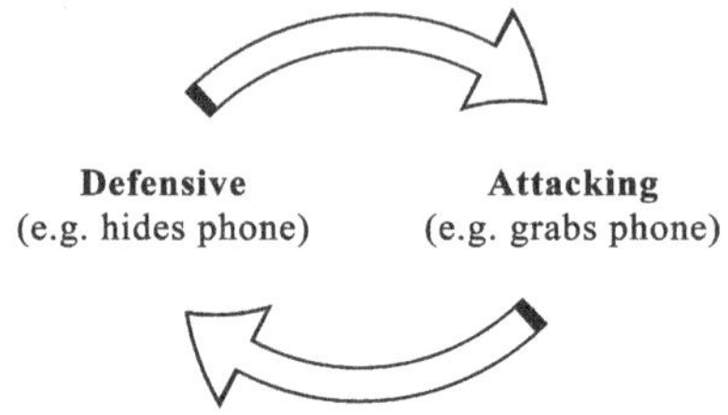

Figure 10.2 Relationship Pattern Diagram

From systemic psychotherapy we integrate into the person-centred model the idea that change in experience can come from change in the relationship. Essentially, this is a reversal of the person-centred framing of change, or a complementary description of change. Change in experience leads to relationship change, and relationship change leads to change in experience (Figure 10.3). In the following example, if the client acted more reassuringly, this would likely change the trust level of her partner. Similarly, if her partner acted with more trust, this would lead to more reassurance. If the client's partner is very traumatised, her reassurance level will have to be so high as to control her freedom. Hence, systemic thinking helps clients evaluate when relationships are damaging.

Systemic psychotherapy views individual wellbeing as part of relationships. Using communication, we interact with others. They interpret us and communicate back – this is called 'feedback'. The feedback we receive shapes our experience, and these communication cycles become repeated patterns. Our emotions and experience motivate us to act and relate to others in ways that establish some kind of 'normality'.

But where do these norms come from?

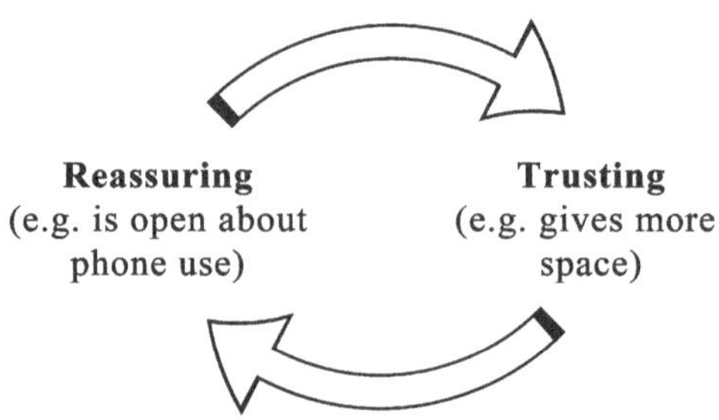

Figure 10.3 Systemic Change in Jealousy

The Influence of the Family

Children brought up in the same household by the same parents have quite different experiences. The puzzle of why this happens was solved in the 1970s. An Argentinian-born family therapist, Salvador Minuchin, who practiced mostly in America, found out why.

He had children observe their parents in a stressful interview while monitoring their stress hormones. The children could not interact with the parents at first; they watched from behind a screen. Then they were asked to join their parents. What did Minuchin find?

In a case example, a family of four, the mother and father's stress levels fluctuate throughout the interview. But they stayed reasonably similar, mirroring each other's stress levels. The younger child's stress increased a little but returned to normal during the experiment. Fascinatingly, the older child's stress hormones skyrocketed and never fully came back down.

The behaviour of the older child, Dede, was interesting. When she joined her parents, she became involved in the disagreement between her parents. Each parent attempted to recruit Dede to their point of view. Violet, the younger child, was not encouraged to take sides or enter into the argument. What's interesting is that when Dede interrupted the argument, the parents began to parent her, and their stress levels reduced.

The stress experience served a complicated function in the family. It transferred from the parents to the child, who, as a result, was left with the most stress at the end. One of the main systemic contributions to psychotherapy is how presenting issues like anorexia, psychosis, depression, anxiety, and schizophrenia can be explained by the scapegoat principle – one person in the family becoming emotionally unwell to preserve the breakdown of the family.

Minuchin and his colleagues concluded that personal experience is interdependent with family dynamics. Each person's emotional health is predicated on the role they take in family interactions. Children like Violet, whose stress isn't needed to rescue arguing parents, are freer to experience conflict without feeling caught in the middle.

Minuchin and other family therapists noticed that the roles people take tend to clump in threes. Something like, one person instigates an argument, another reciprocates, and a third calms down the situation. To acknowledge this pattern, family therapists coined the term 'triangulation'. As well as symbolic triangles in families, the triangle is one of the strongest geometric

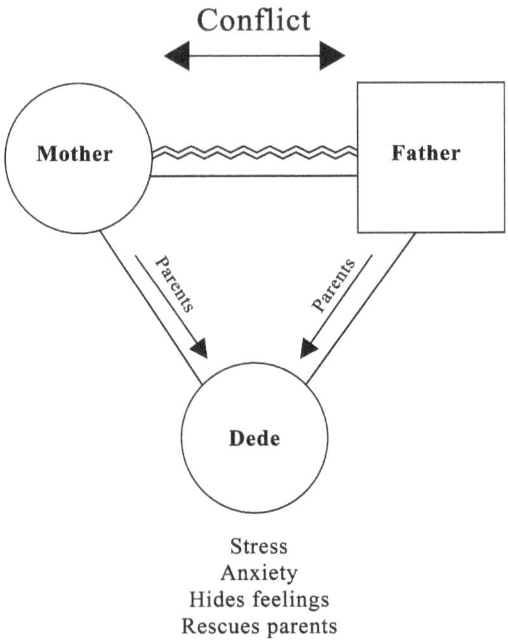

Figure 10.4 Triangulation Map

shapes in all of nature. In a similar way, family members stabilise relationships by creating triangles, even when one person 'loses' by becoming mentally unwell (Figure 10.4).

The importance of this for person-centred counselling is clear. We adopt the perspective that experience has some kind of family or social function, and we explore relationships with clients. We use 'how' questions and 'when' questions to map family interactions. Such as asking Dede, "How do you feel about your parents arguing?," or "When you feel stressed about your parents arguing, what do you do?," or "When you step in to calm them down, how does this affect you?." Systemic questions link experience to family interactions.

Using systemic ideas in a person-centred way means focusing on how experience motivates people into social roles. There is a specific theory about this, called positioning theory, developed by Rom Harré and Luk Van Langenhove. They studied social roles and found that communication positions someone into a storyline or way of perceiving the relationship. The person accepts the position, rejects the position, redefines the position, or challenges it. The family history of the person, the roles they took with their siblings and parents, shape the positions they take. So, a female partner hiding her smartphone screen, for example, invites her boyfriend into a position. Something like, 'accept my privacy'. He rejects this position with an aggressive 'no' and throws her phone. This positions her in the storyline, 'privacy is forbidden'.

Family Development

Minuchin modelled his research into a school of family therapy called structural family therapy. He noticed that a family is basically a web of biologically, emotionally, and economically connected relationships held together by a dynamic structure. Each family has its unwritten rulebook for its different roles, which are learned and negotiated through interaction and experience.

Minuchin theorised that people come to therapy because the family structure is problematic. For this idea, he gets a lot of criticism from modern family therapists; it seems to imply there is a 'correct' family structure, like the nuclear family with a male breadwinner and female caregiver. But structural family therapy merely describes the link between a family structure and the psychological health of family members.

Family therapists see people together because of a huge problem with individual change. If you remember from Dede's family, her parents became less stressed when she became more stressed – and Dede was far from stress-free at the end of the contact. Counselling an individual to improve their psychological health often means passing the emotional buck to someone else in the relationship chain. This feels moral because usually other people constrain the client. But the systemic model notices unintended consequences to individual counselling.

Recently, I was speaking with my clinical supervisor, Conny Kerman, about this. I brought up the issue of a client's defence mechanism. When my client felt annoyed with her mother, she made jokes and changed the topic. Conny had the idea that the defence mechanism was a relationship pattern between me and the client. While I modelled the defence in an experience frame, Conny saw a systemic frame. I went into an emotion, and my client backed off; I tried to go into an emotion, and my client backed off further; revealing a relationship pattern rather than a defence solely in my client (Figure 10.5).

The case was linked with anxiety. The client was triangulated with her parents, forming a coalition with mum against dad. When dad was drunk, he ridiculed mum and became verbally abusive. Daughter, my client,

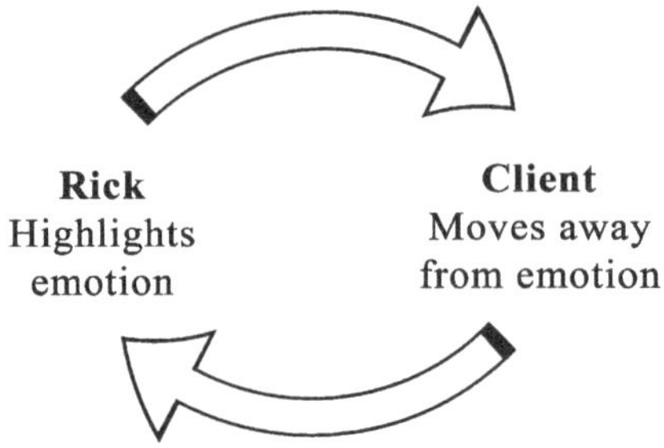

Figure 10.5 A Defence Mechanism as Relationship Pattern

stepped in to defend mum. Often, they would cuddle and hold each other while mum cried – until dad left or calmed down.

The therapy helped the client be less of a comfort blanket to mum. She started therapy saying she couldn't feel her real emotions but began to be emotionally aware and expressive. But this positive change led her to being less available for mum, and she started to socialise more with dad. Her mum resented their relationship and ultimately cut contact with her for two weeks. This dramatic communication led the client to go back and comfort her mother, expressing how sorry she was – and hence the family structure was back in place, especially after mum listed the most recent incidents with dad. Here, the triangulation, and the client's psychological symptoms, reappeared.

My experience-based perspective shielded me from the systemic pattern. Conny highlighted how important it was, in our therapy together, to focus on how being in touch with the client's experience led to negative changes in mum-and-daughter relationship. Hence, I saw a 'defence' in the client but missed the importance of preserving her parental relationship. This became a central theme – how do my client and I create space for her experience without alienating her mother? The client was clear; she did not want to lose this close relationship. When the client experienced my appreciation of her relationship with mum, there were fewer defences.

The Transitional Crisis

So far, we have talked about families as though they were static. Clearly families change with time. Homeostasis – family stability – acknowledges that families remain reasonably structured while continually changing.

Change in families is fairly sequential. The lifecycle of a family begins with an individual leaving home. Then they marry. Then come the children. Then the children grow and have some autonomy. Adolescence hits. And, back to the start of the cycle, with the children being 'launched' like chicks from a nest into adulthood to find partners as the grandparents grow old. Of course, not all relationships work this way. Some cultures arrange marriage. Some sexual orientations exclude marriage or having children. Other people are not biologically able to conceive. Death brings a sudden and tragic end to parts of the lifecycle. But in the general case, families move – within a culture – through reasonably predictable cycles (Figure 10.6).

An insight from systemic therapy is that psychological issues happen during transitional phases. The introduction of a new child. The union of two people into marriage or coupledom. Each change causes a shift in family rules and boundaries.

When a relationship goes through a transition – through a lifecycle stage – there are three factors that influence how people adapt. These are communication, bonding, and flexibility of roles. Seeing an individual for counselling misses this systemic picture.

In Dede's case, from Minuchin's study earlier in the chapter, if we worked with her father, we'd see a small slice of the systemic situation. His presenting

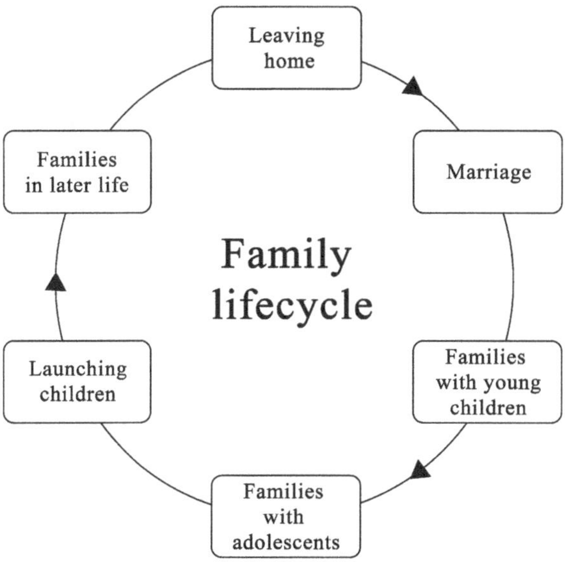

Figure 10.6 Family Lifecycles

issue might look like a lack of confidence. His perspective might be that his wife undermines his role as a father, and when he tries to parent, Dede and her take sides. He tells us that he didn't speak up for himself against his domineering mother as a child. We might support him to sit with his discomfort around conflict. This might develop more self-esteem. He might learn to hear his wife without defending himself. If this creates more flexibility, bonding, and communication, the family manages conflict and change successfully. Hence, systemic change and experiential change are interdependent.

However, if we have merely joined the father's perspective, with our empathy and unconditional positive regard, we may reinforce the family structure. Without change in the family structure, he will return to older ways of behaving. For example, he might be calmer and more able to withstand his wife's perceived attacks. In the current family structure, his lack of a response could be perceived as fuel to the fire – as a direct instigation of conflict. Hence, his wife becomes more agitated and critical of him, until he reaches breaking point. We might empathise with him without spotting the systemic influence of our work. When he returns to therapy unhappy again, we are unclear why and often get drawn into trying to 'remind' him of the progress. The person-centred model doesn't really have a theory of regression or relapse, but the systemic model notices that when people change, they get coerced into old relationship positions.

The learning here is that valuing the perspective of one person in a relationship can unintentionally invalidate the other perspective. In a person-centred model, we don't notice this. In a systemic model, we see that experience and perspective service the relationship. People's feelings are part of the dynamic. Thus, the integrative person-centred model encourages counsellors to take on the perspectives within the client's significant relationships. We help transport the client into other people's psychological worlds. We focus on transitional changes, on the rules and boundaries of the relationship, and on the perspectives of each person in the system. We ask, "How does your wife experience your lack of response?" We explore, "What perspective does your daughter have of your lack of response?"

Taking the other's perspective risks taking sides against the client. We lose our unconditional positive regard. But congruence is a way of overcoming this. That is, putting ourselves, our intentions, and our feelings into the question or statement can communicate congruence with the client. For example, "I can really feel you trying to be calmer. I'm wondering how this looks to your family. How does your wife experience your lack of response?"

In this systemic question is a person-centred core. My value for the client is there, so too is my focus on his autonomy, but I bring some expertise myself – the awareness of the relationship system.

In the 1980s, a very influential school of family therapy in Milan named these kinds of questions circular and neutral. That is, we attempt to be neutral to the truth in our questions. Rather than seeing some perspectives as valid only, we see that all experiences and perspectives are valid. This helps clients perceive relationships differently. Circular questions encourage clients to think relationship without losing their experience. It is when we contradict the experience of the client, and when we fight someone else's corner, I think, that causes clients to feel we are not on their side.

Meaningful Change

The systemic model says that human experience is interdependent with family and social systems (Figure 10.7). The individual takes a role in a family dynamic, and this creates unique experiences. Experiential change is superficial if the family doesn't redefine the individual's role.

Gregory Bateson is one of the early pioneers of family therapy. He said that a difference or a change in an individual is not enough to hope for continued success. He said that therapy looks for "the difference that makes a difference." He meant a 'systemic' difference.

The systemic model sees change on two levels. The first level is behaviour and experience. A person may be happy, sad, excited, and stressed – all in one afternoon! These first-order changes crystallise into family patterns where, for example, happiness is ridiculed (hence sadness comes), and sadness is cured with humour (hence excitement comes), and emotional avoidance kicks in (hence stress). The difference that makes a difference is one that changes the overall pattern – the rules of family life. This is a second level of change called 'second-order change'.

Second-order change is a change in the definition of the relationship. In a family example, two parents treat their teenager as 10 years old. No matter what they do, they create a pattern around this definition. The teenager, who is biologically 16, tries to meet friends and become more autonomous, but the parents prevent them. When the teenager cannot do basic tasks like feed or dress themself properly, like a four-year-old, the parents lecture them to be more independent. Hence, the definition of the 10-year-old organises the family.

Figure 10.7 The Individual Problem as a Family Problem

First-order change (experience and behaviour) happens constantly, but unless the family breaks out of the mindset that their 16-year-old is 10, they won't move forward. Helping the 16-year-old be consistently more mature, helping the parents permit more autonomy, for example, might be the difference that makes a difference – the whole family sees a young adult emerge. Around this new definition, the family structure is more conducive to positive wellbeing.

We call this 'reframing' in systems theory. We change the frame that the client or system puts over their relationships. In doing so, something new is there. They see differently and act in accordance with that new reality. A lifecycle is a time where the family must reframe their relationships, and hence troubles occur.

Meaning and Social Graces

A family is an emotional system, but it is also a meaning system. And the family doesn't create meaning in a vacuum. The final piece of the systemic model is the influence of society on the family.

Vernon Cronen and Barnett Pearce, two communication theorists, showed that a hierarchy of meaning moves through the culture to the family dynamics and onto the individual's experience. For instance, Dede experiences stress because of her parents' dynamic. But her parents' dynamic is the result of wider cultural norms around male–female roles and parental expectations. For example, let's imagine the meaning her mum makes from the disagreement is (1) a woman must stand up to her husband and (2) parents must stick together and show care towards their children. The first belief frames the argument and the second, when Dede enters into the argument, overrides it. Hence families are structured by cultural beliefs. If the family lived in a different culture with different values, they would not act in the same way. As R. D. Laing pointed out, this is the politics of experience.

The biological layer is important to stress. People enter the world with genetic temperaments, being more or less able to tolerate stress physiologically. But the individual's temperament is responded to by people in the family. Are people close enough to notice early signs of stress? Are people so close that reactions override early signs of stress? Hence, family dynamics shape the role an individual takes when feeling stressed.

The culture teaches the family what is important to notice inside the home. If a girl is not supposed to show anger, for instance, then her early signs of stress are undetected – and girls learn to internalise anger, being more likely to self-harm and take on caring roles.

Social scripts are written and re-written with new family generations, holding society's beliefs together. Culture is made up from beliefs about people's identities, which can be broken down into fluid identity categories – like being a boy or girl. John Burnham and Alison Roper-Hall call this the Social Graces model. A person's Gender, Race, Age, Class, Education-level, and Sexual Orientation (GRACES) shape how they are positioned in relationships. Also, Geography, Religion, Ability, Culture, Ethnicity, and Spirituality (GRACES) influence family dynamics. Kimberlé Crenshaw, an American civil rights activist, emphasises that the social graces 'intersect'. That is, when one adds race and gender together, for example, they have a deeper understanding of someone than seeing them through one identify factor alone.

Intersectionality says that dominant ideas in society shape family and individual experience. And this returns us to Salma, from the beginning of this chapter, and her experience with the security guard.

Salma's feelings about the hotel interaction are shared amongst many people in her social groups. Women, Muslims, black people, second-generation immigrants (and, in many respects, northerners!) experience ethnic, racial, gender-based, and classist tension. A phenomenon like this cannot only be explained by a humanistic psychology, particularly where some individuals receive more discrimination than others. For example, being Islamic and going to a British university might create forms of discrimination otherwise unseen.

This brings the politics of experience right into the counselling room. It highlights the therapist and the university lecturer as a part of the cultural process that establishes social norms. My social graces interact with Salma's, including all students and clients. The systemic model invites us to reflect on power embedded in our interactions. While personally I might not be coming from a white-dominance perspective, my actions as a white person in coordination with the class might replicate white dominance by excluding racist experiences. That is, my person-centred lecture assumed that the route to change was experience. Ignoring the disparity in Salma's power would serve the privilege I hold in that context.

Narrative Theory

Michael White and David Epston modelled the way a social system creates power over citizens, students, and therapy clients. They showed how interactions on a one-to-one basis confirm and shape cultural stories. Influenced by Michel Foucault and the idea of the dominant discourse, their model is largely linguistic. Words are like cultural perspectives that divide reality into narratives. In communication, narratives tell people which roles are possible, and thus afford some people privilege over others.

In narrative theory, experience comes from societal, cultural, and family storylines. The more people play into the storyline, the more it becomes social reality. Hence, a culture partially built from Christianity, racism, and sexism creates pejorative dominant stories about Islam, non-white people, and women.

We *can* model Salma's personal experience as a subjective thing. But my argument, ethically, is that we ought to include the social context and power into the model. Recognising this alerts us to the patterns of experience within marginalised groups. Although the experience of a black client and a white client can be described in person-centred ways, the lack of attention to privilege misses why one experience is more distressing than another in some contexts.

Some person-centred counsellors argue that empathy for experience combats racism in therapy, which is probably true. But my argument is why not take on the concepts that help us explore social issues in more depth? I also think that it's tough to empathise with issues outside our awareness. What we lose is a focus on the individual, but we gain a collective and interconnected understanding of the client's difficulty. I think this is more humanistic than person-centred therapy. It puts human beings at the centre of our moral outlook, promoting rights of individuals in the social situation of therapy.

Another insight from narrative theory is an answer to the question of why people change personalities in different contexts. While sometimes this is due to adopting a persona, as Jung describes, it is also because people are defined differently across contexts. I am reminded of a client from a black Caribbean background who drew his dominant narratives as words on a page. When he was in white-dominated spaces, such as school, his language shifted to more pejorative and negative-sounding words – words like 'loud' and 'causes trouble'. When in predominantly black groups, including in his family, he had some negative labels but many more appreciative words, like 'funny', 'thoughtful', and 'clever'. Narrative theory highlights that social context evokes identities, and our experience comes out of this. My client's experience was drastically different according to the environment he was in.

To make use of narrative theory in integrative therapy, we focus on the descriptions and narratives a person brings into the room. We are curious about the meaning of words and the impact the words have on the client. Systemically, this follows from the idea of second-order change where the therapist works on how the client defines themself. The narrative approach encourages the therapist to take the lead on naming social identity features like race, religion, and class – addressing the political elephant in the room.

Summary

The integrative person-centred model has lacked a description of the environment related to personal experience. In this chapter, we showed that experience is interdependent with relationship. Family relationships and wider social relationships are formed emotionally from roles, beliefs, and meaning in the surrounding culture. Hence, the integrative person-centred therapist explores the meaning a client brings to therapy, seeing each word and utterance as part of a personal, familial, and sociopolitical context. Power was viewed as a social construct and became an important part of how we understand the client's subjectivity.

Finally, we addressed a situation in class. A student challenged the person-centred model for its bias towards individual responsibility. In a society of social injustice, how can this be moral? Thinking with Salma about racism on campus, we have tried to show how systemic thinking might explore experiences of social injustice. Here I would like to check in with Salma at the end of the chapter. On the one hand, it's about sitting with experience and not trying to force growth. On the other, it's about evaluating our therapy clinics, universities, and social spaces to consider how they discriminate against marginalised groups, including those related to race, class, religion, gender, sexuality, and disability.

Rick: "Salma, your question seems to be how, in a society of injustice, can we place responsibility for change on the individual? I have two thoughts: (1) I think that working on how you experience racism may give you more power in the moment, so you feel less apologetic and coerced into feeling the need to explain yourself. (2) This is easy for a white male to say, not having to experience racism personally. Hence, thinking about my role in the university, do you want me to address this with the security team? It's on us as a university to take responsibility for the racism you encounter here."

Salma: "The question of responsibility for change in a society of injustice is deeply personal to me. As both a trainee psychotherapist and a Somali wellbeing development worker, being the main contact point for many people in my community, I'm constantly navigating the tension between empowering individuals and addressing systemic barriers. In the hotel lobby, I did everything 'right'. I stayed calm, explained myself, and even had the foresight to set up a support package to eliminate situations like this. But none of that stopped the interrogation, the humiliation, or the dismissal. I was left questioning whether there was anything I could have done differently – or if the system was designed to make me feel powerless no matter what."

"One of my classmates asked if I could've avoided over-explaining myself and demonstrated assertiveness. I appreciated her question but explained that the reality is more complicated. If I hadn't explained myself the way I did, it could've fed into preconceived stereotypes and escalated the situation. If I'd responded with anger or frustration, it would've backfired, placing all the blame on me. Trauma leaves you with no 'safe' response, but only calculated survival tactics."

"Regarding (white) authority figures, I was taught growing up to 'answer every question that they ask you and do not forget to smile.' This advice is rooted in the fear of the dehumanisation we tend to experience, but this anxiety-driven generational response is not a healthy one to live by all the time as it kept me from connecting with white peers wholeheartedly."

"Rick, you shared a story in class about standing your ground, and it made us reflect on the concept of privilege. As a white male, we talked about how your assertiveness was more likely to be respected or understood by authority. For me, I explained that my assertiveness can be perceived as aggression, forcing me to overcompensate to appear non-threatening."

"My work with the Somali community gives me a broader perspective on these patterns. I see how systemic oppression plays out daily, from children being misunderstood in schools no matter the effort, to Somali women disregarded in healthcare settings. My role is to advocate for these individuals, helping them navigate systems that were never designed with them in mind. But living through these injustices myself is exhausting. It's a constant battle to maintain resilience, knowing that my advocacy work can't protect everyone, and won't always protect me."

"Person-centred therapy is invaluable in helping clients build self-awareness, resilience, and personal growth by creating a safe, non-judgemental space. Its focus on individual empowerment enables clients to gain a sense of control over their internal experiences and how they navigate their world. However, when systemic oppression shapes a person's reality, this inward focus can feel limiting. While the approach excels at supporting emotional understanding and personal agency, it struggles to account for the external structural forces that perpetuate injustice. Recognising these limitations does not diminish its value but rather situates its strengths within the broader complexities of clients' lives, shaped by internal and external realities."

"My personal therapist is culturally competent, and she validates the powerlessness involved in these discriminatory experiences. Sadly, this is an experience I am used to navigating. I have reported it to my university mentor and don't want you to take any further action. I am not comfortable revisiting that experience again with the security."

"I will say, I am incredibly thankful for this suggestion and for being part of the case study. It has shown me that my experiences don't have to be hidden, invisible, or forgotten, and people will understand. This is a reality faced by many, and upon reflection, it's essential that therapists take these lived experiences into account as part of their clients' positions and identities. These moments of systemic injustice have a profound impact on self-esteem and are reasons why people try to gain control in unhealthy ways. Recognising and validating these experiences is a crucial step in supporting clients holistically, addressing the internal and external forces that shape their mental health and wellbeing."

Further Reading

Bateson, G. (1972). *Steps to an Ecology of Mind*. San Francisco: Chandler.

Burnham, J. (1986). *Family Therapy*. London: Routledge.

Carr, A. (2014). The evidence-base for family therapy and systemic interventions for child focused problems. *Journal of Family Therapy* 36: 107–157.

Cecchin, G. (1987). Hypothesizing, circularity and neutrality revisited. An invitation to curiosity. *Family Process* 24 (1): 15–25.

Minuchin, S. (1974). *Families and Family Therapy*. Abingdon: Routledge.

Rogers, C. (2003). *Client-Centred Therapy*, 70e. London: Robinson.

Tomm, K.M. (1991). Beginnings of a "HIPs and PIPs" approach to psychiatric assessment. *The Calgary Participator* 1 (2): 21–24.

11

Conclusion

As therapists, we find ourselves in an unknown world. We want to reach out and help those suffering from psychological torments. We ask ourselves: What happened for this person to get into this headspace? How do we help them find a more fulfilling state of mind?

To understand a person's distress, we try our best to model their reality. Each model views a person's mental life from a healing perspective but has many blind spots. The view that the way someone thinks determines their well being misses the influence of social context. The view that social context determines well being misses the infinite depth of experience.

In our attempts to model psychological reality, we have separated into therapy tribes. I have tried to bring the village elders into a conversation, combining the salient knowledge from each person's model into one book. What we have discovered is that psychotherapy speaks many languages, yes, but it has a core of like-minded concepts.

Therapy jargon can be like a fog machine in a library. The books become engulfed by smoke. I have tried to clear the way, a little, to show how even the foggiest concept fits neatly into psychotherapy. In this final chapter, we bring together the key ideas of the book. Once finished, I hope to show that combining models of therapy into one form sketches a useful picture of reality, and one that best serves our clients.

Daughter of fire

the love for a parent is like water
it is a mysterious thing
it can turn to rain

Integrative Person-Centred Counselling: The Combined Model of Counselling and Psychotherapy, First Edition. Rick Murphy.

it can be vapour
it can be ice
it can be snow
it can be many forms
it is all water
but it can never disappear.

Think for a moment. What is this poem about? What model of reality best suits the mind of the poet? What feelings or relationships are being evoked? What thoughts or needs are identifiable? How is culture or attachment relevant?

Emma, who wrote this poem, is one of my therapy clients. The poem was sent in a Christmas card to her father. Carl Rogers invites me to be open to Emma's experience. To try and feel what it's like to be her, understanding her words from inside her perspective.

The person-centred model tries to avoid making assumptions about what the poem means. We accept the subjective experience that love for a parent is like water. It can be rain, vapour, ice, or snow, but it can never disappear. In highlighting this experience back to Emma, we sit with her in what gets evoked. There is a humanity to the person-centred model unrivalled by others. We form a strong relationship based on empathy and acceptance. Our model tells us that forming this relationship creates more hope. But in losing ourselves in the experience of the other, we miss out on seeing the person from the outside. Our senses are attuned to life inside an experience, and we lose focus of the wider picture.

Emma's poem evolves into an unsent story, which she has allowed us to read. Let's pick up on a different perspective to consider her poem. It continues:

> Seeing a suffering father is suffering within the daughter. Seeing a father choose to give up on life, before his time, is impending grief within the daughter, but she believes she can save him. Seeing a father leave his body and stop caring for it, makes the child care harder for the father's body, in spite of herself.

With this passage, Emma connects us with something deeply personal. She loves her father but feels she must abandon herself to save him. The person-centred model that Carl Rogers uses is like a warm and safe room for this experience to sit in. We hear it, tolerate it, face it, and grow from it. We hope that by noticing the conflict in self-abandonment, Emma learns from it emotionally, being more in touch with her needs.

While there is a great deal of humanity in this first model, Sigmund Freud comes at the poem from a different angle. In his view, we missed something important, which is that Emma expresses unconscious wishes by writing her poetry. She fulfils unmet needs, confronts a harsh reality, and explores her internal judge. In this model, a therapist is useful to Emma by highlighting the wishes in her story, drawing attention to the conflict between her hidden hopes and her harsher reality. When we join these two models together, we notice more about the client. As well as taking us on the subjective journey of her inner world, her words reveal childhood experiences of abandonment that have translated into unconscious rules about feelings:

> Seeing a father who has left in spirit, is near existential abandonment .... She must not show him her fears.

In Freud's model, Emma's childhood convinces her not to communicate her emotions, and she replays her abandonment in other relationships. She uses poetry to control an uncontrollable world. That is, in her imagination she exists for a moment in a world where she can "show him her fears." Sometimes, accepting an experience at face value colludes with psychological defences. In real life, it has felt emotionally impossible to communicate fears. The real-life self-policing causes her to abandon her feelings. Hence, bringing out themes from the unconscious level, the poem symbolises her wish for a restored father, the pain of accepting a "father leaving his body," and the reality of shutting down emotions. But, in this new idea, we know to see double: to see the experience and the way the surface experience buries feelings. Had we only looked at the words, without Freud's angle, we would have experienced Emma without feeling the deeper, more heartfelt yearning.

Freud's model notices how Emma injects feelings into poetry, putting stored-up psychological energy into fantasy. In fantasy, we can right the wrongs of our past and live more confidently than in the real world. But this leads to a diminished sense of reality, one we defend against by being anxious, depressed, funny, or even poetic. Emma continues:

> In her dreams, she turned into vapour, floated to the clouds, formed into hard thick, heavy ice, and rained down in a furious storm. As the flow melted from anger to grief, it poured with tropical thunder and put out the fire. She hoped that the fire in her father's heart had been ignited again, by her love.

While profoundly expressive, creative acts like poetry hide raw emotion with imagination and false hope. Carl Jung modelled this from a different angle, saying that people who hide raw emotion anchor themselves to roles, to personas, where their sense of self gets entangled with trying (and failing) to correct childhood experiences. That is, from a Freudian point of view we did not notice the universality of Emma's struggle, how she re-enacts the collective unconscious, the human story, by taking on the role of carer.

Emma sees this herself; she takes on the ultimate caregiver role, the person who sacrifices herself for the other. We know this is unsustainable. At some point, the caregiver must confront her needs:

> But in reality, she had only turned to vapour. She learned a great many things from the new perspective. She took her time understanding, seeking guidance, integrating, growing, drawing power to cut off the things which held her back. They no longer served. She found meaning, purpose, self-love, healing, and unconditional love for all others. She rested alone. She learned how aloneness is different from loneliness and drew them both in … She used everything she had learned from her father about the nature of the world and fought with courage rarely seen. A tool made from self-sacrifice. She won, only to have survived and feel an existential need to rest and grieve for all she had lost in the fight.

Awareness of the self-sacrifice led to "drawing power to cut off the things which held her back." What a powerful expression of Carl Rogers' fundamental idea that sitting with experience generates hope. But Freud's model arrived at the same conclusion. He said that facing reality against the fantasy or defence of hidden emotions, that challenging the inner policewoman, leads to growth-inducing insights. Hence, the models are not incompatible; they draw attention to different aspects of a bigger picture. Jung simply widens the picture further, seeing how experience sits above an unconscious, and an unconscious sits above the human tendency to replicate psychological themes like the 'hero' and 'caregiver'.

Melanie Klein, in developing Freud's model, focused more on Emma's internalisation of the good and bad. Klein sees how Emma attaches negative emotions onto the father's experience. She internalises this into a self-image, someone who alleviates her suffering by 'saving' her father. Thus, showing how Jung's theory happens in reality – the self-image forms into an archetype, a common human role. Klein notices Emma's growth in changing from dividing up the world into good and bad, to one that is more realistic. That is, she is good and bad, and so is her father. To cope in her early life, she saw her needs as 'bad' and abandoned them. After self-discovery, she saw the goodness in her needs, being able to self-heal.

Notice what Klein adds to the therapy model. She draws attention to how clients like Emma absorb the **positive** and <u>negative</u> into themselves and their view of others:

> And in the **restful nest**, felt the **fire in her heart**, which her **father had given her**, such a long time ago. She would have <u>fought to the death</u> for **what was right for her** life. **Her life**. And <u>so she had</u>. <u>Depleted, isolated, grieving, wounded</u>, **but alive**, she **rested in the dwindling fire** of her heart whilst **Spirit danced all around her, resourcing her.**

Klein views the integration of positive and negative elements, of grief and appreciation, as true maturity. In this way, we are taking concepts from different psychotherapy models. We look through each prism, noticing something new about the client. We aren't forcing ourselves to overly theorise the client's problem. Our model is to stay focused on their experience, to be humanely with them in the therapy space, listening to them and caring about what they say. But our listening ear brings about unique blind spots, which we resolve when adopting another vantage point.

John Bowlby offered another point of view. He added that Emma's internal representation of the self and the father is an accurate picture sketched from childhood. Klein notices the process of dividing the world into good and bad things, but Bowlby cuts a bit deeper.

Bowlby's attachment model asks why Emma hopes to save her father, and why she abandons herself. How can the therapist or the poem help her to care for herself?

Bowlby's view teaches us that Emma's human need to form close emotional bonds is greatly instinctual from birth. From an attachment model, we find new questions, like "What is Emma's internal representation of help?" Sadly, to me at least, it is one in which she cannot rely on others. She can try and save others, to hope for a time where the other is available to save her. But, even in fantasy, we see that "she rested alone. She learned how aloneness is different from loneliness and drew them both in. She flew against the wind and storms again and again, to stay put. She survived harder than she could ever imagine." Her internal representation of the father is someone who needs looking after. Her internal representation of the self is of someone who is not looked after and must find her way alone. Though "she had learned from her father about the nature of the world" to fight for herself, it was a "tool made from self-sacrifice." Hence, the attachment model reminds us to be with Emma in a reliable and trustworthy relationship. Cutting out the interpretations of other models, we go back to the importance of being someone who is there unconditionally for Emma and her experience. Our relationship creates a secure base for her to go and explore the world, always having a safe place to return. This is especially important in her role as a mother of three children, which comes out in the next section:

> But in reality, not the dream, three small ones were watching her too, needing her. Learning from her ... Understanding how she had unknowingly passed shadows on to the children, filled her with shame. And so, she sat there, nearly overcome, wondering what to do, when she remembered the vapour had shown her the shadows: self-sacrifice, emotional detachment, and repression, which all led to future dis-ease and suffering. Spirit danced with her and showed her, her ancestral lineage, full of love, support, and suffering. Then Spirit showed her her descendants, all weighed down and suffering with the shadows. Then she realised, the shadows were the way forward. The sun came out. It had always been there, above the clouds. It lit up the shadows. They became instructions. Love yourself, feel it all and freedom will flow from the heart with abundant love. She showed her children.

The themes of isolation, meaning, life, and death come through in this passage. Yalom, Frankl, and Van Deurzen say that existential themes were lurking behind all of Emma's experience. She was exploring existential issues throughout the poem, but our model missed them. She discussed existential insight such as that "being alone is different from being lonely," or the notion of "saving" her father from "leaving his body." On reviewing this chapter, Emma tells me this was not meant to literally mean 'death', but when we discussed this further she did say underneath the intention is an ultimate fear of her father's death. Hence the existential theme may be the origin of a present concern.

Although the aforementioned therapists, the great tribal leaders, provided answers to the question of why people have mental health issues, they missed the existential point, that life stops. Human progress can only ever take us so far. In five billion years, the sun will expand and engulf the Earth, rendering all human experience, the fruits of every civilisation, the memories, traumas, and moments of joy, as brief encounters in the history of the universe. Coping with our existence and the punishing lack of justice in the world is part of the human burden. Emma picks up on this theme, in the spirit of existential acceptance:

> So in reality, she did not save her father. She took everything she had learned from him and went on the hero's journey. To save the one's she could save.

The existential theme casts a new light on Emma's poem. She is finding meaning, exploring existential isolation, and using poetry to express her purpose and optimism. The cognitive thinkers, people like Aaron T. Beck, notice how the existential quest shows itself in thoughts, feelings, and behaviours. We see an Emma who is more self-appreciative, someone who is 'courageous', someone who can 'create the future'. Carl Rogers sees this as self-actualisation – Emma tolerating her experience and growing from it. But the cognitive viewpoint helps us notice exactly where the change occurred, in the way Emma thinks and acts. Her thinking leads her to be more autonomous. While she begins the poem with self-abandonment, she ends with acceptance and a sense of autonomy:

> In her new dreams, her father saw her rise like a phoenix and realised, she had got it all from him. For he was also a phoenix. But in reality, the choice to rise is his, for now. His whole family (wife, sons, daughters, granddaughters, grandsons, brothers, aunts, cousins, father, and ancestors), regardless of their own self-awareness, had an abundance of love waiting for him. Courage could reveal the beauty in everything he had created, if only he looked to a higher perspective. But only he could choose to look.

This is the end of Emma's story, and the end of the book. Emma, in Fritz Perls' language, completes a gestalt. That is, she closes the puzzle of her saviour complex by recognising her father's responsibility. Each turn in a poem, story, or client's words, gives us an opportunity to see them from a different perspective. So often are we trained into one-track-mindedness, by being therapists who see from one angle.

In this book, I have encouraged you to take on multiple perspectives, to lean on other ideas when clients start to seem one-dimensional. Hence, if the therapy is creating the change that Emma has created here for herself, there is no need for other ideas, though we might be needed to help her live this change in her life. Integration happens when new ideas are needed to relate to the client.

In the final passage of her story, Emma unknowingly brought in the last perspective we have explored, which is the systemic impact of family and ancestry, culture and meaning, on the people we become. We are part of a human lineage that transcends our present experience. The hundreds of thousands of years of human culture, change, and pilgrimage have led to a fairly stable world society in which our individual experiences are interdependent. Without looking at gender, race, religion, social class, and any social aspect, we miss the politics of experience that lead the client to therapy (or to write poetry!). My sense is that seeing the person through the different lenses is more humanising than pure person-centred approaches. This is because the more we see the more we are capable of seeing. And seeing, experiencing, perceiving, and relating are really the only tools we have to help people out of distressing realities.

I am thankful to Emma and all the clients, colleagues, family members, and others who have contributed to this book. My philosophy has been to view human experience through the variety of models that exist on the psychotherapy bookshelves. My attitude has been one of taking what is useful, that more eyes and ears are best. I am reminded of a quote from Albert Einstein, which, at the end of this long journey, I think sums up my thoughts about the creativity of counselling and psychotherapy. It is something about seeing the opportunities in each way of looking at a counselling problem:

> "In the middle of difficulty lies opportunity."
>
> *Albert Einstein*

References

Ainsworth, M.D. and Wittig, B.A. (1969). Attachment and exploratory behavior of one-year-olds in a strange situation. In: *Determinants of Infant Behavior*, vol. 4 (ed. B.M. Foss), 113–136. London: Methuen.

Ainsworth, M.D.S., Blehar, M., Waters, E., and Wall, S. (1978). *Patterns of Attachment: A Psychological Study of the Strange Situation*. Hillsdale, NJ: Erlbaum Associates.

Baker, R., Owens, M., Thomas, S. et al. (2012). Does CBT facilitate emotional processing? *Behavioural and Cognitive Psychotherapy* 40 (1): 19–37.

Bateson, G. (1972). *Steps to an Ecology of Mind*. San Francisco: Chandler.

Beck, J. (1995). *Cognitive Therapy: Basics and Beyond*. New York: Guilford.

Beck, J.S. and Fleming, S. (2021). A brief history of Aaron T. Beck, MD, and cognitive behavior therapy. *Clinical Psychology in Europe* 3 (2): 1–7.

Bischof, M. and Bassetti, C.L. (2004). Total dream loss: a distinct neuropsychological dysfunction after bilateral PCA stroke. *Annals of Neurology* 56: 583–586. https://doi.org/10.1002/ana.20246.

Bisson, J.I., Roberts, N.P., Andrew, M. et al. (2013). Psychological therapies for chronic post-traumatic stress disorder (PTSD) in adults. *Cochrane Database of Systematic Reviews* (12): CD003388.

Bowlby, J. (1969). *Attachment: Attachment and Loss: Vol. 1: Loss*. New York, NY: Basic Books.

Bowlby, J. (1988). *A Secure Base: Clinical Applications of Attachment Theory*. Hove: Brunner-Routledge.

Brown, L.S. and Wright, J. (2001). Attachment theory in adolescence and its relevance to developmental psychopathology. *Clinical Psychology & Psychotherapy: An International Journal of Theory & Practice* 8 (1): 15–32.

Integrative Person-Centred Counselling: The Combined Model of Counselling and Psychotherapy, First Edition. Rick Murphy.

Burnham, J. (1986). *Family Therapy*. London: Routledge.

Burnham, J. (2005). *Relational Reflexivity: A Tool for Socially Constructing Therapeutic Relationships in "The Space Between"* (ed. C. Flaskas, B. Mason, and A. Perlerz). London: Karnac Pubs.

Calverley, R.M., Fischer, K.W., and Ayoub, C. (1994). Complex splitting of self-representations in sexually abused adolescent girls. *Development and Psychopathology* 6 (1): 195–213. https://doi.org/10.1017/S0954579400005952.

Canty, N. and Gould, J.L. (1995). The hawk/goose experiment: sources of variability. *Animal Behaviour* 50 (4): 1091–1095. https://doi.org/10.1016/0003-3472(95)80108-1.

Carr, A. (2014). The evidence-base for family therapy and systemic interventions for child focused problems. *Journal of Family Therapy* 36: 107–157.

Cecchin, G. (1987). Hypothesizing, circularity and neutrality revisited. *An Invitation to Curiosity. Family Process.* 24 (1): 15–25.

Cooper, M. (2010). *Essential Research Findings in Counselling and Psychotherapy: The Facts are Friendly*. London: Sage publications LTD.

Cooper, M. (2017). *Existential Therapies*, 2e. London: Sage Publications.

Cornelius-White, J.H., Motschnig-Pitrik, R., and Lux, M. (2013). *Interdisciplinary Applications of the Person-Centered Approach*. New York: Springer.

Crittenden, P.M. (1981). Abusing, neglecting, problematic, and adequate dyads: differentiating by patterns of interaction. *Merrill-Palmer Quarterly of Behavior and Development* 27: 201–218.

Crittenden, P.M. (2006). A dynamic-maturational model of attachment. *Australian and New Zealand Journal of Family Therapy* 27 (2): 105–115.

Crittenden, P.M. (2013). Attachment and psychopathology. In: *Attachment Theory: Social, Developmental, and Clinical Perspectives* (ed. S. Goldberg, R. Muir, and J. Kerr), 367–406. Hillsdale, NJ: The Analytic Press.

Cuijpers, P., Driessen, E., Hollon, S.D. et al. (2012). The efficacy of non-directive supportive therapy for adult depression: a meta-analysis. *Clinical Psychology Review* 2012 32 (4): 280–291. https://doi.org/10.1016/j.cpr.2012.01.003.

Farias, M. and Wikholm, C. (2015). *The Buddha Pill.* Can Meditation Change You? Watkins.

Dryden, W. (2012). The therapeutic relationship in CBT. In: *The CBT Handbook* (ed. W. Dryden and R. Branch), 83–100. London: Sage.

Ellis, A. (2003). Early theories and practices of rational emotive behavior theory and how they have been augmented and revised during the last three decades. *Journal of Rational-Emotive & Cognitive-Behavior Therapy* 21 (3/4): 219–243.

Faris, A. and Van Ooijen, E. (2012). *Integrative Counselling and Psychotherapy: A Textbook*. London: Routledge.

Farnfield, S. (2014). From preschool to school age: Narrative story stems. In: *The Routledge Handbook of Attachment: Assessment* (ed. S. Farnfield and P. Holmes), 81–101. Routledge/Taylor & Francis Group.

Fischer, H., Wik, G., and Fredrikson, M. (1997). Extraversion, neuroticism and brain function: a pet study of personality. *Personality and Individual Differences* 23 (2): 345–352. https://doi.org/10.1016/S0191-8869(97)00027-5.

Fordham, B., Sugavanam, T., Edwards, K. et al. (2021). The evidence for cognitive behavioural therapy in any condition, population or context: a meta-review of systematic reviews and panoramic meta-analysis. *Psychological Medicine* 51 (1): 21–29. https://doi.org/10.1017/S0033291720005292.

Frankl, V. (1959). *Man's Search For Meaning*. London: Penguin Random House UK.

Freud, S. (1913). *The interpretation of dreams*. London: MacMillan Co.

Freud, S. (2005). *The Essentials of Psycho-Analysis*. New York: Vintage Classics.

Gendlin, E.T. (1961). Experiencing: a variable in the process of therapeutic change. *American Journal of Psychotherapy* 1961 (15): 233–245.

Ghafoori, B., Wolf, M.G., Nylund-Gibson, K., and Felix, E.D. (2019). A naturalistic study exploring mental health outcomes following trauma-focused treatment among diverse survivors of crime and violence. *Journal of Affective Disorders* 245: 617–625.

Goldberg, S.B., Tucker, R.P., Greene, P.A. et al. (2018). Mindfulness-based interventions for psychiatric disorders: a systematic review and meta-analysis. *Clinical Psychology Review* 59: 52–60. https://doi.org/10.1016/j.cpr.2017.10.011m.

Goldsmith, D.F. (2010). The emotional dance of attachment. *Clinical Social Work Journal* 38 (1): 4–7.

Gomez, L. (1997). *An Introduction to Object Relations*. London: Free Association Books.

Goss, P. (2015). *Jung: A Complete Introduction: Teach Yourself*. Mobius.

Gosselt, J., Van Hoof, J., Gent, B., and Fox, J. (2015). Violent frames: analyzing internet movie database reviewers' text descriptions of media violence and gender differences from 39 years of U.S. Action, Thriller, Crime, and Adventure Movies. *International Journal of Communication* 9 (2015): 547–567.

Green, R., Carr, W., and Green, M. (1968). The hawk:goose phenomenon: further confirmation and a search for the releaser. *Journal of Psychology* 69: 271–276.

Greiger, R. (2018). *On Becoming a Cognitive Behavioural Therapist*. London: Routledge.

Hall, J., Kellett, S., Berrios, R. et al. (2016). Efficacy of cognitive behavioral therapy for generalized anxiety disorder in older adults: systematic review, meta-analysis, and meta-regression. *American Journal of Geriatric Psychiatry* 2016 24 (11): 1063–1073.

Harris, R. (2019). *ACT Made Simple*, 2e. New Harbinger.

Hazan, C. and Shaver, P.R. (1987). Romantic love conceptualized as an attachment process. *Journal of Personality and Social Psychology* 52: 511–524.

Hill, C. (2009). *Helping Skills in Practice: A Three-Stage Model*. American Psychological Association [DVD].

Hill, C. (2017). Therapists' perspectives about working with meaning in life in psychotherapy: a survey. *Counselling Psychology Quarterly* 30 (4): 373–391.

Huppert, F.A. (2009). Psychological well-being: evidence regarding its causes and consequences†. *Applied Psychology: Health and Well-Being* 1 (2): 137–164. https://doi.org/10.1111/j.1758-0854.2009.01008.x.

Husserl, E. (1989). *Ideas Pertaining to a Pure Phenomenology and to a Phenomenological Philosophy*. Boston: Springer.

James, W. (1890). *The Principles of Psychology*, vol. 1. Henry Holt and Co. https://doi.org/10.1037/10538-000.

Johnson, D.L., Wiebe, J.S., Gold, S.M. et al. (1999). Cerebral blood flow and personality: a positron emission tomography study. *American Journal of Psychiatry* 156 (2): 252–257. https://doi.org/10.1176/ajp.156.2.252.

Josefowitz, N. and Myran, D. (2005). Towards a person-centred cognitive behaviour therapy. *Counselling Psychology Quarterly* 18 (4): 329–336. https://doi.org/10.1080/09515070500473600.

Joseph, S. (2017). *The Handbook of Person-Centred Therapy and Mental Health: Theory, Research and Practice*. PCCS Books.

Kang, L. and Pendersen, N. (2017). *Quackery: A Brief History of the Worst Ways to Cure Everything*. New York: Workman Publishing.

Jung, C. (1923). *Psychological Types*. Brace: Harcourt.

Jung, C. (1958). *The Undiscovered Self*. London: Routledge.

Jung, C. (1995). *Memories, Dreams, Reflections* (trans. R. Winston and C. Winston). Fontana Press.

Kelly, K. (2017). *Basic Counselling Skills: A Student Guide*. Warrington: Counselling Tutor.

Kiley, D. (1997). *The Peter Pan Syndrome: Men who have never grown up*. New York: Dodd, Mead & Co.

King, M., Sibbald, B., Ward, E. et al. (2000). Randomised control trials of non-directive counselling, cognitive-behaviour therapy and usual general practitioner care in the management of depression as well as mixed anxiety and depression in primary care. *Health Technology Assessment* 19 (1): 1–83.

Kocur, M., Dechant, M., Wolff, C. et al. (2021). Computer-assisted avatar-based treatment for dysfunctional beliefs in depressive inpatients: a pilot study. *Frontiers in Psychiatry* 12: https://doi.org/10.3389/fpsyt.2021.608997.

Kohut, H. (2009). *The Restoration of the Self*. University of Chicago Press.

Korkmaz, B. (2011). Theory of mind and neurodevelopmental disorders of childhood. *Pediatric Research* 69: 101–108. https://doi.org/10.1203/PDR.0b013e318212c177.

Langevin, R., Cossette, L., and Hébert, M. (2019). Emotion dysregulation in sexually abused preschoolers: insights from a story completion task. *Journal of Child Sexual Abuse* 29 (4): 468–489. https://doi.org/10.1080/10538712.2019.1678542.

Lapworth, P. and Sills, C. (2009). *Integration in Counselling & Psychotherapy*. London: Sage.

Lazarus, A.A. (1989). *The Practice of Multimodal Therapy*. Baltimore: Johns Hopkins University Press.

Leichsenring, F., Hiller, W., Weissberg, M., and Leibing, E. (2006). Cognitive-behavioral therapy and psychodynamic psychotherapy: techniques, efficacy, and indications. *American Journal of Psychotherapy* 60 (3): 233–259.

Mariani, R., Musetti, A., Di Monte, C. et al. (2021). Maladaptive daydreaming in relation to linguistic features and attachment style. *International Journal of Environmental Research and Public Health* 19 (1): 386. https://doi.org/10.3390/ijerph19010386.

Liotti, G. (2006). A model of dissociation based on attachment theory and research. *Journal of Trauma & Dissociation* 7 (4): 55–73.

Main, M. and Solomon, J. (1986). Discovery of a new, insecure-disorganized/disoriented attachment pattern. In: *Affective Development in Infancy* (ed. M. Yogman and T.B. Brazelton), 95–124. Norwood, NJ: Ablex.

Marie Curie. (2024). Public attitudes to death, dying and bereavement in the UK re-visited: 2023 survey Summary report. Available online: https://www.mariecurie.org.uk/globalassets/media/documents/policy/policy-publications/2024/n401_padd_report_final.pdf (accessed 21 April 2025)

Marzano, C., Ferrara, M., Mauro, F. et al. (2011). Recalling and forgetting dreams: theta and alpha oscillations during sleep predict subsequent dream recall. *Journal of Neuroscience* 31 (18): 6674–6683. https://doi.org/10.1523/JNEUROSCI.0412-11.2011.

Maslow, A.H. (1943). A theory of human motivation. *Psychological Review* 50 (4): 370–396.

Mason, B. (1993). Towards positions of safe uncertainty. *Human Systems* 4 (3–4): 189–200.

Merry, T. (2014). *Learning and Being in Person-Centred Counselling, Ross on Wye.* PCCS Books.

Mesman, J., van Ijzendoorn, M., and Bakermans-Kranenburg, M. (2009). The many faces of the still-face paradigm: a review and meta-analysis. *Developmental Review.* 30: 120–162. https://doi.org/10.1016/j.dr.2009.02.001.

Merry, T. and Lusty, B. (1993). *What Is Person-Centred Therapy?* Loughton, Essex: Gale Centre Publications.

Meyer, T.D. and Hautzinger, M. (2012). Cognitive behaviour therapy and supportive therapy for bipolar disorders: relapse rates for treatment period and 2-year follow-up. *Psychological Medicine* 42 (7): 1429–1439.

Minuchin, S. (1974). *Families and Family Therapy*. Abingdon: Routledge.

Moodley, R., Sutherland, P., and Oulanova, O. (2008). Traditional healing, the body and mind in psychotherapy. *Counseling Psychology Quarterly* 21 (2): 153–165. https://doi.org/10.1080/09515070802066870.

Moreno, J. (1994). *Psychodrama Since Moreno* (ed. M. Karp and M. Watson). Routledge.

Morgan, D. (2003). Mindfulness-based cognitive therapy for depression: a new approach to preventing relapse. *Psychotherapy Research* 13 (1): 123–125. https://doi.org/10.1080/713869628.

Murphy, R. (2024). *A Systemic Approach to Integrative Counselling*. Abingdon: Routledge.

Norcross, J.C. and Lambert, M.J. (ed.) (2019). *Psychotherapy Relationships That Work: Evidence-Based Therapist Contributions*, 3e. Oxford University Press.

Otway, L. and Carnelley, K. (2013). Exploring the associations between adult attachment security and self-actualisation and self-transcendence. *Self and Identity* 12: 217–230. https://doi.org/10.1080/15298868.2012.667570.

Pavot, W., Diener, E., Colvin, C.R., and Sandvik, E. (1991). Further validation of the Satisfaction with Life Scale: evidence for the cross-method convergence of well-being measures. *Journal of Personality Assessment* 57 (1): 149–161. https://doi.org/10.1207/s15327752jpa5701_17. 1920028.

Perls, F. (1969). *Ego, Hunger, and Aggression; the Beginning of Gestalt Therapy*. New York: Random House.

Perls, F. (1973). *The Gestalt Approach & Eye Witness to Therapy*. California: Science and behavior books.

Perls, F. (2015). Madeline's Dream. [Video file]. https://www.youtube.com/watch?v=TFqhPe5DR98&list=PLcEd0IYai8aSoVldXdUbUKPjvtN_OJUjZ&index=5

Perls, F. (2016). Fritz Perls explains Gestalt Therapy. [Video file]. https://www.youtube.com/watch?v=2hhtNjjBAhA&list=PLcEd0IYai8aSoVldXdUbUKPjvtN_OJUjZ

Perls, F., Hefferline, R., and Goodman, P. (1951). *Gestalt Therapy: Excitement and Growth in the Human Personality*. New York: Dell.

Raskin, N.J. and Rogers, C.R. (2005). Person-centered therapy. In: *Current Psychotherapies* (7, instr. ed. (ed. R.J. Corsini and D. Wedding), 130–165. Thomson Brooks/Cole Publishing Co.

Rogers, C.R. (1951). *Client-Centered Therapy*. London: Constable.

Rogers, C.R. (1957). The necessary and sufficient conditions of therapeutic personality change. *Journal of Consulting Psychology* 21: 95–103.

Rogers, C. (1959). A theory of therapy, personality, and interpersonal relationships, as developed in the client-centered framework. In: *Psychology: A Study of a Science. Study 1, Volume 3: Formulations of the Person and the Social Context* (ed. S. Koch), 184–256. McGraw-Hill.

Rogers, C. (1963). The actualising tendency. In: *Nebraska Symposium on Motivation* (ed. M. Jones). University of Nebraska Press.

Rogers, C. (1971). My way of facilitating a group. *American Journal of Nursing* 71 (2): 275–279.

Rogers, C. (2003). *Client-Centered Therapy*. 70th Anniversary Edition. Robinson Publishing.

Rose, S. (2015). The Quentin Tarantino race debate isn't black and white. The Guardian. https://www.theguardian.com/film/2015/oct/13/tarantino-race-debate-isnt-black-and-white

Rosenthal, H. (2016). The Gloria Films. Psychotherapy.Net. [Available online] https://www.psychotherapy.net/blog/title/the-gloria-films-candid-answers-to-questions-therapists-ask-most#:~:text=In%20the%20movie%2C%20Rogers%20comes,Perls

Rowan, J. and Jacobs, M. (2002). *The Therapist's Use of Self.* Berkshire: Open University Press.

Russell, W., Breunlin, D., and Sahebi, B. (2022). *Integrative Systemic Therapy.* London: Routledge.

Sanders, P. (2003). *The Tribes of the Person-centred Nation: A Guide to the Schools of Therapy Associated with the Person-centred Approach.* PCCS Books.

Shostrom, E.L. (1965). Three approaches to psychotherapy (Part I) [Film]. In: *Psychological Films. Adapted from the Transcripts of Carl Rogers' Therapy Sessions* (ed. B.T. Brodley and G. Lietaer). Orange, CA: [online]: https://anamartinspsicoterapiaacp.files.wordpress.com/2016/04/brodley-transcripts-of-carl-rogers-therapy-sessions.pdf.

Skinner, B.F. (1988). *About Behaviourism.* New York: Random House.

Stern, J.A., Fraley, R.C., Jones, J.D. et al. (2018). Developmental processes across the first two years of parenthood: Stability and change in adult attachment style. *Developmental psychology* 54 (5): 975.

Taylor, J., Lauder, W., Moy, M., and Corlett, J. (2009). Practitioner assessments of 'good enough' parenting: factorial survey. *Journal of Clinical Nursing* 18: 1180–1189.

Tomm, K.M. (1991). Beginnings of a "HIPs and PIPs" approach to psychiatric assessment. *The Calgary Participator* 1 (2): 21–24.

Tronick, E. (2003). Things still to be done on the still-face effect. *Infancy* 4: 475–482.

Tudor, K. and Merry, T. (2006). *Dictionary of Person-Centred Psychology, Ross on Wye.* PCCS Books.

Van Deurzen, E. (2012). *Existential Counselling & Psychotherapy in Practice,* 3e. London: Sage Publications.

Van Deurzen, E. and Adams, M. (2016). *Skills in Existential Counselling & Psychotherapy,* 2e. London: Sage Publications.

Van Ijzendoorn, M.H. and Kroonberg, P.M. (1988). Cross-cultural patterns of attachment: a meta-analysis of the strange situation. *Child Development* 59 (1): 147–156.

Wallin, D. (2013). We are the tools of our trade. In: *Attachment Theory in Adult Mental Health: A Guide to Clinical Practice* (ed. A. Danquah and K. Berry), 225–240. Routledge.

Wachtel, P.L. (2011). *Therapeutic Communication: Knowing What to Say When.* Guilford Press.

Weinrach, S. (1990). Rogers and Gloria: the controversial film and the enduring relationship. *Psychotherapy* 27 (2): 282–290.

White, M. (2020). An exploration of 'earned-secure' attachment and the role of attachment-informed psychotherapy. [Higher diploma thesis, Dublin Business School]. Dublin. https://esource.dbs.ie/server/api/core/bitstreams/5a219e4a-327f-4c33-bae0-9ce51f1126f0/content (accessed 21 April 2025).

Williams, M., Teasdale, J., Segal, Z., and Kabat-Zinn, J. (2007). *The Mindful Way Through Depression: Freeing Yourself from Chronic Unhappiness*. New York, NY: Guilford.

Winnicott, D.W. (1971). *Playing and Reality*. London: Routledge.

World Health Organization (2022). *Mental Health: Strengthening Our Response*. Geneva: World Health Organization https://www.who.int/news-room/fact-sheets/detail/mental-health-strengthening-our-response (accessed 08 October 2024).

Wosket, V. (2002). *The Therapeutic Use of Self: Counselling Practice, Research and Supervision*. London: Routledge.

Worsley, R. (2007). *The Integrative Counselling Primer*. Monmouth: PCCS Books Ltd.

Wright, J.H., Owen, J., Eells, T.D. et al. (2022). Effect of computer-assisted cognitive behaviour therapy vs usual care on depression among adults in primary care: a randomized clinical trial. *JAMA Network Open* 5 (2): e2146716. https://doi.org/10.1001/jamanetworkopen.2021.46716.

Yalom, I. (1980). *Existential Psychotherapy*. USA: Basic Books.

Yalom, I. (2008). *Staring at the sun. Overcoming the Dread of Death*. London: Piatkus.

Yalom, I. (2017). *Becoming Myself. A Psychiatrist's Memoir*. New York: Basic Books.

Index

Integrative Person-Centred Counselling: The Combined Model of Counselling and Psychotherapy, First Edition. Rick Murphy.